CLIMBING FROM
DESPAIR
—— *to* ——
GRACE

*An Empowerment Ladder for Healing the Hearts of
Mothers with Special Needs Children*

KAREN HASSELO

CLIMBING FROM DESPAIR TO GRACE

*An Empowerment Ladder for Healing the Hearts of
Mothers with Special Needs Children*

Copyright © 2023. Karen Hasselo

Book Design by
Transcendent Publishing
www.transcendentpublishing.com

ISBN: 979-8-9878728-7-1

This book is a memoir and reflects the author's present recollections over time. Some names, locations, and institutions have been changed; events have been compressed; and some dialogue has been recreated.

Medical Disclaimer: The following information is intended for general information purposes only. Individuals should always consult their health care providers before administering any suggestions made in this book. Any application of the material set forth in the following pages is at the reader's discretion and is his or her sole responsibility.

Printed in the United States of America.

To the *Divine Sisterhood* of mothers who are advanced alchemists; rather than transforming base metals into gold, they weave their pain into a higher awareness that infuses everything they touch, resulting in a deeply meaningful and majestic tapestry of life.

And to my courageous son Mark – who gave permission to share our story so that others could more easily walk their transformational paths.

TABLE OF CONTENTS

RUNG ONE

SHOCK AND DESPAIR

"More tears are shed over answered prayers
than unanswered ones."

Truman Capote

It was November 22, 1994. I sat alone on the cold hardwood floor in my kitchen in total darkness, replaying the pronouncement from earlier in the day. My mind flashed back to hearing that shattering word – *AUTISM,* followed by three professionals crunching numbers that came from their prolonged psychological assessments. My mind had processed their words as though they were speaking through a long tunnel with sounds fading in and out.

Abruptly, my foggy intellect latched onto the phrase, "expressive language at a four-month level."

I felt lightheaded. It seemed that my brain was trying to speed up to catch the fast- flying words that were rushing past. Out of the corner of my eye, I observed my beautiful, charming, towheaded, twenty-one-month-old toddler Mark, grasping the handlebars of his stroller and crashing his mode of transport into the office furniture in a repetitive manner.

In the next moments, I'd lost all focus regarding what the psychologist was uttering and thought, *Why am I here* alone *with my son without any forewarning that today would be the day to hear this life-shattering diagnosis?*

Dr. L. had mentioned that she would complete my son's assessment; however, I was never informed that I would be given the results on the same day. Since my husband and I had attended two prior appointments, I just assumed that we would be together when given the diagnostic results and future recommendations. Another part of my mind commanded me to return to this precipitous moment and concentrate on the import of what was being said.

Another thought floated into my head: what about my planned hysterectomy that was under consideration following the New Year? When there was a brief pause in the flow of words, I asked a question related to the advisability of having upcoming surgery.

The answer echoed into the room. "Well, that decision we'll leave up to you."

Next, I heard my hesitant, wooden "Okay..." after which I fell mute.

My sluggish brain then formulated a better question. "How am I going to keep Mark engaged in meaningful social interaction throughout the day?"

Dr. L. stood up and reached for a bright, shiny, red, remote-control car as a sample of the type of toy that would engage Mark.

Inside my mind, I heard, *That will work for about seven seconds.* Taking naptime into account, there are only fourteen more hours of the remaining day that need to be filled. I asked for a list of resources, professionals to consult, and books to read.

The response was a memorable one. "We don't have anything like that."

Dr. L. did recommend two books: a well-known memoir, published in 1967, detailing a mother's journey with her daughter with autism; the other, a book of research summarizing interventions with preschool-aged children on the spectrum.

Were these books going to provide a foundation for charting a course forward? Was I actually on my way out of one of the top diagnostic centers in the country – a center that labeled children with one of the most serious and devastating disorders of our time, without any concrete, effective, actionable steps to take? My mind was silently screaming, *This can't be my life. This can't be my life.*

Later, as I stood on the sidewalk waiting for my car at the hospital valet parking, I observed a middle-aged man accompanied by a young woman with Down syndrome who by all appearances looked to be his daughter. With no one else in sight, they were literally standing within a few feet of me. I saw myself, in my mind's eye, running over invading the father's personal space and shouting at the top of my lungs, *How have you done it…how have you done it?* Possessing a shred of rationality, I ordered myself to focus on steadying my trembling hands while getting Mark buckled safely into the car.

Much, much later, I would discover that there was a phrase for what I faced every single day after November 22, 1994. I believed that I had been drafted, against my will, into my *new normal.* All my carefully crafted plans were decimated. The life that I had known was, effectively, over. There would never be an end result to match what my mind originally demanded. Dramatic, sweeping, unexpected, and surprising changes that couldn't be fathomed at the beginning of my journey would be an outgrowth of this new normal. Another was my hyper-focus on the need for balance, first within myself and later within my daily practices.

My new normal also placed the spotlight squarely on my marriage. One of the tenets of a successful marriage is that only one partner at a time has permission to be in crisis, with the other available to support them. Usually, as time goes on, these roles switch back and forth; however, when autism or any lifelong, impactful diagnosis is involved, that seesaw dynamic is no longer viable. Both parties are in excruciating pain simultaneously. It is akin to a death; the death of all the couple's hopes and dreams for what their child would become, milestones that would be celebrated, joyful moments that would be commemorated, and the bittersweet day their child would be launched into adult independence. However, there is not a single societal ritual to mark the death of these parenting dreams.

Our culture hasn't created avenues that support ways for mothers of newly diagnosed children to grieve. There are no established rituals of comfort (i.e., meals brought to the house); there is no guaranteed paid leave-of-absence from work. This child and his siblings will still be there, waking up the next morning hungry with their attendant needs. The day after the diagnosis, it is likely the mother who must gather the necessary strength to provide quality nurturing, while beginning the exhaustive efforts to ensure that appropriate resources are garnered to meet the needs of the disabled child.

Three months prior to being diagnosed with autism, Mark had already begun early intervention. When he was fifteen to seventeen months of age, I realized that his development had drastically careened off course and immediately resigned from my sixteen-year career as a psychotherapist. Soon I was taking him to three professionals a week, hoping his developmental lags could be addressed.

The morning after the diagnosis Mark was scheduled to see his speech and language therapist. My heightened sense of urgency and over-responsibility drove me to keep the appointment. After absorbing such a body blow, a mother with self-compassion would have stayed home and given herself a twenty-four-hour cushion. My misguided notion that Mark could never feel abandoned at this critical juncture had completely overtaken my life. En route, I felt an incredible level of depersonalization, as though I was driving to this appointment with my head floating somewhere above my groundless body.

I explained in a flat and mechanical manner that a mere twenty hours earlier my son had been saddled with the autism diagnosis.

I received the following response from Mark's speech therapist: "Well, you suspected as much, so now that it's been confirmed it should be a relief. Don't waste any time feeling upset. This diagnosis is in fact a blessing because you can now move forward."

Once those words were spoken, I wished to remain completely outside of my body. Instead, I was jolted back momentarily to a muted form of reality. Tears began to slide down my face. Nevertheless, I experienced it as though it was happening to someone else.

I will never forget the words that came next. "Whatever you do, you've got to keep it fun; keep it spontaneous; be playful with him. Don't you realize that he can pick up on your sadness? There's no room for sadness in his life right now. The clock is ticking. He needs you right now and *you've got to be at your best!*"

There was a tiny ember of anger starting to glow inside of me. It seemed to me that a very sick karmic joke had been instigated. Would a mother whose child had been diagnosed with life-threatening cancer twenty-four hours prior be admonished against showing sadness and told instead to be an exuberant full-time play buddy? I didn't think so and yet what good would it do to compare? Also, I know now my level of shock kept me safe in a protective yoke that quickly extinguished my anger. I knelt next to Mark on the floor of that office certain of only one thing: I would never have another genuinely joyful moment again. I couldn't entertain the idea that someone else was suggesting that I would.

I also couldn't come to grips with a professional tossing down the guilt card. In this game of life, I had already been dealt many hands of guilt – along with despair, self-sacrifice, and stoicism – and I had learned that it was up to me how I played them.

The words kept reverberating… "Keep it fun, keep it spontaneous, be playful with him and *you've got to be at your best.*"

I was convinced that my best days were behind me. My wedding day seventeen years earlier; the summer-long sabbatical that my husband and I had shared a few years prior; the day that infant Mark had been placed in my arms at the hospital; our twentieth-anniversary party attended by our circle of friends that validated the arc of our relationship; the day we moved into our newly built dream home bordering an exquisite pond. We had waited a long time to have Mark. The adoption process alone had been an arduous journey. However, it was not the only reason that I had once questioned whether motherhood would ever be a part of my path.

For most of my life, in the recesses of my heart, I didn't see myself as mother material. During my twenties, I didn't want the responsibility that came with round-the-clock caregiving and I had been extremely anxious about being the primary caregiver while my husband regularly traveled for work. The deeper reason, however, came from somewhere else. It was a paralyzing fear born during the first eight years of my childhood.

I grew up on a safe, tree-lined street with many, many material advantages. But I did not live with a mother who knew how to provide a nurturing relationship. Through no fault of her own, my mother did not know how to offer comfort through physical touch, or loving and nurturing words. "I love you" was never spoken out loud. She was unable to do so as she had never received those gifts during her own fractured childhood. My father also came into the marriage with his own buried traumas. He spent the vast majority of his time away from the home, making his mark on the world. My mother followed suit by often escaping the home and her parenting responsibilities. When my parents were together, my father's drinking was front and center and there was plenty of heightened drama to keep soap opera fans on the edge of their seats.

By commenting on this cycle, I am not blaming or condemning my parents or anyone else's, their parents, our own children, or any of us. I am attempting to shed light on the following fact: not all of us entered into motherhood with a strong foundation for fulfilling our roles; in fact, some of us did so with a seriously flawed foundation or almost no foundation at all. Some of us chose parenting while still coping with the vestiges of codependency in our marital and/or family or origin relationships.

Codependency is a form of enmeshment where our partner or someone close to us *is expected to fulfill the missing elements inside of us*. It is often a desperate, empty search for wholeness, lovability, visibility, and worth based on someone else's ability to fill those voids. Codependency is also characterized by a dance where one or both parties are overly invested in the relationship and are compensating for the wounded behavior(s) of the other, by getting an emotional payoff for being in the role of giver or taker. The traits that go hand-in-hand with codependency can range from mild to incapacitating. The roots typically stretch back to childhood.

Here is a salient question for you to consider: As a child, were you trapped in an obligatory role that required you to frequently put your own needs on the back burner because something or someone else took precedence in your family of origin? That something else might have been a parent's addiction; enmeshed boundaries between your caregivers and/or overt and heightened conflict between them; some level of instability or physical or mental illness on the part of a caregiver; an absent or self-absorbed caregiver; an explosive caregiver; a single-parent household in which you were forced to take on adult responsibilities before it was developmentally appropriate; or a household marred by continual chaos.

As a daughter in one of these families, your *emotional dependency needs*[1] were not optimally met. A need is a *requirement* that must be fulfilled in order for you to optimally thrive in adulthood. Having your emotional dependency needs met at each and every developmental stage of childhood is not a luxury or an extravagance. In my case, I felt the strain of trying to keep my primary caregiver (my mother) stable and content. I existed as a tool to regulate her emotions. I learned in early childhood to adapt by being compliant, pleasant, and accommodating. I clung to a mirage of safety and security, continually gauging my own behavioral responses in tandem with my mother's emotional thermometer, via the practice of hypervigilance.

> Since the parent, especially the mother, is the child's sole source of survival, the child strives to please, fearing disapproval, or abandonment. Thus, the child sublimates his needs for the parent's. Roles reverse and the child frequently takes on the parent's responsibility as emotional caregiver. This impedes the growth of a child's true identity, and a "loss of self" frequently occurs. The child adapts by not "feeling" his own needs, and develops finely tuned antennae, focusing intensely on the needs of the all-important other.
>
> ~Alice Miller, *The Drama of the Gifted Child:*
> *The Search for the True Self*[2]

My self-worth was established externally as a survival strategy. I grasped for any crumb of validation that existed outside of myself and thus I began my lifelong chase for approval, lovability, and worth, running forevermore on a hamster wheel. Once I entered adulthood, I was not completely aware of the parts of myself that I had disavowed that mirrored my mother or the ways in which my ego drove me to overcompensate for those parts. It was second nature for me to deny my own emotional truths and instead focus on the needs of others or project my unrealistic expectations onto others, hoping they would fulfill my chasm of unmet needs.

Some of us enter into adulthood having learned to ignore our own perceptions while holding the family secrets and automatically suppressing, repressing, and minimizing *our own* needs and feelings by projecting a façade of independence, competence, and self-reliance into the world. Worst of all, we may not even be aware that we are engaged in these survival strategies, nor the repercussions of them. We have gained this education while living in a childhood minefield. Without healing our minds, bodies, and spirits, we might unconsciously continue some form of this legacy during adulthood. I know that I did. As Spiritual Teacher and Therapist, Robert Burney, writes in *Codependence: The Dance of Wounded Souls, A Cosmic Perspective of Codependence and the Human Condition,*

> The war we were born into, the battlefield each of us grew up in, was not in some foreign country against some identified "enemy" it was in the "homes" which were supposed to be our safe haven with our parents whom we loved and trusted to take care of us. It was not for a year or two or three, it was for sixteen, or seventeen, or eighteen years. We experienced what is called "sanctuary trauma" – our safest place to be was not safe and we experienced it on a daily basis for years and years. Some of the greatest damage was done to us in subtle ways on a daily basis because our sanctuary was a battlefield. It was not a battlefield because our parents were wrong or bad – it was a battlefield because *they were born into the middle of a war.*[3]

I realized that as a child, I was caught in a no-win, double-bind circumstance. No matter how much I fulfilled the role of "perfect child," by turning myself inside out to please my emotionally absent mother, I would continue to be viewed as a disappointment. For my sister, it was even worse. She took on the role of the out-of-control, tyrannical child, who stepped into the shoes of the family scapegoat. However, both of us experienced the environment described below in Ross Rosenberg's 2013 book, *The Human Magnet Syndrome: Why We Love People Who Hurt Us.*

> Without warmth, acceptance, safety and unconditional love, this child eventually learns that she is essentially unlovable, unworthy and that the world is an unsafe place. Humiliation, shame and anger accumulate as she realizes that the abuse and neglect may never stop and unconditional love will never come. To temper the child's loss of hope and despair, and to survive

her living nightmare, she will need a psychological strategy to protect her from the stark realities of her life. [4]

Even though I spent my childhood years enacting an obsession with *looking perfect on the outside*, I believed that my mother knew I had been saddled with "the unlovable seed" and was therefore deserving of her disdain and her intermittent rage attacks. These kinds of conditioned family patterns can be absorbed into our unconscious minds and even our DNA, only to be transferred trans-generationally in a never-ending cycle of heartache that, as mentioned above, Robert Burney labels as "warfare" inside our home fronts.

Unless healing occurs to interrupt this cycle, these childhood remnants will be reenacted as we either undercompensate or overcompensate for our wounds. When a special needs child graces the family with his or her presence, a glaring spotlight will shine on any cracked, damaged, or non-existent foundation within each party and between the couple, potentially shattering any remaining illusions or fantasies.

As a woman and mother, I am still examining these shameful parts of myself that I would rather lock away in a dark closet. I would like to pretend that the young girl inside of me, who grew up needing to coerce and control others in order to feel safe, who tried to mask her pain with a false veneer of overachieving and perfectionism, the girl who ran furiously away from a core of self-loathing and shame, didn't exact this same emotional toll on her husband and ultimately, her son. *Unfortunately, running from the truth always leads back to recreating companion results and often a heightened version of them!*

As a highly sensitive woman who came into adulthood having lost touch with parts of my emotional life, many of my own emotional needs and preferences, my connection to my body, the capacity to fully trust God, and healthy tools to fill my self-love cup and live my life in balance, I was far from prepared to adapt when the Universe asked me to fulfill my soul contract as Mark's mother. It is vital to look at the truth, to understand the truth, and at the same time view my inner child personas with compassion and the woman I became with self-forgiveness. As the proverb states, "Tout comprendre, c'est tout pardoner," or, "To understand everything is to forgive everything."

As an adult, I lived with what Robert Burney termed "delayed stress syndrome," which bubbled to the surface when the conditions were ripe, most often when I was feeling emotionally abandoned or feared censure of some kind. Indeed, the severe wounds of my child-hood had resulted in emotional storms in my relationship with my husband. I had the profile to occasionally react with vicious words to what wasn't truly there on the outside, but did exist from the inside, based upon the perspective of my wounded inner child personas. I didn't completely know how to freely give emotional and sexual inti-macy in a marriage, and I didn't completely possess the capacity to have a mature loving adult relationship that was reciprocal in nature. At the same time, I was committed to self-improvement. After explor-ing some of these dynamics during psychotherapy sessions from years seven to ten of our marriage, these storm clouds didn't form as often. My ego tried to convince me that for the most part, the turbulent weather was behind me.

The truth was that I had been needing and relying upon my hus-band's love and approval to make me feel whole for years. After autism, gale-force winds were brewing. Something very real and traumatic was there on the outside and something very real and damaged was also there on the inside. Without the emotional devastation that accompa-nies having a child with autism, I might have been able to continue to delude myself by minimizing my shadow personas, as well as the flaws in my marriage. From outward appearances, my life appeared to be ideal.

My long-term friends agreed that they had never seen me as ful-filled and joyful as they did during Mark's first year of life. All of that was true. However, once the black silent hole called autism swept in, any neglected cracks in my life's foundation became insurmount-able craters that eventually imploded the family. After all, no one ever exits a black hole without being shredded and having every aspect of life dismantled.

In the beginning, I wouldn't allow myself to see this level of truth. Once it became official that my son had autism, my mind mercilessly drove me to ignore much of my own pain, at the expense of my body, mind, and soul. I had internalized this pattern of self-protection during childhood: "When things get tough, the tough get going." The tougher my exterior, the more my ego insisted that I was protected. I had mastered being the ultimate workhorse, at the expense of having much balance and peace in my life. My subconscious mind demanded that I behave as the perfect mother who didn't abandon her child during his most urgent time of need. My mind couldn't tolerate any suggestion that I might be capable of throwing my son away emotionally, in the same callous manner I believed I had been treated.

Portia Nelson, author of *There's a Hole in My Sidewalk: The Romance of Self-Discovery*, beautifully articulates the stages we potentially progress through as we build our spiritual muscles.[5] I have adapted them slightly for the purposes of this book. **Stage One (Childhood):** I walk down a street. There is a deep hole in the sidewalk. I fall in. I am lost. I feel helpless. I think it's my fault. It takes forever to find a way out. **Stage Two (Adulthood, Trial and Error):** I walk down an almost identical street with a different name. There is a deep hole in the sidewalk. I pretend I don't see it. I fall in again! I can't believe I am in the same place, yet this time I am questioning whether it is my fault or someone else's. It still takes a long time to get out because I am just beginning to master the tools to do so. **Stage Three *(Adult Empowerment is taking hold)*:** I walk down the same street. There is a deep hole in the sidewalk. I see it there. I still fall in because I've developed a long-standing habit of doing so, but I now have the insight to understand why I fell in – and the ability to get out quickly. *I realize that it isn't my fault or anyone else's fault. At the same time, I know and accept that it is my total responsibility to get out.* **Stage Four** *(Solidifying Empowerment)*: I walk down the same street. There is a deep hole in the sidewalk. I walk around it because I have released any and all patterns that drew me to holes in the first place. ***Stage Five*** *(Alignment with My Purpose for Living):* I walk down a new safe, well-lit street, full of grace and ease because I now know how to choose the street that feels right for me, as I AM a self-empowered, emotionally mature woman.

I'm going to tell you honestly and courageously about many of the holes I got lost in on my way toward self-empowerment and ease. I'm going to share with you how I added to my life challenges by digging even deeper holes and living under the crushing weight of suffocating dirt. My intention is that you may benefit from my experience and side-step these cavernous holes. My hope is that you will choose a shorter path to wellness, wholeness, and freedom. I took the long, arduous path because that was what I needed to do to awaken to my higher truths.

There is no right or wrong way to "seek," as long as you continue to seek *your* truth. It's perfectly reasonable to stay down in your hole for some time; to find comfort in that hole because it's what you recognize, and to even temporarily hold onto the belief that you deserve the hole. It's reasonable to be so far down in the hole that you no longer believe in the light of day. That's what happened to me. Nevertheless, I eventually learned that the hole was my teacher. The outer hole that swallowed me alive was a mirror for the hole inside of me that was crying for my attention. I am living proof that conscious awareness paves the way to surmounting life's holes.

It doesn't happen overnight and it does take effort – but it can be done. *The Universe (God) doesn't make mistakes!* As challenging as it was for me to accept, every single experience was placed in my life for a reason. Those reasons were not obvious or apparent when I was down at the bottom of my dark hole; however, everything eventually worked, and continues to work, for the greater good. That doesn't mean that it felt good or even tolerable when I was in the middle of it. In fact, I felt despair. I felt terminal sorrow. I believed that I couldn't recover. At points, I even lost my will to continue. I want to gently suggest that no matter where you are in your journey, it's never too late to stop digging a deeper hole or to make peace with the hole. It's never too late to assign a new perception to your struggle and to reassign those new meanings again and again.

I now recognize that absolutely everything that happened opened me up to a rich and fulfilling healing experience that allowed me to stretch myself further than I would have ever believed possible. I know with certainty that I would not be the woman I am today – one who is far wiser, more empowered, more authentically self-sufficient, and more courageous than the thirty-eight-year-old me who sat in Dr. L.'s office on that fateful day back in 1994, listening to the pronouncement of autism. I know now that I experienced a profound longing after I lost the child I had imagined I would raise to adulthood. I so yearned to have my idealized child back.

WHAT I KNOW NOW THAT I DIDN'T KNOW THEN: YEARNING IS A FORM OF STRUGGLE THAT DENIES US THE SUPER-ABUNDANCE OF THE UNIVERSE. IT IMBUES OUR ENERGY FIELD AND OUR ACTIONS WITH FEAR.

Thus I began an obsessive and exhaustive mission to recover my son from autism. I felt such emptiness and desperation because *my ego* believed that my bond with Mark was permanently shattered. I felt terrified of the future – my biggest fear being that my son would never know love; that he would never know the gut-level, primal, deep, abiding love that I felt for him; that he would move through his life never being able to freely receive love or give love to others. I felt devastated when I considered that he would be looked upon by others as "less than." My most catastrophic fear was that he would be expendable, languishing away in a facility for the forgotten.

I carried a deep abiding yearning for Mark to know me; to look into my eyes, to be able to say "Mom" as he threw his arms around my neck; to sit by my side while I read to him; to seek my comfort; to belly laugh in my presence; and to ask me why the stars burned brightly in the night sky. I yearned to know Mark – what he was thinking, what he was feeling, what he would be interested in, what he would be drawn to, who his intimate circle would be, and how he would interface with his world.

Yearning is an affirmation of lack and scarcity because the moment your mind desires something beyond what currently exists, your mind has taken you into separation from your full powers as a Divine creator being. Your mind has thrown you into a state of continual preoccupation with what you don't have – and unconsciously propelled the very things you so desperately wish to obtain further away. It's a way of "placing an order" in the Universe for what you *don't* want: more circumstances that place you in a state of yearning.

I now know that I held the power to quiet my mind; center my energy; trust in God's abiding love; and BE in faith that whatever the future held, Mark and I were Divinely protected. What I wish I had done then was give myself permission to actually feel my sorrow, instead of masking it with workaholism and perfectionism. What I wish I had done then was ground myself energetically before I charged in with my "take no prisoners" stance. I wish I had brought more LOVE into my interactions, rather than FEAR that oozed out of my every pore.

I remember consciously thinking that I would bulldoze over anyone who didn't share my vision for Mark. As a *warrior mother,*[6] my vision prescribed that within a few short years Mark would join the children who had "recovered," meaning they no longer consciously remembered the sting of autism and were now indistinguishable from their neurotypical peers. *I wish I had known that warring against anything in life, most especially ourselves, pushes our desires further and further from the finish line.*

If anyone dared to interfere with fulfilling this vision, they were disposable. I jumped in and expected my husband to be on board and to have unwavering faith in my ability to recover our son. I expected the paraprofessionals to see therapy with Mark as a "calling," rather than a job for which they were compensated a bit above minimum wage. I expected the mothers in Mark's playgroup to cease their marathon gossip circles so that they could support his social interactions. My ego was running amok with myriad ways for me *to control* what had happened while assuring myself that a positive outcome was within my grasp.

What I truly wish I had known was my capacity to move toward accepting my son, myself, and my husband, and each circumstance as it unfolded, while simultaneously holding a strong and unwavering vision for Mark to reach *his* fullest potential as I navigated the middle path. But that wasn't the way I approached my life. I wish I had known how to *BE* the patience I was seeking. I wish I had known that I could *choose* to *BE* at peace with myself, significant others, and the *lawful unfoldment* of life. I wish I had opened to my Source within, where all answers were available to me.

FEAR AND GUILT

"Adversity is the first path to truth."

Lord Byron

Before Mark reached twenty-six months, his father and I flew to Los Angeles to attend a three-day Applied Behavioral Analysis (ABA) conference featuring Dr. Ivar Lovaas, the "Godfather" of Discrete Trial Training (DTT) for children with autism. Discrete Trial Training is a method of teaching children with autism that takes complex skills and breaks them down into a step-by-step process of chained skills that builds one upon another – using "discrete trials" or short teaching segments.[7] In the beginning, a discrete trial learning segment typically lasted about three minutes, with Mark being rewarded for every single instance of a correct response or an approximation of a correct response.

Mark had also begun taking Dr. Bernard Rimland's protocol of high doses of B6 and magnesium. Dr. Rimland, who founded the Autism Research Institute in 1967, debunked the accepted theory that autism was caused by cold/uncaring, "refrigerator mothers" and replaced it with a neurobiological cause for the condition. I continued to drive Mark to his therapy appointments three times a week; spent countless hours on the phone securing resources; advertised for and interviewed paraprofessionals to implement a home therapy program; and devoted every possible waking moment to teaching Mark how to match and sort objects, scribble, attend to books with sounds, and any other skill sets for children with autism.

Mark was also attending a two-hour weekly playgroup for toddlers. During playgroup, he spent most of his time toe-walking[8] in a daze and disconnected from the parallel play that his peers engaged in. Mark was mute, with the exception of one vowel sound: *"Eee."* I was there by his side, physically coaxing him back to his peer group and investing "my all" to get him to focus on any interaction that could potentially be meaningful.

One memorable day, I decreed that before the day was out Mark would master waving. I brought his "preferred objects" and his lunch into my very large master bathroom and geared up for a session that would surely conclude with the achievement of a major milestone. I also had data from the behaviorist showing that Mark had an average attention span of four to eight seconds; however, that did not in any way deter me. I had learned during my career as a psychotherapist that a clinician always begins exactly where the client is. I was adamant that Mark would greet his dad with a wave.

I brought all of my passion, immense love, and resources into that bathroom. I was animated, fun, entertaining, and creative. With sweat pouring off my body, I continued to attempt one inspired strategy after the next. When the session finally came to a close *six hours later,* Mark was seemingly no closer to mastering the conventional social greeting and I was left with nothing but abject physical and mental exhaustion, combined with raw grief.

Every single day, my ego-mind drove me to thrust Mark into my world, to give him a life where he could receive love and, someday, return it.

During this same time period, a friendly acquaintance suggested that it would be a good idea for Mark to "just look at the clouds, as they rolled by."

As soon as she uttered her comment, rage surged through my body. My reaction was along the lines of, "He doesn't even know what a f★★king cloud is right now. I'll let him look at the clouds after he has mastered some basic prerequisites for life. Until that time, I don't have time to waste staring at clouds and wishing on stars. He's going to sit in his therapy chair until he knows how to process our world."

As an aside, this type of intensity and demeanor on my part did not lead to warm and fuzzy interactions with the few friends who were still reaching out to me!

Mark was languishing on the waiting list to begin forty hours of weekly ABA home-based therapy. Mindi, our consultant, was ambivalent about starting Mark, as she had never worked with a two-year-old. When I discovered that Mindi had begun work with a child who was assigned to the waiting list after Mark, I began a concerted campaign to change her mind. After a month of outreach went unanswered by her and the overseeing administrators, I secured her home address through a mutual contact and immediately fired off an impassioned plea on Mark's behalf. I knew it was a huge risk to send a letter to her home, and in this case, my ego-mind was rewarded. Upon receiving my letter, Mindi reconsidered her decision and training dates were immediately scheduled.

Mark belonged to the first wave of children diagnosed with autism on the cusp of the burgeoning expansion of the condition. Circumstances were quite different during the tail end of 1994 and the beginning of 1995. I did not yet own a personal computer, and hardly anyone had a cell phone or knew what a search engine was, let alone relied on them for information. It was also not yet standard for professionals to use e-mail as a form of communication. Instead, speaking with them was done the old-fashioned way – talking over the home landline while scribbling furiously on a notepad. Then, sometime during that first year of ABA, we purchased a home computer and I became a member of the Me-List, a private online support group for parents and professionals dedicated to ABA.

No amount of effort was enough, and would never be enough, until there was no perceptible difference between Mark and his typical peers. I refused to let him, and therefore myself, be held hostage to autism – waiting and waiting as he traced all the license plate letters and numbers on every single parked car in the lot, or stood, frozen, for interminable periods of time in front of a park sign rather than enjoying the benefits of play; walking along carpet lines, rather than joining his peers at an indoor play arena; leaning sideways from his stroller as he fixated on shadows, rather than participating in events at the pumpkin farm; running back and forth with his head cocked to the side, any time he experienced an unstructured moment; or having to leave a birthday party because he couldn't cope with the sensory overload. If I interfered with any of Mark's fixations, I could confidently predict that a tantrum would follow and I didn't want a lifelong job of managing meltdowns.

I read *Let Me Hear Your Voice: A Family's Triumph Over Autism* by Catherine Maurice[9] countless times. At the time, Maurice was one of the few voices of light amidst many of fatalism and doom. In today's world, *some* professionals view ABA as the gold standard of intervention for children with autism. Back in 1995, implementing ABA was still deemed highly controversial. It had been tainted by the use of aversive methods during the 1970s. Additionally, many professionals were convinced that ABA "turned children into robots." In fact, Mark's speech therapist held that exact view and did everything within her means to convince me to abandon the prospect of ABA.

The lower vibrational states of fear and toxic guilt had pervaded my mind, body, and soul. I was at war – with the pathways in Mark's brain, with his compromised immune system, with anyone or anything that stood in the way of progress, and primarily with myself. I couldn't submit to my own human frailty and vulnerability. I didn't have time for chitchat, trivialities, socialization, leisure pursuits, or watching TV. I wasn't available for more than going through the motions of any kind of intimacy with my husband. My defenses were becoming more and more brittle with "scheduled time off" for monthly crying bouts.

Mothers want the best for their children and will go to great lengths to ensure that they have appropriate care and resources. This stance is understandable and greatly magnified for special needs mothers. We're familiar with the notion that a mother's protective instincts emerge when her child is under threat. However, in my case, other unconscious influences were at work. Because I had not yet learned to actively nurture my own wounded inner children, who had experienced feeling rejected, unloved, and unwanted, these personas came rushing to the forefront and were in large measure "commandeering the ship" in their misguided attempts to safeguard Mark from experiencing my same level of wounding.

Andrew Solomon, in *Far from the Tree: Parents, Children and the Search for Identity*,[10] espoused a similar view. *"Perhaps the immutable error of parenthood is that we give our children what we wanted, whether they want it or not. We heal our wounds with the love we wish we'd received, but are blind to the wounds we inflict."* That's a pretty strong dose of truth that I would have avoided swallowing, even when accompanied by Mary Poppin's heaping spoonful of sugar. These same personas were replaying what I had experienced during childhood, by reacting to the trauma of 1994 and 1995 as though it was 1960-something and I was back in my small Dutch colonial house on a tree-lined street.

Thus, my present painful emotions were reminiscent of my buried, automatic, conditioned, paranoid-filled, beliefs and childlike reactions of the past. My ego-mind was transmitting an old story of survival on an endless feedback loop with the attendant good guys and bad guys. This old movie replaying in my energy field would have deleterious consequences down the road, but at the time, I was too blind to see it. Instead, my ego had me barrel ahead with ABA, while pushing my terror down into the deeper recesses of my mind.

With Mindi at the helm, Mark weathered the intensive, two-day, staff training. Irrespective of the fear that I felt at the start of Mark's home program, I was committed to single-handedly implementing Mark's twenty hours of weekly therapy myself, while supervising a team of paraprofessionals that were facilitating the other twenty hours weekly. As the leader of the team, I felt it was imperative that I erect an optimistic façade. Truth be told, the night before his program officially began my mind played out scenario after scenario as my stomach churned with acute nausea.

The clock had been running ever so slowly for eight long months as we waited for Mark to take his seat at the ABA table. Now that the day – and an inexperienced paraprofessional named Jeanine – had arrived, she reported for work with her own fear and trepidation. I believed that unless the team could wrench Mark back from the precipice called autism, my life with my life partner would not be salvaged and God only knew the level of suffering ahead for both of us. I didn't want to show any of these cracks in my armor.

I felt angry with all of the naysayers who had discouraged me from investing any hope into ABA. I was staunchly determined to prove every single one of them wrong. Once Mark's first ABA session began, my psyche focused on his every tantrum, his whimpers, and any positive giggle and interaction emitted from the therapy room. My psyche was in that room willing Mark to pay attention, to learn, and to benefit from this program. I was ultra-invested in every selected command, prompt, and reinforcement, as well as Mark's capacity to participate and give the correct responses. From my perspective, this method *had* to work, as there wasn't any other viable way forward.

Within two weeks of beginning intensive ABA, Mark mastered more skills than he had learned in the previous eight months. Before the start of ABA, he understood only twelve nouns receptively and spent close to all of his unstructured time engaged in a wide repertoire of self-stimulatory behaviors. Children with autism frequently engage in repetitive body movements, repetitive production of sounds, or repetitive movement of objects, termed self-stimulation, as a way of soothing themselves. In the first month, with the structured therapy and the specialized methods employed, his learning soared, including, surprisingly, mastering the universal wave hello. When Mindi returned for the monthly consultation, she was extremely impressed with Mark's progress and the implementation of the home program, and he was assigned four new skills to master during the month ahead.

At the same time we started ABA, an earthbound angel named Pat also walked through my door. Pat was an experienced Speech and Language Therapist who specialized in working with preschool children on the autism spectrum. Over the next three years Pat would pour her heart and soul into helping Mark acquire a foundation for language. Without her expertise, in conjunction with the specialized methods of ABA, he never would have gone on to speak his first three-word sentence by age two and a half. Every single time Mark hit a roadblock in learning, Pat found a novel way to help him grasp the skill via her special brand of therapy, and she typically did so during a single session.

Without Pat's incredible experience, creativity, and dedication, the team would have regularly put a number of teaching segments on hold. Pat was the master problem-solver, which buoyed my hopes for Mark's future; she also spent an inordinate amount of time listening to me vent about all of the stressors in my life. During this journey, Pat was one of the most important people that Mark and I crossed paths with and I will forever feel indebted to her for all that she did for us.

There isn't any definitive playbook that tells us how to mother and there certainly isn't one for parenting a special needs child. I was formulating my own customized cocktail, made up of equal parts control, perfectionism, grandiosity, martyrdom, and toxic guilt. I was starting to rely on this drink to get myself through each day, not seeing the poisonous results. I wouldn't encourage my worst enemy to drink such a ruinous drink. Nevertheless, at the time this cocktail was familiar – it took the edge off my inconsolable sorrow and it allowed me to put one foot in front of the other.

There are two kinds of guilt: appropriate, healthy guilt, and inappropriate, toxic guilt. Appropriate guilt helps us recognize when we have violated our own or someone else's boundaries because it leaves us with a feeling of remorse. It helps us live a life that is congruent with our values because we are in tune with our authentic selves. It allows us to course-correct at the soonest point in time by accepting our missteps, potentially making amends to the injured party, and letting go.

In contrast, inappropriate guilt is harmful because it is an irrational response to a circumstance that creates a burden of over-responsibility, over-care, over-love, and over-identification with someone else's pain, *at the expense of our own well-being.* This kind of inappropriate guilt is often learned during childhood at the unwitting hands of our caregivers who were rigid, controlling, disengaged, or a combination of all three. When we choose to internalize unhealthy guilt, we often marry ourselves to perfectionism, while chasing unreasonable, unrealistic, and unattainable standards. We believe we have to *earn* a place in our children's hearts through our deeds, obligations, and duties.

Not only does our ego dictate that we carry the burden of over-responsibility for our special needs children but it also hammers us continually with toxic guilt related to the myriad ways we are neglecting the needs of our neurotypical children or our spouses. Nothing we do is ever enough for anyone, beginning with our own impossible standards for ourselves. Needing to wield control, to judge our mothering acts through an unforgiving lens, to take up the mantle of making our children whole through *our will alone,* offers nothing more than a mirage of safety and an empty illusion. A future toll will be exacted. It is a house of playing cards that will inevitably topple down, with disastrous results.

WHAT I KNOW NOW THAT I DIDN'T KNOW THEN: UNIVERSAL INTELLIGENCE GOVERNS VIA THE LAW OF CREATION.

The Law of Creation is **Be, Do, Have.** It holds that it is in our best interests to become consciously aware of our vibrational states, because *we attract our life circumstances based on who we are*, not necessarily what we claim we want. I now understand that I was holding onto a lifetime of toxic influences that were stopping me from **Be**coming a match for what I wanted to experience. I had not yet awakened to a strong communication with my Higher Self so that I could gently be guided to **Do** the things that aligned with the truth of my Divine blueprint. Had I been able to identify with the *I AM* flame within – the part of myself that can never be lost, that exists eternally, the part that is also multi-dimensional[11] – I would have begun embodying the **Law of Be, Do, Have**. Via the process of **Being, followed** by inspired **Doing**, I would then have been able to come closer to **Having** what it was I envisioned, without resistance and struggle, as long as the outcome was part of my Divine plan.

As Wayne Dyer asserted, "Abundance does not need to be earned or acquired. Rather, it is a vibrational match that we have the opportunity to tune into." Spiritual abundance is love energy made manifest in the form of spiritual relationships, psychological wholeness, optimal health, a joyful existence, and a state of mind that exemplifies gratitude, focused presence, and a reverence for life. A prerequisite to creating abundance would have entailed transcending my unconscious limiting beliefs, releasing emotional blocks, and unlearning self-sabotaging habits.

Back in 1995, I was not yet a student of the Law of Be, Do, Have; in fact, it was still many, many years away. I hadn't been taught that abundance, like oxygen, is always present and available to us. Indeed, many of us live our lives chasing abundance, with a deep-seated core belief that we'll never truly find it, and in my case the struggle also limited my spiritual abundance. After Mark's autism diagnosis, this frenzied vibrational state was how I conducted my life. I raced fast and furiously ahead, trying to secure the outcomes that my ego-mind demanded: a child indistinguishable from his typical peers.

Within months of Mark's second birthday, I was operating under the grossly mistaken assumption that his life map, my map, and even parts of my husband's map were ultimately under my control and my responsibility to procure. I was also operating under the mistaken assumption that I could singlehandedly force a raging river to flow in my own predetermined direction, even if that direction was not necessarily in harmony with what God or Universal Love intended. I didn't offer myself the grace and time to feel and process my ongoing sorrow, my terror, my rage, my despair, or my despondency. Instead, I unconsciously rehashed my "feel sorry for me" storylines to anyone who had the patience to listen.

I now know that repeatedly retelling a story is not synonymous with feeling and releasing trapped and toxic energy stored in one's body. In fact, doing so is a recipe for inviting in more experiences that would magnify the same energy. On the surface, I was mastering the autism literature, making sound educational decisions for Mark and taking some very proactive steps to assist my family, but all of it was imbued with FEAR energy. All of it was imbued with TOXIC GUILT. My frenzy was coming from a place of "not being enough" and as my terror descended, it enticed me into believing that irrespective of any actions I took on Mark's behalf, he would be relegated to *my same fate* – never being good enough.

He would be viewed as damaged goods, barred from a meaningful entry into societal participation and potentially even an adult throw-away. My ego kept promising that if I did everything exactly as the literature and the trusted professionals dictated; brought my unyielding passion for healing Mark into every moment of my day; and left no stone unturned, Mark would be among the recovered children.

I subscribed to the philosophy espoused by Catherine Maurice's mother and quoted in *Let Me Hear Your Voice*. I'm paraphrasing here, but basically it meant praying as if everything depended on God and working as though everything depended upon me. If Mark's outcomes were dependent upon my willingness to work, Mark would eventually recover, because no one would push harder than I would. I couldn't entertain the notion that after all I had lived through fate would sentence my son to carrying the burdens my ego claimed were inherent with autism. I was living under the false assumption that *Do, Do, Do,* was the answer to *Have, Have, Have.*

My prayers were the prayers of a mother petitioning God from her foxhole, without much attendant faith that my prayers would be answered. My ego held me hostage to the idea that the locus of control and the outcomes were within my grasp. What folly! I had not yet learned what Eckhart Tolle espouses; "Suffering cracks open the shell of the ego and then comes a point where it has served its purpose. Suffering is necessary until it's unnecessary." There would be years of suffering ahead. The shell of my ego hadn't yet been pierced. It was still fully intact.

RUNG THREE

OVERWHELMING GRIEF AND UNBALANCED SELF-SACRIFICE

"Self-development is a higher duty than self-sacrifice."

Elizabeth Cady Stanton

I can't count the number of times that someone trotted out the self-care cliché about the mother on an airplane who placed her own oxygen mask before attending to her children. Later, I was given a drawing of an empty carafe that was perched over the lip of a glass devoid of water because the carafe had nothing left to pour. Different delivery method -- same message. Fast forward to the day when I was told the story of a child drowning in a raging current and joined by his mother who jumped off a bridge to save him. Her desperation had blinded her to the choice of staying on safe ground where she could have potentially mounted a response that saved his life without risking her own. Were all of these well-intentioned people and their metaphors misguided? From my vantage point, some salient aspects were missing from these equations.

Other people couldn't appreciate that "the airplane" had already gone down countless times through the years. My life was like the movie *Groundhog Day*. I awoke to rerun a version of prior events with the plane repeatedly going down again, no matter the order of masks. Furthermore, others were blind to the fact that my child had been drowning in the raging river for years and when I called for help from the bank, often the response had been nonexistent, negligible, or blaming. They were oblivious to the idea that my carafe was empty in part because the water supply was unavailable or would require a twenty-mile trek that I was now too depleted to even consider doing again.

Given the fact that our responsibilities for our children are forever, these easy prescriptions are far from ideal. Our relationships with our children are not characterized by one acute event that fosters a turning point and charts a course forward, for better or worse. Our tour of duty will not be up after a finite period. Our tour of duty continues until our incapacitation or our death and then it is either handed over to our child's sibling(s), another relative, or God forbid, a state social service system.

However, at the outset of my son's diagnosis, I could not begin to process the *long-term impact* of being a caregiver. In the beginning, I felt energized, carried a façade of optimism, and was ready to "slay the beast of autism." In my mind, this trek into the wilderness would last for approximately three years. I told myself that I could *do anything* for a three-year period.

I vividly recall several months later visiting a support group for parents of children with autism – and being shocked and disturbed by what I observed there. The members of this group were middle-aged mothers who were caring for developmentally disabled teens. There were no fathers in attendance. I immediately noticed that these mothers "had let themselves go." They were overweight, had grey, unkempt hair, were wearing outdated "stretch pants" and brought a frazzled energy into the meeting. They looked like they had just come from a day of cleaning the garage!

I recall one mother recounting that her son spent much of his time chewing the drapes in the living room, while she spent most of her time locked in a power struggle with him over this compulsion. The visiting speaker recommended an "environmental intervention": removal of the drapes from the windows and simultaneously offering him "chew toys" to provide the sensory input he was seeking. My racing and judgmental mind couldn't fathom how an experienced mother could miss such a simple solution. What had happened to these mothers? Had their thinking faculties left them too?

I made a solemn vow right then and there. Under no circumstances would I ever return to this so-called "support group"; nor (I added this part with a glance at my perfectly manicured fingertips) would I ever allow myself to end up like one of those women! What I offer my readers from my current vantage point is this: be very, very, careful of all pronouncements made in the aftermath of any significant trauma or loss by the ego. This is not the appropriate point in the story to own up to my neglected, cracked nails or my dreaded stretch pants, sweatpants, overalls, yoga pants, or any other similarities between myself and these women.

There was a similarly shocking and disturbing phone conversation, with the president of a local autism advocacy group that will forever be etched in my mind. After telling me that she was the sole caregiver for her young adult son, she revealed that a group of friends had recently *staged an intervention* at her home. They were so concerned for her welfare that they decided to "kidnap" her and take her away for four days so that she could regain her equilibrium, while two other friends managed her son. Apparently they had been offering to do so for years but she had steadfastly refused, insisting that she was the only person capable of appropriately meeting his needs. She believed that without her presence her son's welfare would be in jeopardy. She shared with me that she was still enraged with her friends for removing her from her home against her will. She did not find her time away beneficial and in fact it had created untold stress.

The whole time I kept asking for clarification because the entire scenario left me incredulous. How could this woman be in charge of a large advocacy group, come across as extremely articulate and educated, and at the same time be so incapable of acting in her own self-interests? At that time, I had no reference point to relate to her experience. I just knew that this particular conversation, in tandem with the support group meeting that happened during the same period, jarred and frightened me.

My way of coping with these experiences was to have my ego assert that none of these circumstances applied to me. I was different from these women, and I would never end up in their shoes – end of story. At the time, I couldn't begin to appreciate the *long-term impact* of caregiving that would so significantly erode my capacity to *make myself matter*, to adapt, to think flexibly, and to create novel solutions.

I couldn't comprehend how a mother would allow herself to fall into such a deep rut – a pattern of behavior that no longer served her own interests or her child's. Somewhere deep inside, I attempted to squelch these unsettled thoughts and feelings. My ego's storyline would not allow me to be humbled. I was entrenched in creating the perfect early intervention program for my son that would opt me out of ever having to entertain the dilemmas these mothers faced. My ego kept me unconscious to the fact that I had already begun navigating a very slippery slope.

By mastering the parable of the frog we can avoid the descent of the slippery slope, so I will turn to that parable now. Once upon a time, a mother frog happily rested upon her lily pad, sunning herself in her heavenly pond. All felt right in her world. Then without any forewarning, her life abruptly changed course. She was taken from that idyllic pond and thrown into an uncovered pot of water on a stove. The moment she left her natural surroundings, shock set in. She slammed into the sides of this hard, dark, unfamiliar and constricting pot.

Even while grieving for her baby frogs, she realized that she needed to adapt to her *new normal – life in the pot.* At first the temperature felt tolerable. It felt warm, certainly warmer than the life she had known in the pond – but it was passable. As she navigated life in the pot, she was unaware that the water temperature was ever so imperceptibly being raised. She adapted, as all mother frogs do. After all, she was still dreaming of the day when she would be reunited with her children. She kept adapting as the temperature increased, not realizing the harm that would eventually befall her. Life in that pot felt draining. Eventually, she encountered the moment when the water was boiling over. She questioned her capacity to save herself. Was it too late? It required every last ounce of courage and fortitude that she possessed to scale the heights of the pot. Yes, she was finally free, but at what cost to herself and her children? Life in the pot did not leave her unscathed.

This parable illustrates the often insidious and invisible forces that shape our lives with our children. It is so easy to fall asleep to the seductive allure of life in the pot. I barely escaped my pot alive. My entire saga is about how to avoid the oblivion of the pot! As a mother frog, remember, you have been given four legs for a reason! You hold the power in any moment to jump from your pot and re-enter the swim of life.

Because I was not yet a student of the frog's tale, I had already "ceased to notice" the way my ego was treating my body as a machine. This addictive pattern was a forerunner to the very alarming dynamics that I had observed in these middle-aged women. I was supervising a team of paraprofessionals, making the assigned flashcards into the wee hours, keeping the therapy room stocked with supplies, filling in whenever a home therapist canceled, driving back and forth to appointments, and facilitating half the therapy hours myself. I was also facilitating a weekly socialization group for Mark. On my "off hours," I tried to generalize Mark's skills into the home environment.[12]

In the midst of this all-encompassing routine, Mark was found to be severely food intolerant, necessitating a gluten/casein-free diet. I worked closely with Kelly, an expert nutritionist who recommended an eating plan and supplements that would support Mark's gut and immune system. Unfortunately, based on his test results, I had to wean him off of every single food in his repertoire and introduce foods that he found extremely noxious.

During the first year of ABA therapy, we flew to California to see one of the top DAN (Defeat Autism Now)[13] doctors to address Mark's long list of chronic immune, digestive and bowel symptoms. In 1994, DAN was a fledgling organization, with no more than fifteen dedicated, pioneering doctors. Mark had previously undergone the traumatic Brainstem Auditory Evoked Response Test, several audiological evaluations, a brain MRI and an EEG, not to mention a plethora of assessments from a host of health care professionals. Now he was required to undergo an outpatient blood draw with multiple needle sticks because this West Coast physician, Dr. G., insisted that he needed nineteen vials of blood! I listened, my heart breaking, to my two-year-old's wracking sobs, as he underwent this painful procedure, his playschool cassette player clutched in one hand.

After examining Mark and viewing these lab results, Dr. G. asserted that he was in the "high optimistic group" of children. His first order of business was to prescribe a medication to treat Mark's yeast overgrowth syndrome, a condition that had flourished after he had been plied with rounds and months of antibiotics for chronic ear infections. Unfortunately, the die-off reaction that Mark experienced was an unmitigated disaster. It was a Herxheimer reaction[14] of enormous proportions, occurring because toxins completely overran Mark's fragile body. Thirty-two days later, after an untold number of phone calls for medical advice, I called a halt to this treatment. Mark experienced rashes, chronic diarrhea, continual crying jags and, worst of all, an unchecked ravenous appetite. He spent almost every waking moment behaving like a wounded animal on a desperate prowl famished for any morsel of food that he could wolf down. When the vomiting set in, I felt there had to be a better way to proceed. It would take Mark close to eight months to return to his prior baseline of functioning.

"If you discontinue his treatment protocol," Dr. G. haughtily responded to my decision, "you will be leaving Mark in a *permanent brain shutdown* for the rest of his life."

Here was another instance of a professional tossing the guilt card while arrogantly attempting to coerce me into doing his bidding. I didn't need his condemnation because my ego was already in overdrive, blaming me for Mark's long-lasting Herxheimer response.

Because many of the biomedical interventions for children with autism were under the umbrella of holistic medicine, there were no set protocols for treating a child with chronic bowel inflammation, strange rashes, bouts of staggering where he appeared drunk and in a mental stupor, episodes of self-abuse that appeared to be driven by chronic pain, immune deficiency making him prone to chronic viral assaults and either extreme hypo-sensitivities or hyper-sensitivities to sensory input, to name just a few examples. Parents who have disposable income to put toward biomedical interventions are left with four choices: 1.) Participate in trial-and-error interventions that offer a level of reward yet also pose a certain level of risk; 2.) Go down the road of conventional psychotropic medications; 3.) Do a combination of options one and two; or 4.) Do nothing.

At that time, my failed attempt to eradicate Mark's yeast overgrowth and my frenetic actions toward making him indistinguishable from neurotypical children were unable to wholly anesthetize my overwhelming grief and sorrow. One of, if not the most, accurate depictions of what I was feeling can be found in Jane Taylor McDonnell's arresting memoir *News from the Border: A Mother's Memoir of Her Autistic Son.*

> [Mine] is a story of grief, yes, and of loss. But it is a different kind of grief from the one brought by the death of a child. For one thing the child isn't gone; he or she is *right there* flooding the backyard, screaming from the top of a tree, or pouring maple syrup all over the carpet and vacuuming it up… And the

terrible, extra burden that befalls parents of [disabled] children is that they have no time to grieve… They are caught up from the beginning in a perpetual crisis that leaves them no time to reflect, no time to even feel their feelings for themselves. They must always be rushing to attend to a child in distress. [15]

Dr. Pauline Boss, a marriage and family therapist and researcher examining complicated, unrelenting grief, coined the term "ambiguous loss," to capture exactly what Jane McDonnell so eloquently describes. Dr. Boss asserts that ambiguous loss is the most unimaginable kind because the long-range consequences remain unclear and indeterminate. According to Dr. Boss, ambiguous loss shatters the caregiver's beliefs in a fair, orderly, and manageable world while simultaneously eroding any confidence to control and master circumstances. In the case of autism, the child's body is still present but his or her developmental trajectory is drastically altered. Portia Iverson, co-founder of the former organization, Cure Autism Now wrote, "It's as if someone has stolen into the house during the night and left your child's bewildered body behind." As one of the parents subjected to this scenario, whom could I appeal to demand that my delightful, cherished, idealized child be returned?

I likened it to the famous nursery rhyme: "All the king's horses and all the king's men couldn't put Humpty (Dumpty) together again." But, damn it, my ego was in fix-it mode and was assuredly going to pull off the feat, irrespective of the failure of the king's knights. This passage from *Ambiguous Loss: Learning to Live With Unresolved Grief* (1999) best describes what I was feeling at the time:

Ambiguous loss is typically a long-term situation that traumatizes and immobilizes, not a single event that later has flashback effects. The outcomes of PTSD are similar, though not identical to outcomes of long-term ambiguous loss. Both can result in depression, anxiety, psychic numbing, distressing dreams, and guilt. But ambiguous loss is unique in that the trauma goes on and on in what families describe as a rollercoaster ride, during which they alternate between hope and hopelessness…Hopes are raised and dashed so many times that psychically people no longer react. Just as animals lay down in their cages and no longer tried to avoid the pain in early experiments of erratically places electric shocks, people experiencing trauma out of which they can't make sense feel helpless and no longer act.[16]

In 2007, Tricia Regan premiered a documentary titled *Autism: The Musical*. This documentary follows five families as their ASD children mount a live musical production. It also plaintively captures the parents' ongoing sorrow as they push to give their children a better quality of life. Years ago, while watching this film, I was struck by the poignancy of one of the father's words.

[There's] the crazed Mom of a disabled kid. That may be a category of person. You see an awful lot of single moms of autistic kids. There are a lot of reasons that men leave women. Women overlook that *they* may have been a factor, but it may not be the only factor. *They* may have been a factor for being so maniacal or self-involved with their kid. The world revolves around their getting that one last ounce of information to apply to their kid's environment or learning or whatever. [17]

It was like a punch to my gut when I reluctantly recognized myself in his characterization of mothers of children with autism. Via my observations of families in the aftermath of the diagnosis, I have concluded that a vicious cycle of polarization frequently occurs. In pattern one, the more a father denies the child's challenges, detaches, disassociates, and uses depersonalization to numb the emotional pain, the more the mother becomes obsessively consumed by a life purpose filled with achieving her child's benchmark goals and milestones. I don't know which dynamic comes first, the mother's obsessive pursuits or the father's increasing withdrawal, but soon this pattern of polarization takes on a life of its own, as the parents drift further and further apart, increasingly unable to share any kind of collaborative perspective and approach on behalf of their child.

In pattern two, the father's anger and frustration often erupt and spill over onto the child and his wife, who he perceives to be coddling and shielding the child. Many fathers believe that they are impotent when it comes to altering the family dynamics for the better, leaving them with chronic feelings of inadequacy and helplessness. Our culture teaches men to be in charge by providing leadership. The more a father feels that his leadership is being usurped, the more he potentially lashes out at the child and the more the mother's protective instincts are activated, resulting in an ever-widening gulf of separation between the couple.

The kind of raw sorrow that parents experience when one or more of their children have special needs is not something that they quickly manage to move on from. Time, in and of itself, never heals sorrow. Phase one of the mourning process is twofold: mourning the child who potentially *should* have stood in for the child who is here now and mourning for the one who is still here – the child who shows up day in and day out to navigate his way in what is often perceived as a very harsh world.

And just as there was no one to petition to return the fantasy child in whom I invested my glorified projections of the future, who could I petition to reclaim the parts of myself that were irretrievably lost? Who could I petition to reclaim the marriage that once was? Given all these tandem losses, whom could I turn to for help integrating and assigning new meaning in my life? As Alison Nappi wrote, "The truth is there are losses you never get over. They break you to pieces and you can never go back to the original shape you once were, and so you will grieve *your own death* with that of your beloved lost."[18]

WHAT I KNOW NOW THAT I DIDN'T KNOW THEN: FOLLOWING OUR DIVINE NATURE MEANS ALLOWING THE UNCOMFORTABLE ENERGIES TO PASS THROUGH, SO THAT WE MAY ACCESS OUR POINT OF BALANCE. I know now that a different kind of path exists – one that did not demand that I go into *continual self-sacrifice* in order to provide for my son. This path is not necessarily easy to master, because our egos potentially prompt us to go unconscious to our *own* needs while putting ourselves at risk for unknowingly sacrificing critical aspects of ourselves, including our health, well-being and, potentially, our longevity.

Do we continually need to awaken to the knowledge that a Universal anchor is located inside each of us, perpetually pointing us in the right spiritual direction? Yes. Do we continually need to remember that this guidance system is *forever present inside our children*? Yes. After all, they are Spiritual Beings, first and foremost, who are having human experiences, irrespective of their bodies and minds.

Wayne Dyer taught that a flower, if left alone to follow its Divine nature, develops easily from a seedling. It unfolds without struggle because it has been programmed with ALL that is required. What puts a flower at risk? Coaxing, over-tilling the dirt, over-watering, over-feeding, and over-pruning – in short, hovering and interfering with Divine Intelligence. Is ushering a special needs child through life as simplistic as tending to a flower? Absolutely not!

However, we can reclaim our power as guardians by not investing our energy into the extremes. I borrow my teaching metaphor from Michael A. Singer, author of *The Untethered Soul: The Journey Beyond Yourself.* [19] Think of a desk pendulum with steel balance balls. If one steel ball on the left side is activated at thirty degrees, the right side of the pendulum will activate a thirty-degree counter position. An opposing counterbalance of force to match the arc of the pendulum will always exist. The counterbalancing of opposing forces is a law of physics and Universal truth. Everything has its yin and yang energy.

The only way to create balance within our families is to first create balance from inside us.

Similar is the Taoist philosophy, which is based on the belief that life is full of seeming opposites, dualities, or paradoxes. The challenge for all of us is to find the place where the energies balance quietly in harmony while acknowledging that they are continually exposed to forces that are never fixed or static. *This harmonious "sweet spot" is a resting point in dynamic equilibrium.* In order to live a masterful life, we are required to adapt to the forces around us. Mastery of life sometimes means finding our way to the eye of the storm, as forces rage, while balancing doing and not doing for our children and for ourselves.

I invariably put myself at risk when I didn't rest in the sweet spot – when my ego had me resist doing so. Whenever we feed the extremes, life exacts a price, consistent with the *Law of Sowing and Reaping.* Like all universal laws, the effects are not intended to be personal, nor a penance – they just are. If I allowed my arc to activate to seventy percent, let's say through binging on food and drink, eventually nature would purge everything in order for me to regain my equilibrium. I would then need to release the toxicity throughout my alimentary canal. After rest and recuperation, my body would more than likely recover and come back into balance. The salient question is, what will I do next? Will I immediately listen to my body's wisdom and eat when I feel the sensation of hunger and nourish it through mindful eating, portion control, and nutrient-dense foods?

For most of us, learning this balance point isn't as simple as binging and purging one time. Even though purging is Spirit's way of bringing the body/mind/spirit back into balance, there are other forces that will likely shape our future behavior. What emotional, social and learned behaviors shape our eating habits, under what conditions, and when do they occur? Aspects from our history and our intergenerational conditioned programming will likely drive us to live out of balance and will do so without our conscious awareness or consent, unless and until we become highly observant of our patterns of self-sabotage.

This counterbalancing force asks us to develop conscious awareness and to let go and trust that all will unfold and be revealed as Source intends. The corollary is the following: as a mother I don't have to make it my life's mission to steer the river; I don't have to control it all; I don't have to have all the answers; I don't have to reshape the world so it treats my child with compassion; and I don't have to carry an unbearable weight on my shoulders. However, when I do feed the extremes with fear while overexerting my will, a state of emotional, social, cognitive, physical or spiritual deficit existed, exacting a future price.

Again, I didn't know any of this back then and thus often found myself experiencing the consequences of this deficit. I became immobilized. I didn't *choose* to rest, relax and recuperate. I collapsed for portions of days. I lived in survival mode and later could barely access the person I once knew myself to be. I felt increasingly numb and indifferent to my own pain and other people's pain. I eventually entered the "dark night of the soul." [20]

Letting go does not mean that I am coerced to give up, to acquiesce, and to do nothing to improve my circumstances. Letting go means that I potentially permit myself to see my child as already whole and perfect in spirit form while trusting that he is already imbued with his own inner guidance system and safeguarded by the following higher truth; *He came into physical form with a blueprint for his soul's path!* I believe that every single special needs child, at any given time, potentially has access to this guidance and their higher soul plan, irrespective of how they may present in their bodies. My child's connection to his higher knowing *does not in any way negate me* from having the opportunity to support, encourage, advocate, teach, hold space on his behalf while guiding him through life.

However, I will more easily discover alignment with the highest potential by adapting and allowing the uncomfortable extreme energies to pass through me in order to locate my middle balancing point. Like a tree that bends in the storm to preserve itself, yielding to the storm allows the energy to move through without doing permanent damage. I can choose to rigidly feed the insatiable energy of the extremes, acknowledging that a high price will always be exacted on the long path or I can relax, release, and let go as I find my way into the center of the storm where, paradoxically, calm, peace, and the short path grabs hold under my feet.

RUNG FOUR

HOPELESSNESS AND FEELING TRAPPED

"Above all, be the heroine of your life, not the victim."

Nora Ephron

Through the examination of roles or archetypes played out on the earth plane, we are able to gain insights into our behavioral patterns, beliefs, feelings, and the motivations underpinning our psyches. Each archetype possesses a pattern of strength and aspects that we would rather avoid, deny or disavow – termed our "shadow leanings. Carl Gustav Jung, the founder of analytical psychology, added to Plato's original work on archetypes by proposing twelve fundamental patterns, characterizing overarching themes of the human experience. No matter whose framework for personalities typing you lean toward, your objective is to integrate and bring both your assets and shadow leanings into unification.

During my "dark night of the soul" I found myself entrenched in identification with the victim's archetype. I suspect that as special needs mothers, we do not readily play out the Jester's curriculum! As I have outlined in Rung One, this victim identification began during my early childhood wounding and continued to be an enveloping contaminant that pervaded my life. My mind reinforced the idea that I was trapped in this circumstance, unable to turn back time to Mark's first year of life – a time seemingly filled with awe and wondrous possibilities. Victimhood represents disempowerment, attachment to suffering, and a sentence of despair. We cannot choose *all* of our life circumstances but we can decide whether to foster or forego our own suffering. As holocaust survivor Viktor E. Frankl wrote, "Everything can be taken from a man but one thing: the last of human freedoms – to choose one's attitude in any given set of circumstances, to choose one's own way."

I ascribed to that philosophy on an intellectual level; however, after undergoing so many losses and traumatic events compressed into such a short window of time my ego dragged me into playing out a victim/martyr role. I found myself looking to others to enable my wallowing. I was enmeshed in the egoic block of self-pity, playing out accompanying storylines that reinforced this identification. During the time that I was doing so, I wasn't conscious of my need to gain support and attention via my storylines.

For four long years, while buffering back and forth between states of bravado, self-pity and everything in between, I was treading water amidst the choppy waves and had managed to keep myself afloat... one single event pulled me into the undertow. This event removed any traces of bravado and instead left me entrenched in the belief that my recovery was insurmountable and sealed my identity as a victim for years to come.

However, before that event could unfold and before I encountered my breaking point, there was much emotional battering to come. My ego still drove me to ward off some level of victimhood by permanently immersing myself in workhorse, fix-it mode. After the treatment with the DAN physician failed, I actively searched for another physician who could successfully treat Mark's chronic bowel disorder and chronic immune deficiency. After returning from the West Coast, we were told that Mark, now aged three had severe hypothyroidism. Three endocrinologists at a major Chicago Children's Hospital were highly suspicious of this diagnosis; however, a simple blood test unequivocally proved the point. Mark was immediately prescribed a replacement hormone that precipitated extreme agitation and self-abusive behaviors. For the first time ever, Mark engaged in face-slapping and hand-biting. It wasn't until seven months later, after being weaned down to one-twelfth of the originally prescribed dose, that his behavior stabilized.

Also at age three, Mark was put through aversive tests, ordered by Dr. D., a local physician. Dr. D.'s willingness to prescribe a milder medication to treat Mark's yeast overgrowth had led me, albeit reluctantly, to agree to this testing. However, even the milder medication proved to be way too aggressive for Mark's fragile body, sending him into a lengthy time span of cognitive and behavioral regression. After the test results came back, I returned to this physician who cavalierly informed me that my son had been *poisoned* and would likely go on to develop terminal cancer.

With absolute conviction he stated, "You need to move out of your home immediately. It is life-threatening for Mark to remain there. I will be launching a full environmental investigation into the nature of Mark's poisoning, and I have already consulted with another physician about it. Has Mark been drinking well water?"

I exclaimed, "No! We drink city water and we live in a brand-new, state-of-the-art home in an upscale suburb."

"Well, during my thirty years of practice I have never seen such elevated levels of metal toxicity in a child, and the only other child with this level of poisoning was poisoned by a well."

Hearing this, I became so overwhelmed and distraught that I felt incapable of adequately functioning. Worse yet, my spouse was in Florida for business, and I was grateful for a friend who came to stay the night with me. I cried for most of it while waves of nausea overtook my body. It took three days of recovery for me to decide to initiate contact with Mark's nationally prominent consulting nutritionist, Kelly.

She reviewed Mark's heavy metal findings and informed me that these highly elevated numbers were typical of almost every child with autism on her caseload! Based upon these labs, she added, Mark was not at risk to develop a terminal illness, and there were ways to support Mark's detoxification pathways. Needless to say, my relationship with Dr. D. came to an abrupt halt.

Although I am sharing my own unique set of challenges, I want to convey that most of us ushering these children through life learn to lurch from crisis to crisis. While doing so, it is exceedingly difficult to discern which crises require a mounted response and which ones are in fact manufactured dramas. I no longer walked around in an invisible bubble believing I led a charmed life that insulated me from catastrophic events. Rather, I believed that I had been drafted into the card-carrying army of the walking wounded.

In fact, over time, my mind began to sit in wait for other enemies and dangerous threats to appear. At the same time, I became totally immune to the repercussions of living in constant combat mode. I believed that I was forced to adapt to doing so. I was simultaneously blinded to the impact of the chronic stress on my walnut-sized adrenals.[21] My ego no longer allowed me to recognize the toll that was being exacted on my child, the entire family and, most importantly, myself.

During Mark's exhaustive medical odyssey, we also visited an out-of-state physician who treated children dually diagnosed with autism and immune suppression. Dr. H. was a proponent of the treatment regimen of Dr. Sudhir Gupta, a well-regarded immunologist. Dr. Gupta, via a "happy accident," had recently discovered that immune-compromised children on the autism spectrum could benefit from pre-scribed IVIG (IV Gamma Globulin). A small number of physicians in the country subscribed to his protocol by ordering the monthly six-hour Gamma Globulin infusions for children with autism.

My hope in pursuing this course of treatment would soon turn to confusion and frustration. Months passed, with Dr. H. refusing to schedule the procedure as promised. Whenever I followed up to learn the reason for the delay, no one from his office bothered to tell me that he had reversed his decision and was no longer willing to treat Mark. Demoralization set in as I realized it was time to resume the exhaustive search for a new physician.

Finally, when Mark was close to four and a half years old, we found ourselves at Cincinnati Children's Hospital with a rheumatologist experienced in treating children on the spectrum with IVIG. It was a five-hour commute by car to reach his location. Nevertheless, once Dr. L. completed his assessment and was able to convince our insurance company to pay for the exorbitantly expensive infusions, Mark began his series of treatments.

Rather than allowing gratitude to wash through me, I instead felt terrified of the potential side effects that came along with IVIG. I recall hyperventilating and having my first-ever panic attack in the car on the way to Mark's first procedure. Once the dreaded IV was inserted, things seemed to go relatively smoothly. Mark spent his time in bed interacting with a host of new toys, while watching preferred videos. A major impetus for treating Mark with IVIG was the hope that he would eventually be able to attend school and participate in community outings without succumbing to every virus present in the environment. I quote from a letter that I sent Dr. L. at the beginning of our relationship.

Mark has been ill much of the time since late January of 1997. His sleep, sensory system and capacity to learn are significantly compromised with these viruses. The bottom line is that when my son leaves the house, he usually gets sick and stays sick for weeks. Unfortunately, these stressors on his immune system have impeded his therapy progress. During his first illness this winter he was even unable to recognize his own mother the day prior to running a fever and showing signs of intestinal illness and vomiting. He also lost a set of concepts that we had been working on for five months. This circumstance has been repeated on numerous occasions following illness. He also experiences depression after being ill.

That last sentence was a foreboding of what was ahead. As a three- and four-year-old child, Mark coped with viral assaults followed by a number of month-long depressive episodes. He would become lethargic, lose interest in previously enjoyed activities and exhibit extreme irritability in conjunction with long crying jags.

After undergoing his first IV infusion, Mark immediately displayed some atypical behaviors. For portions of a day, his gait was staggered, as he appeared disoriented and drunk, a probable sign of a yeast die-off reaction. He also fell asleep during the course of several days, which never occurred unless he fell ill with a high fever. On a positive note, Mark's therapy response rate and eye contact greatly improved. Within a week of his first infusion, he was no longer as dazed and spaced out as he had been prior to the treatment. Further, he began to engage in spontaneous playful imitations of typical household routines. His language acquisition rate and socialization skills also improved. He spent less time felled by virus after virus.

However, a new side effect was about to rear its ugly head. Prior to the infusions, he had consistently slept from 9:30 p.m. to 6:30 a.m. and, unless ill, did not have night awakenings. But that circumstance was about to change! After the second monthly infusion, Mark slept on average three hours nightly. Following a terrible reaction to melatonin used to improve this sleep disturbance, Mark's disrupted sleep patterns continued unabated. During the night hours, Mark's mind raced. He ran back and forth for hours on end, body slamming into the crib and spouting rapid-fire speech.

I called the treating physician and shared that Mark's behavior appeared to be "manic." I distinctly recall using that word, without truly appreciating the implications or the gravity of my statement.

He responded, "These are central nervous system effects from the IVIG." Upon further exploration on my part, he added, "These effects aren't typical of the other nineteen children we have previously treated."

The doctor, while kind, had no solutions to offer, though he did posit that the sleeplessness and agitation might end when the series of IVIG infusions concluded. Due to the overwhelmingly positive effects on Mark's autism, I was willing to assume that risk.

Facilitating Mark's therapy; keeping the program afloat; the inordinate stress associated with toilet training; planning and shopping for the monthly commute to the hospital; packing for all of Mark's special needs; and being confined to a hotel for two nights – all in addition to undergoing the infusions themselves – was very, very, draining.

My husband and I were depleted from the long-term ongoing stress and the chronic lack of sleep, and all of these stressors were accelerating the demise of our marriage. Occasionally we went through the motions of putting a band-aide on our hemorrhaging relationship; however, the reality was that it was beyond repair.

My continual criticisms aimed at my life partner, my need for control, my obsessive and exhaustive chase to recover Mark from autism and my overt verbal escalations felled a twenty-five-year relationship. My ego was trapped in blame and holding recriminations, as Mark's father exited stage left. At the time, I was in large measure blinded to the weight of the repercussions of our split upon Mark. Later, my ego mercilessly attacked me for the suffering that I believed I had inflicted upon our innocent child.

WHAT I KNOW NOW THAT I DIDN'T KNOW THEN: WE HAVE ALL BEEN GIVEN THE POWER TO CHOOSE EITHER OUR MIND'S HISTORICAL CONDITIONING OR MASTERY OVER OUR EGOS. According to Eckhart Tolle, "suffering does not diminish when we make it unconscious." In fact, our suffering compounds as we continue to suppress it. We can either create our lives by *default,* via an unconscious involuntary replication of old patterns that we internalized during our fractured childhoods, *or* we can awaken to the opportunity to release the programming that no longer serves us so that we may create our experiences consciously by *design.* Because I was not yet a student of ego mastery, mine held me in the grip of a severely dysfunctional mind-identified state of victimhood – telling me that I was forever caught in a permanent disempowerment trap. Our unconscious, involuntary default replications have been passed down to us trans-generationally, via core patterns of abandonment, scapegoating, the illusion of control, and enmeshed codependent boundaries. Victim identification consistently creates a mirage filled with restrictions, pain, and loss.

My downward spiral was tied to my Unconscious Victim Identification that pushed me to either suppress my emotional pain or express it in less-than-healthy ways. My ego-based survival identity rationalized more and more of my harmful acts toward my husband and myself. When had I crossed that invisible line in my marriage where the cumulative effects of my harmful acts were beyond repair? The more harmful verbal outbursts my ego pushed me to commit toward my spouse, the more justifications my mind created to support this unhealthy legacy, while ignoring the emotional first-aid that would have been a balm to my soul. The more I avoided responsibility for my own *Self-betrayals,* the more I sabotaged having my longstanding partner's loyalty and compassion.

I want to emphasize the notion of *Self-betrayal.* Anytime our egos turn us into emotional *reactors* rather than *responders,* we have disempowered ourselves by actively participating in a form of Self-betrayal that exacts a karmic debt in our outer relationships. Thus, I allowed myself to go out of loving communication with the very person I valued the most – my husband. How could I possibly *BE* a receiver of emotional support from my partner when my ego blinded me to **GIV-ING MYSELF** the steady measure of emotional support I so deserved? Many of my primary physical and emotional needs were still as invisible to me as they had been to my caregivers in childhood. Oh, what a "tangled web [the ego] weaves" as "we deceive" ourselves by masking our higher truths.[22]

I now know the myriad ways the ego entices us with rational lies. It will use any means necessary to help us to survive, even if the thoughts are immature, defensive, and paranoid. Eckhart Tolle teaches that mind-identification illness is "a form of socially acceptable insanity." My ego was having me tap dance pretty quickly to keep up with suppressing my emotional pain, all the while haranguing me with dire warnings that I was on the brink of losing everything I had previously built. Listening to the ego's grim proclamations, while taking on that fear-based energy, seals a self-fulfilling prophecy in place.

In 1998, I was the mother of a chronically ill child who lived with a compromised digestive system, who had manic bursts of energy that prevented him from sleeping more than three hours nightly and who was assigned a team of daytime paraprofessionals that I supervised. I had left my career behind, been cut off from most of my long-term friends, and was now on the precipice of losing my soul mate, who held me in sway longer than I was under the wing of my parents' influence. Without my husband's partnership, I would find myself alone to carry the bulk of the responsibility and, simultaneously, be forced to leave our dream home behind. This meant leaving Mark's dream team behind as well, and starting over in a new suburb where I knew no one. I felt completely adrift.

I now know that many of us find our light in the clearing after walking through the dark forest. Many of us need to face that terrifying forest in order to receive the gifts of the illuminated clearing, as they are both intertwined. But the forest isn't merely an experience outside of us; rather, the forest is born in our minds. It is the place where all of our so-called fractured, ugly parts reside and thus it takes emotional courage to look within and to fully face all that is lurking there.

Harnessing our light is a process that often begins by standing naked in the darkness, testing ourselves there, seeing what it is we are being called to heal and overcome, and eventually stepping into our light-filled clearings. This magical synthesis is our daily process of life.

DEPRESSION AND UNWORTHINESS

"You have to keep breaking your heart until it opens."

Rumi

On Memorial Day weekend of 1998, my life partner removed his designated furniture from our home. The life that I had known would never be the same. During April and May, Mark felt despondent and engaged in long crying jags both at school and at home. His obsessive-compulsive behaviors were more prominent. Furthermore, he had become increasingly resistant to participating in ABA therapy. During the marital separation, my ego minimized the impact for Mark, but I soon realized that I was deluding myself. My attempt to cushion Mark's pain did not prevent him from sobbing inconsolably when he felt his father's absence during bath time.

Nor did it prevent Mark from sobbing inconsolably at nighttime and wanting to share my bed. Although Mark's father now spent time in the family home at set times, by the fall's approach, Mark's behaviors were unmanageable during extracurricular activities.

I also greatly minimized the impact of my own lower vibrational emotional state on Mark, who absorbed it like a sponge. Further, there was no precedent for processing these changes with a child who had limited abstract language and emotional regulation. At the time, sitting Mark down to have the "divorce talk" would have been ludicrous. Mark rarely sat still and was quite confused about the use of pronouns conversationally, as well as the discrimination of who, what, where, when, and why questions in conversation.

As a consequence of Mark's increasing resistance to therapy, I sent twelve hours of videotape to Scott, the out-of-state ABA supervisor. After his programmatic review, he asserted that no adjustments were necessary. I could either continue with the ABA program as it currently existed or I could instead enroll Mark in special education classes. After much soul-searching, I decided to withdraw Mark from ABA and create my own preschool curriculum. During the summer, Mark continued to attend inclusion preschool five mornings a week. He also participated in semi-structured therapy for three hours each weekday, as well as twelve hours on the weekends.

Pat, Mark's speech and language therapist, conducted twice-weekly sessions that were more "natural" in bent. He continued to attend weekly occupational therapy appointments. Frequent community outings and his socialization group were also part of his therapy schedule. It took an inordinate amount of time to outline over twenty hours a week of teaching activities. I continued to facilitate many of those hours myself. At my direction, the team allowed Mark to initiate more of his own desires. Mark was no longer required to sit in a therapy chair. His therapy was still loosely outlined, but much more fluid and free-flowing. Mark seemed to benefit from the autonomy.

In the midst of all this change, realtors were bringing prospective buyers in and out of the home. I relocated the therapy program to the finished basement and, during these showings, scrambled to rectify any neglected area of the house and whisked Mark away to a temporary landing site. Any moment not spent on his therapy was taken up preparing for a move to a home half the size of my current residence.

But, most significant of all, during the last year of my marriage my body was felled by an Epstein-Barr-like virus. I spent the better part of a month in bed, and even after I resumed my schedule I never embodied optimal stamina and vitality again. In fact, my muscles were considerably weakened. I was at the mercy of what I termed "fatigue attacks," typically lasting six hours daily, one day per week. These attacks came on without forewarning and abruptly stopped me from functioning. I vividly recall collapsing in the upstairs hallway for hours, too weak and exhausted to move. Because I had carried the bulk of the responsibilities related to my son, these attacks posed quite the obstacle!

Temporary insanity ensued as my ego adapted by moving a cot into the secluded office, inserting earplugs, and sleeping during some of Mark's daytime therapy shifts. Did I consider making radical changes to my schedule or to my lifestyle? No. Did I consider seeing a physician for an evaluation? No. Did I believe that this circumstance was temporary and that I would eventually recover? Yes. Was my mind creating a state of massive denial? Yes.

The Universe was upping my pain quotient, but I barreled ahead as though this circumstance was a temporary setback that would magically resolve itself. Part of the reason I did so came from two decades of compensating for severe physical pain bouts associated with endometriosis. Other than surgery interruptions, I had developed a pattern of compensating for continual pain and temporary days of incapacitation while functioning essentially as though my life was unchanged. My ego decided that my single-minded focus on recovering Mark from autism would not be derailed by an upcoming divorce or the loss of my health!

My pervasive denial, coupled with my stubborn insistence that nothing interfere with Mark's treatment, precipitated a long, arduous, and exceedingly painful road back to *partially* recovering my health. Had

I implemented some drastic changes in my self-care routines, coupled with getting aggressive holistic intervention for my fatigue and malaise, my future global incapacitation *might* have been avoided. Instead, my ego blinded me to the reality at hand and even now it wants to judge me for my unwise, foolish, and self-destructive choices. I still want to shout at my forty-two-year-old self, "**WAKE UP BEFORE IT'S TOO LATE!**"

Maybe a couple of harsh face slaps might have been in order, with the admonition, "Snap out of it!" Or maybe if someone had doused me with a tub of ice-cold water, I might have roused myself from my delusional stupor. No, it would have probably taken the "ghost of the future" to come down and show me detailed scenes of my upcoming years spent listless in bed.

This all-knowing presence would have needed to shout at me, "Look at these scenes in front of you. LISTEN CAREFULLY: you're consigning your son to live with an incapacitated mother for the remainder of his childhood. Is that circumstance in *his* best interests? Is that circumstance in *your* best interests?"

Even better, maybe my guardian angel could have visited, wrapped her lofty wings around me and whispered in her angelic voice; "It's time for you to learn to love yourself unconditionally. I know why you have struggled to do so. Remember, you are not required to *earn* anyone's love or allegiance. It's time for *you to shower yourself* with unlimited and bountiful love."

Why didn't I see the truth? The gaping blind spots left over from childhood were corrupting my choices. For six long years, while orchestrating Mark's therapy program, my self-image was totally dependent upon the addictive actions of a devoted mother. Following Mark's autism diagnosis, the most formidable influence driving my behavior was the wound of childhood emotional abandonment and my fixation on Mark not feeling the same level of abandonment. However, I couldn't appreciate the ways that I was still abandoning *my own* physical, emotional, intellectual, and spiritual needs while chasing this illusionary attachment to how Mark's life *should* unfold.

In the Hindu tradition, seven spinning energy centers or chakras are part of the etheric energy body, providing us with an energetic map to reach our highest potential. When a chakra is blocked, we experience a host of physical, mental and spiritual challenges. Due to the blockage in my heart chakra, I wasn't able to freely give myself the self-compassion, self-nurturing, radical self-care, self-forgiveness, and self-love that I so deserved? Instead, my ego wielded a battering rod. I treated myself as though I was a high-level performance machine that was worthy only so long as it performed at its peak. Lying down on the job wasn't acceptable. And yet the reality was that I *was* beginning to lie down on the job. I was beginning to experience physical incapacitation. In Rung One, I disclosed that I would courageously share the holes that I stepped in on my way toward Self-discovery. At the time of my marital separation, I stepped into a massive hole that hadn't yet become a crater.

As I stood at that crucial crossroads, my future actions could have made all the difference. Nevertheless, my ego wouldn't allow me to choose a healthy path of self-love. Shakti Gawain admonishes us; "Every time you don't follow your inner guidance, you [will] feel a loss of energy, loss of power, a sense of spiritual deadness." Cheryl Richardson admonishes us, "Life sends us messages all the time and when we don't hear the message, we get a lesson. When we don't hear the lesson, we then get a problem. And if we don't hear the problem, we get a full-blown crisis." The Universe sent numerous warning messages that my ego chose to ignore. I had become habituated to lurching from crisis to crisis, while my needs remained insignificant.

I now understand a great deal more about why I fell into this crater of my own making. From 1995 to 1997, the Kaiser Permanente Health Maintenance Organization and the CDC conducted a study with more than 17,000 white, college-educated, and employed participants. The study found an irrefutable association between childhood trauma or Adverse Childhood Experiences (ACES) and the future probability of individuals engaging in risky behaviors and/or substance abuse and/or those same individuals experiencing *chronic depression, chronic disease,* and *even premature death.*[23] The identified ACES in the study were physical abuse, sexual abuse, emotional abuse, physical neglect, intimate partner violence, mothers treated violently, alcohol and substance abuse in the household, parental separation or divorce, and the incarceration of a household member. Two-thirds of the participants had experienced at least one ACE. With a score of 4 or more, the likelihood of chronic disease, depression, and suicide rose exponentially.

Does this mean that our fate is sealed if we have lived through multiple kinds of developmental trauma? I don't believe so. But it does mean that we need to be especially cognizant of the potential ways in which our unconscious programming might potentially hijack our capacity to act in ways that support our highest good. My story is a cautionary tale of living unconsciously by default. Don't wait. Ask for help. Keep asking for help. Find the coaches, healers and practitioners who fit your needs. Find the kind of help that *feels* right for you. Open your arms to receive the help that is offered. *Put yourself at the top of your own priority list and know that when you do so, you are honoring your child with the deepest reverence imaginable.*

Then and only then, might you be able to avoid some of the following circumstances. By December of 1998, I had uprooted Mark to a new community; hired a team of four paraprofessionals who required ongoing training; enrolled Mark in a new preschool; and was in the midst of navigating a divorce. Mark's behaviors escalated to the point that I regularly restrained him, something I had never had to do prior to the marital separation.

When I visited the new preschool to observe through a two-way mirror, I felt shocked and saddened to see the level of deterioration in Mark's functioning. The school didn't appreciate the difference in Mark's behavior as compared to most of the prior school year. Mark was withdrawn, sullen, and non–compliant and broke down in tears for no observable reason. My ego wouldn't allow me to acknowledge the following factors: the divorce, the move, the loss of his former staff members, the loss of his preschool and the seemingly healthy mother he had come to depend on might have been part of the equation!

As the winter wore on, Mark demanded that I place his portable TV in the darkened bathroom so that he could sit alone for hours watching his preferred programs. He slept three to four hours nightly and was almost impossible to arouse in the morning. All of my attempts to have Mark evaluated for a sleep disorder had been summarily rejected. Every facility told me that the root of the problem was obvious... autism. Because Mark had slept peacefully prior to the administration of the IVIG, their answer infuriated me. Yet, there was nothing I could do to force their hands.

Mark also spent daytime hours immobilized on the living room carpet – a pattern that shocked and disturbed me as he had been a child with the energy of ten children, endlessly running, jumping, spinning. One of his favorite activities had been springing onto the sofa and flipping upside down into a headstand using the back of the sofa for support. Now he spent hours frozen on the floor, mute and motionless. When I spoke to the school social worker about my concerns, she could not appreciate the gravity of what I was sharing.

She responded, "Why *can't* you just give Mark some downtime when he comes home from school? He doesn't need to be pushed all of the time."

Once again, I heard an implication that my relentless actions were in part responsible for Mark's shutdown. I felt very alone with the weight of my fears.

In February, I sought an evaluation through a professional trained in Dr. Stanley Greenspan's Developmental, Individual Differences, Relationship-Based Model (DIR), commonly referred to as Floortime. The evaluation showed that Mark was functioning at Dr. Greenspan's fourth stage of development, with emotional constrictions within earlier stages. A neurotypical child who was developmentally on track and with a comparable chronological age would have already mastered the model's stage six. At that time, there were many barriers to finding the right Greenspan specialist for Mark.

In April, I was immediately brought up short when the third-in-line Greenspan practitioner, Michelle, asserted that Mark's clinic hours be summarily increased to five days a week. Implementing that recommendation would have required a large financial commitment and a substantial time investment that included commuting to her home office. There was a vast difference between paying Michelle's fees out-of-pocket and implementing the therapy myself at no cost. It might be hard to imagine now, but back in the 1990s, autism-related services were *excluded* from health insurance policies!

During this particular bi-weekly DIR therapy appointment, I sat on the floor with my back against the wall undergoing the aftereffects of the flu. Without my active participation, it suddenly dawned on Michelle that Mark was not functioning anywhere near the level she had originally conceived. Having worked with Mark for so many years, I intuitively knew how to support him in sessions, which inadvertently overinflated his presentation of cognitive, motor, and problem-solving skills.

This recommendation for intensive therapy hours came on the heels of the Columbine high school massacre. I felt astounded and appalled to overhear Michelle assert that without Mark's participation in this intensive intervention under *her* supervision, he could potentially grow up to commit a similarly heinous act. As I sat against the wall, I knew with complete certainty that my son was never going to share a profile with a murderer. In this instance, she had flung the entire fifty-two-deck of guilt cards at my feet! Prior to that event, I had liked, trusted, and respected her. Yet, suddenly out of nowhere, Michelle wielded the sledgehammer of guilt.

I felt sick at heart, realizing that I had to immediately sever ties with her. With the gift of hindsight, I now believe she was a well-intentioned, adept practitioner. However, her ill-advised, fear-driven comments were completely unacceptable and ungrounded, resulting in a complete rupture of the confidence that I had placed in her.

Not only was I faced with locating a new Greenspan consultant pronto but I also had to continually screen approximately one hundred paraprofessional candidates in order to hire one Floortime therapist with potential. It then took approximately three months of concentrated training on my part for that individual to facilitate Mark's therapy independently. Although I had spent years implementing play therapy with children, the Greenspan model was different in a number of respects. It took a great deal of creativity, enthusiasm, and emotional attunement to the child, as well as a sophisticated understanding of the theoretical model's underpinnings, to make a highly competent Floortime specialist.

With a sense of urgency, I called the first Floortime consultant back and literally begged her to assume responsibility for Mark's case. Because I lived sixty miles from her location, she was understandably reluctant to do so. In order for the team to receive more support and training, I agreed to commute there one Saturday per month, which, shortly thereafter, increased to twice monthly so Mark could receive occupational therapy focused on his significant motor planning deficits. Mark was enrolled at both clinics until he aged out at eight years old.

In mid-June of 1999, approximately six months after moving to my new home and four months after enrolling Mark in Floortime, my divorce was finally granted! It had been mutually decided that the financial agreement would be revisited again and renegotiated eighteen months later. As part of my emotional recovery process, I had begun seeing a psychotherapist, Cynthia, to support me in restructuring my life. Although my physical state was still compromised, Cynthia believed that I had recently shifted into feeling more optimistic, resilient, and confident about my ability to manage my future circumstances. All of that hope, optimism, and resiliency was decimated with one glancing blow. A mere two weeks after the ink was dry on my divorce papers, my body was swept into the freezing oceanic riptide that I alluded to earlier.

My former spouse stood in my kitchen and informed me that he planned to remarry – the wedding scheduled in approximately four months! Blindsided, I was not in any way emotionally prepared to accept this remarriage so soon after the divorce had been finalized. My life was beginning to resemble an age-old cliché, as I played the role of bitter ex-wife. My Spirit shattered into what felt like irretrievably lost pieces and my body, no longer afloat, washed bruised, and beaten to the shoreline.

WHAT I KNOW NOW THAT I DIDN'T KNOW THEN: EVERY SINGLE EXPERIENCE, NO MATTER HOW PAINFUL, HAS BEEN PERFECTLY DESIGNED FOR THE EVOLUTION OF OUR SOULS. From the spiritual perspective, there are no "mistakes" in an ever-expanding and loving Universe. The Universe is forever working *through us* in order to bring about a higher state of consciousness. With the wisdom of hindsight, I now see that my ego was squandering my power reserves by resisting the path under my feet, which took me further away from being and transmitting Universal Source energy.

My ego promulgated the lie of separation by categorizing humans into winners and losers. It also assigned toxic guilt and shame to many of my prior actions. In the midst and aftermath of divorce, the ego swings between self-condemnation and assigning indefensible blame toward our former partners. The truth is that any former spouse is truly gifting us a clearer vision of how to live our divinity and step into the fullness of our authentic and sovereign power as Beings who are having a physical adventure. At the time, a tamer adventure would have been much appreciated!

I now recognize that these painful experiences were designed to teach me to slow down; to go within in order to connect with my Divine answers; to build my trust in a greater organizing intelligence;

and to more powerfully emotionalize my divinity through my daily actions. According to Master Coach Joseph Hu Dalconzo, "What we perceive as *error* is either [our] old karma [lessons] burning off or [our] spiritual evolution manifesting." You may want to consider re-reading that profound statement: "What we perceive as error is either [our] old karma [lessons] burning off or [our] spiritual evolution manifesting."[24] That statement should be posted on every mom's refrigerator as a reminder of the Universal truth serum!

I now recognize that I wasn't being punished in those painful moments. As Wayne Dyer affirmed, "[We] live in a friendly Universe that will support any thing or any desire that is aligned with the universal Source of all." I now know with certainty that every single adversity potentially elevates life, giving us the gift of Divine connection – where universal truths, empowerment, and purpose are revealed. In other words, God hadn't been "playing gotcha" with me.

My spiritual fitness plan was being created with infinite precision. This plan continues to bring me closer and closer to the truth of integrating my wholeness and perfection as a Divine Being. Given those spiritual truths, could the divorce have been avoided? Possibly, had I made a solemn and ongoing commitment to my own emotional/ spiritual and physical healing, in conjunction with a more balanced approach toward Mark's rehabilitation. However, the Universe is forever working to give us another opportunity to look squarely at our blind spots. Even though I often found myself in a state of *egoic temporary amnesia,* my life's plan was unfolding exactly as it had been designed.

After the divorce, my ego kept me immersed in despair, self-pity, guilt, depression, and blame. It convinced me that I wouldn't possibly survive another substantial emotional blow. Consequently, it seduced me into nursing my painful emotional blocks and injuries and prevented me from taking emotional risks for many years to come. I falsely believed that, via willpower alone, I had partially clawed my way up the cliff, only to be thrown back down to begin anew. I believed that it was imperative for me to remain at rock bottom. I knew the comfort that rock bottom brought. Another fall, even a lesser one, could anni-hilate me. If you find yourself at rock bottom, it's perfectly permissible to spend *temporary* time there.

Again, none of our lessons, whether immediately mastered or delayed, are mistakes. I unwittingly chose to delay mine. I have learned to be very, very, patient with myself as I navigate this Mom journey. I now understand that life isn't a pass/fail examination that is continu-ally put in front of us to test our abilities. Failure is an illusion. *There were missed opportunities that my ego had me avoid in its misguided attempts to protect me.*

I'm willing to fold my wounded inner children into my arms and look upon my former actions with pure love and compassion. I now recognize that all of my chosen transformational opportunities were not lost to me. The perfect lessons that are of greatest benefit will be repeatedly presented, until I lovingly embrace them – during this life-time or in other lifetimes in a loving multiverse.

RESIGNATION

"Be patient. Eventually you will see the beauty in your
chaos, the purpose in your pain."

Karen Salmansohn

Mark completed ten IVIG treatments prior to the start of kindergarten. However, once the treatments were concluded, Mark continued to be at the mercy of virus after virus. It was quite taxing caring for a chronically ill, sleep-deprived child who missed school for weeks to a month at a time. During the fall, I had no one to substantially relieve me in the middle of Mark's thirty-two-day siege of chronic illness and hours of inconsolable crying bouts.

Mark was not the only one coping with chronic illness. Concurrent to that event, I received a provisional diagnosis of fibromyalgia. The rheumatologist handed me an antidepressant to pacify my nervous system. As expected, my body was completely unable to cope with the side effects of the medication. Prior experience had demonstrated antidepressants were intolerable for my body. At the time, I was not aware of any local physicians willing to treat me.

In 1999, according to the professional body of rheumatologists, fibromyalgia was not yet a designated health condition. Many physicians were under the assumption that women who presented with chronic fatigue and the "aching all over syndrome" were under stress, malingering, or in need of psychiatric care. I sobbed uncontrollably in the bathroom of Loyola Hospital after seeking out a second opinion and being told by the head of Rheumatology that I did not meet the *full* criteria for expected tender points in fibromyalgia. On that particular day, I was one tender point short!

He opined, "You are under chronic stress. The answer is obvious. You need to place your son in a custodial facility and move on with your life."

This callous and dismissive assertion was bandied about as though it was the 1960s and I was living in the era of the "refrigerator mother."[25] My uncontrolled sobbing was triggered by the insensitivity of this rheumatologist, but also by a prior experience. During the last year of my marriage, I consulted with a psychiatrist in the hopes that an antidepressant would assist me in salvaging my marriage.

This physician proclaimed that Mark's ABA therapy was no more effective than "taking him to Mexico for a bloodletting ritual with chickens." He condescendingly informed me that in order to rescue my marriage I should immediately place my son in a facility. It was inconceivable to me that these physicians believed that "putting Mark away" was akin to returning a faulty automobile.

Given the reality of how things worked in the United States during the 1990s, I felt incredulous when I was on the receiving end of these statements. Relinquishing our parental rights and surrendering our disabled children to the state for custodial care is an area fraught with barriers and the pertinent laws vary from state to state. Irrespective of the law, relinquishing Mark to a facility was *not* something that I was ever going to entertain, as long as I had a shred of stamina left inside of me.

Further, Mark's overall trajectory in therapy had been an upward one, with lots of temporary dips downward, due to his taxing health challenges, his chronic sleep disruption and the many other stressors in his life. *Blessedly, even with his ongoing developmental delays, all of the evaluating professionals placed Mark in the top group of therapy responders.*

After the fiasco with the rheumatologist, a friend suggested that I consult a physician ninety minutes away in Evanston, Illinois. He conceptualized my condition as "yeast overgrowth syndrome" and wanted to immediately have me adhere to the yeast-free diet. He did not have a nutritionist in his office to walk me through the protocol or any additional resources to support me. He suggested I order the "William Crook books"[26] and get started. Shortly after that appointment, he resigned from his position and went elsewhere. At the time, I was so overwhelmed with just slogging through my days that I could not begin to imagine taking on such an all-consuming and labor-intensive diet.

Cooking was not my strong suit and it would have been a very steep learning curve. However, the deeper reason that I didn't implement this diet was my complete inability to *make myself a priority*. I was still in the midst of hiring and training paraprofessionals, facilitating some of Mark's therapy myself, driving to the Greenspan consultants on weekends, volunteering in Mark's classroom (try not to faint), and trying to get Mark through illness after illness, not to mention navigating my new normal as a single mother.

In December of his kindergarten year, while in the company of his father, Mark flew into a rage at a local mall. Mark's rages were certainly not new and transpired with me on a regular basis. During this event, Mark bolted outside and preceded to lie down in front of a moving vehicle in the parking lot. After that car stopped in the nick of time, Mark broke away and proceeded to lie down in front of a second moving vehicle that also stopped before Mark could be harmed. After learning of these events from my former husband, I explored them with Mark the following day.

Mark stated matter-of-factly, "I wanted to die."

Due to his limited abstract language abilities, he was unable to articulate whether he had been thinking about dying for some time or whether he impulsively acted in the moment. He also couldn't tell me if he was still having the wish to die. Although I had paltry information, I decided it was imperative that I consult a child psychiatrist about Mark's worsening mood and behavioral profile. Unimaginably, my six-year-old son had just made his first suicide attempt!

Due to the scarcity of child psychiatrists, I placed Mark on a waiting list to see a doctor fifty miles away and also completed the paperwork for an evaluation with Dr. Stanley Greenspan in Bethesda, Maryland. I did not know whether traveling to see Dr. Greenspan was a realistic option but I decided to cross that bridge if a potential appointment became available.

During the winter, Mark suffered from a virulent flu, followed by six weeks of bronchitis, culminating in a worsening mood profile. The spring brought a different kind of challenge. Mark's environmental allergies were so severe that he suffered another cognitive regression that impacted his learning capacities both at school and at home. Because his cognitive profile was compromised, I decided his formal therapy schedule should be put on hiatus for two months.

It was shocking to witness how a viral assault, even as late as age seven, or an overreaction to "environmental allergens," could so drastically alter his functioning. By the summer following kindergarten, his mood and behaviors had deteriorated even further, requiring me to manage his explosiveness on a daily basis. Reasoning with Mark was completely ineffective and back-end consequences, although rarely used, made things much, much worse.

During the prior summer, our Greenspan consultant, Nikki, opined that Mark was presenting with features of oppositional defiant disorder. Her recommendation included intervening preventatively at the front end of his behaviors and parenting him with more flexibility, as outlined by Dr. Ross Greene in *The Explosive Child: A New Approach for Understanding and Parenting Easily Frustrated, Chronically Inflexible Children*.[27] Dr. Greene's novel approach helped reduce some of Mark's meltdowns.

As a result of seeing some benefits to this approach, I educated the school personnel on the implementation of Dr. Greene's strategies. Nikki also recommended that I increase the number of one-on-one Floortime sessions with Mark, in order to bolster a trusting/nurturing relationship with him. Neither of these strategies was foolproof in helping Mark's emotional regulation.

By the time I saw Dr. F., a child psychiatrist, in June of 2000, I was armed with a copy of *The Bipolar Child: The Definitive and Reassuring Guide to Childhood's Most Misunderstood Disorder* by Demitri Papolos and Janice Papolos.[28] The Papoloses had been featured on *The Oprah Show* after writing what some professionals and parents considered to be the "bible" on early-onset pediatric bipolar disorder. At the time, the book was considered highly controversial because many in the psychiatric field remained unconvinced that any such condition existed. Today, pediatric bipolar disorder is still not listed as a diagnostic category in the DSM-5. [29]

Dr. F. was progressive in his viewpoint. Following the evaluation, he agreed that Mark fit the criteria for bipolar disorder, NOS (Not Otherwise Specified). During the assessments with Dr. F., I described Mark's manic bursts of energy that could exhaust a team of ten; his bouts of elation that could turn into rage at a moment's notice; his tendency to meltdown anytime an expectation was set; the night terrors that worsened with illness; my inability to keep staff employed in the home program (eight of eleven staff quit during a six-month interval); and Mark's numerous subject fixations related to death and dying.

I explained Mark's recent compulsion to enter advertised sweepstakes, and described the disordered thinking that led him to conclude that a life-threatening bomb had been planted in our phone's answering machine, resulting in abject terror and hysteria. I recounted how a settling crack in the wall during a heavy snowstorm brought on an episode where Mark became convinced that the roof of the house was at imminent risk for collapse. These episodes continued for hours, often in the middle of the night. Although I felt in my heart that Mark was experiencing the classic symptoms seen with early-onset bipolar disorder, I still felt shattered when the diagnosis was made.

For five-plus years, I had experienced what seemed like an aviator's disorienting, graveyard spiral, replaying in a never-ending feedback loop. Once autism stealthily invaded, my life irretrievably changed course. My health was irreparably damaged, leaving me to exist as a shadow of my former self. My former soul mate decided to remarry within months of the finalization of our divorce proceedings and *now* one of my most catastrophic fears had been realized. Mark, at seven years and four months old, had been diagnosed with a lifelong mental illness. It seemed that no matter how many compulsive efforts I invested in remediating Mark's autism, he would still be consigned to live out the remainder of his life with this unrelenting and sadistic mental illness. In psychiatric speak, "Bipolar illness could potentially be managed but never cured."

The standard management for bipolar disorder was psychotropic medications, coupled with cognitive/behavioral treatments and coping strategies. In my opinion, Mark was a poor candidate for all of those interventions, given his hypersensitivities to medications and their additives; his lack of abstract language; his short attention span; his brain-based lack of motivation and initiative; and his overall non-compliant stance. How was a seven-year-old child with autism going to effectively use standard psychotherapy methods? Following the psychiatric evaluation where Mark exploded and was again restrained in a doctor's waiting room, I returned home with a prescription for an atypical antipsychotic medication.

Within a few short days of beginning the new medication, Mark developed severe mental confusion and a pronounced tremor in one hand. Thankfully, Dr. F. took a conservative stance and decided to discontinue the medication. Before the second medication could reach a therapeutic level, Mark made another suicide attempt. Following his allergy-related springtime withdrawal from therapy, I required him to resume Floortime sessions with Nikki, precipitating another rage attack. There was an explosive episode just getting him into the car.

Then, en route to the appointment, while I was driving seventy miles an hour on a busy highway, Mark repeatedly screamed, *"I'm going to commit suicide!"*

I was completely stunned because I could not fathom how a child with limited language abilities even knew the meaning or existence of such a phrase. Before I even knew what was afoot, he opened the front passenger sidecar door and attempted to jump from the car. In a split second, I grabbed his wrist, while swerving recklessly on the road. It took every ounce of my strength to manhandle him back into the car.

I drove the car to the berm and informed Mark that someone might use their cell phone to inform the police. At that point, he latched onto the belief that he would likely be jailed and decompensated further, threatening to flee from the car. Another lengthy restraint ensued.

After learning of this episode, Dr. F. wanted to give the next medication an opportunity to work before considering psychiatric hospitalization. At that time, there truly were no psychiatric facilities in existence tailored to treat a dually diagnosed seven-year-old like Mark. In 2000, most professionals were leery of diagnosing a seven-year-old child with bipolar disorder, and I knew no one else personally or via my internet circle that was parenting a child dually diagnosed with *high-functioning* autism and bipolar disorder. The second medication tried was a standard SSRI (selective serotonin reuptake inhibitor) used to treat depression and anxiety.

It took months to notice any improvement in Mark's overall functioning because his doses had to be titrated so slowly. The medication was compounded in a specialty pharmacy, given the risks posed by the long list of inactive ingredients in standard medication – substances like titanium dioxide, ferric oxide red, polyethylene glycol, et cetera. It was a precarious undertaking when considering what compounds could send Mark's body into an allergic reaction or an inflammatory response, impacting his brain and exacerbating his neurological symptoms.

Mark's erratic moods continued through that summer; he also struggled due to the ongoing titration of medication and sleep deprivation. At the time he was spending his weekday afternoons acquiring new language abilities via a computer-based program, and I noticed that after 4 p.m., his behaviors typically were more challenging. At bedtime, he experienced huge energy surges accompanied by racing thoughts and obsessive desires that drove him to attempt grandiose projects.

Unfortunately, his autism-related deficits prevented him from completing his imagined plans. During the wee hours of the night, if I didn't agree to assist him to bring these projects to fruition, he would immediately become enraged. Over the years, I refused to comply with most of his nighttime demands. Nevertheless, my sleep was continually disrupted as I tried to monitor whether Mark remained safe in my home.

By the time first grade began, thankfully, Mark's mood swings were beginning to taper off. Concurrent with the events outlined above, my health challenges were taking center stage. I found myself bedridden with incapacitating fatigue for portions of every single day. In addition, my body was overreacting to household chemicals and scented products.

As winter unfolded, I found myself totally overwhelmed by the agreed-upon financial renegotiation with my "ex." This responsibility was even more time-consuming than the divorce had been. I spent my "downtime" organizing and copying enough paper to eventually fill four medium-sized bins. At the time, I jokingly told my friends that the court was asking me to provide backup documents for every single aspect of my life, other than proving my bra's cup size, and I was awaiting a discovery motion on that aspect too!

I felt forced to hire a new law firm. At the conclusion of my divorce, the dot.com bubble burst, wrecking havoc in the financial markets. My original attorney had not filed essential paperwork in a timely manner, resulting in a loss of $350,000 in my retirement account. Due to my trauma-ridden life, it would be years before I appreciated the magnitude of that loss.

During the winter of first grade, as part of the financial reassessment, Mark was ordered to undergo a psychological evaluation. At that time, Mark was in the process of being weaned off the SSRI, as it was no longer having a positive benefit. After several months on the medication, he experienced what is termed an antidepressant tolerance effect or a so-called "poop-out" effect. Then, after the dose was increased ever so slightly, Mark was thrown into a full-blown manic episode. Such a risk is present in individuals with bipolar illness, who are being treated with an "unopposed antidepressant," or one that is prescribed without an accompanying mood stabilizer.

At the direction of Dr. F., I weaned Mark off the antidepressant over the course of a month. Unfortunately, Mark exhibited the most explosive and irrational behaviors I had ever witnessed to date. Weaning over a four-week period is considered a slow weaning pattern, but in Mark's case, it was not anywhere near slow enough. In the future, I would spend *four to six months* weaning Mark from his psychotropic medications and sometimes longer to titrate a therapeutic dose of medication.

Mark's behaviors were completely unmanageable at home and now his agitation and threats toward others were carrying over into his school day. During these episodes, school personnel described his language as incoherent. For the first time ever, the school needed an assigned aide to spend portions of the day outside of the classroom with Mark.

At home, he was in the midst of frightening two-hour rage attacks that would come on without warning. During one restraint that lasted for an interminable amount of time, Mark attempted to bite me a number of times, a behavior that was totally out of character for him. When the episode was over, Mark looked up at me with such confusion and shock on his face.

He began to sob in my arms while repeating these phrases over and over again, "What's happening to me, what's happening to me, Mom? My brain doesn't work. My brain is out of order. My brain is out of order."

I felt bereft, as I was completely unable to offer him a satisfactory explanation for what was taking place, or any heartfelt guarantees that his life was going to improve or in what timeframe.

At the time, I was completely in the dark regarding what was taking place and so were all the assigned professionals. The school personnel were beginning to ask pointed questions. My impression was that the staff was beginning to suspect that Mark was either being emotionally or physically abused, or both. I called Dr. F. in a panic and asked him whether I could go on record with the school about Mark's diagnosis of bipolar, NOS.

Dr. F. was treading cautiously due to the controversial nature of Mark's bipolar diagnosis, but he agreed that I could inform the school team that he was deciding between a diagnosis of unipolar depression or childhood bipolar disorder. The school personnel seemed highly skeptical of the diagnosis but shelved their immediate concerns related to child abuse. Simultaneous with fending off the school's suspicions, the university team reevaluating Mark strongly disputed any consideration of a bipolar diagnosis, while asserting that Mark's explosive behaviors could easily be explained by his autism.

The lead psychologist told me during a joint session with my former husband, "The problem here is that you are too well-read. You are looking for problems where they don't exist."

My heart began to race, my body surged with rage, as I heard my retort inside my mind: *I certainly don't have to look very f**king far! So, all I need to do now is spend less time at the library!*

As expected, their testing over several sessions confirmed that Mark still had autism. However, his IQ was now in the normal range! It had been in a range of mild intellectual impairment at the time of diagnosis, had increased to 87 at age three and was now assessed to be in the normal range for both verbal and nonverbal performance.

In spite of that fact, Mark and I continued to star in our own daily episode of *The Twilight Zone*. For example, Mark exploded and tried to physically attack me after I flushed his mucus-filled tissue down the toilet. He demanded that I somehow retrieve it. Next, Mark exploded because he did not like a drawing on the refrigerator, ripping it to shreds and flinging every scrap of paper into the wastebasket, only to replace it with a preferred poster. In the not-too-distant past, flushing a toilet and arranging papers on a fridge had been commonplace occurrences that didn't faze him, and I found his behavior perplexing, baffling, and completely unpredictable.

During every community excursion, Mark compulsively collected garbage – candy wrappers, drenched scraps of papers, crushed pop cans, broken-down toys and boxes, rocks, sticks, and even an old rag. If I interfered with this fixation or did not assist him in carrying these objects home, he immediately melted down. Unless I wanted to set Armageddon into motion, I could not discard the stockpiled bags of trash that filled my garage.

During this period, I tried to carry on, in spite of the fact that I felt completely annihilated, both physically and emotionally. One of the most challenging aspects of my parenting experience was my all-consuming state of aloneness. This growing isolation was compounded by the consensus held by many of the professionals; they believed that Mark was not as severely impacted by his condition as what I knew him to be or, alternatively, they believed that my parenting approach was in large measure responsible for Mark's explosive behaviors.

Those of us on the front lines with Mark were scrambling for any approach that would alleviate his suffering. During an occupational therapy session, Mark exploded when the therapist, Jennifer, prevented him from removing a large wooden stake with a pointed tip from their ground's construction site and carrying it to the car. Not only was it a safely issue for him to cart this object away but it may also have been illegal to remove.

When Jennifer rightly insisted that Mark give the object back, all hell broke loose. I was stranded at the appointment for an additional hour as she repeatedly drew pictures of this object on paper in order to provide a transitional object that would help coax him into my car. During the long car ride home, Mark was in a state of complete mental decompensation.

After witnessing his behavior, Jennifer provided the first successful strategy in months that actually helped manage Mark's escalating mood swings. She recommended an approach called "affect matching." She suggested that I immediately try to match his emotional escalation with a similar intensity of affect in tone and movement on my part. However, she admonished me to make sure that I did not in any way inadvertently mock him.

Rather, I should join him during his episode but in an exaggerated playful manner. I immediately implemented this method and it headed off some of his explosions, as he became redirected into watching my antics and possibly feeling validated that he was not so alone with his pain. It temporarily soothed him.

For four very long months, I repeatedly explored the option of having Mark psychiatrically hospitalized, but my multiple pleas fell on deaf ears. In February, I met with two independent psychiatrists about my deep-seated fears related to Mark's risk of self-harm. Both psychiatrists concurred with the dual diagnosis of autism and bipolar disability but neither wanted to assume responsibility for managing such a complicated and high-risk case.

The court-mandated psychologist and psychiatrist, Dr. O., seemed to believe that I was either exaggerating Mark's condition for emotional gain or to hold my former spouse financially hostage. Dr. F. did not want to go on record regarding Mark's bipolar diagnosis. As is typical with mental health professionals, he understandably wanted to steer clear of legal complications between parents.

Dr. O. recommended reinstating Mark's SSRI and that is exactly what happened. In April, following the months of hell related to weaning Mark's medication, we were right back to square one, with Mark resuming the same medication that had originally precipitated his mania!

Dr. F. wisely attempted to add a mood stabilizer to the mix, but once again, Mark experienced extreme side effects, and at the same time, it was a battle of epic proportions to get him to swallow the liquid concoction. Some of the time, he just vomited the solution back up. Mark felt exceedingly anxious about what entered his body, given his history of severe reactions to foods, supplements, and medications.

Dr. F. was also quite constrained by what could be tried, given the fact that Mark was completely unable to swallow pills due to his sensory aversions. The school staff, although well-intentioned, did not really know how to help on the home front. I had already contacted every single local childhood psychiatric hospital myself, only to be told that Mark would absolutely be excluded based on his age, his autism, and his special diet! No one seemed to grasp or appreciate the reality of what Mark and I were being asked to endure for months on end. Things finally came to a head at the beginning of May.

The financial renegotiation was not going in my favor. In fact, my attorney had informed me that there was a high probability that the judge was going to order me to work part-time! I had already been ordered to undergo a lengthy career evaluation at my own expense. I continued to assert that I did not see any viable way to return to clinical social work due to my full-time parenting responsibilities and the state of my health. In addition, I did not know a single physician who would go on record to the court stating that I was, for all practical purposes, disabled with chronic fatigue and malaise, nor had I been able to qualify for disability through the Social Security Administration, as I had missed too many consistent quarters of work by the time I was officially diagnosed with fibromyalgia.

While the threat of resuming paid employment loomed over my head, Caitlin, one of Mark's most promising staff members, abruptly quit without notice, completely reneging on her one-year commitment. I had just completed her three-month intensive training program and she was slated to begin her first shift independently. Instead, she arrived for her first solo session on the Saturday before Mother's Day and quit on the spot.

A paraprofessional's departure from Mark's program was not surprising, but in that moment – and on Mother's Day weekend, no less – it was just too much for me to bear. I had spent months banging on countless doors pleading for someone to assume responsibility for Mark's unrelenting suffering and I had been met with a stonewall of indifference. Beyond the wall was the ever-present implication that I was a malingerer who would use any means necessary to avoid going to work to support my son's financial needs. My isolation, my fruitless attempts to be heard by the professionals, this woman's unanticipated abandonment, combined with the expectation that I resume my former professional life, sent me into a desperate maelstrom of despair and resignation. I felt so invalidated and misunderstood.

It is far from easy for me to write about the dangerous, dark and irrational thoughts that overtook me, as well as the state of abject physical and emotional depletion that consumed me at that time. I was no longer coping. I started to seriously consider ending my life and ending Mark's life as well. My twisted mind began to justify a heinous and irreversible action, and even told me that ending Mark's suffering was an act of mercy. Of course, it would not have been so, and I am forever grateful that I resisted those impulses.

In the United States, at least once per week, a caregiver decides to snuff out their disabled child's life – and often their own as well. Disability rights advocates assert that the largest contributing factors to these tragedies is the devaluing of disabled people's lives in our society and the limited community resources for parents. I agree on both counts: people with disabilities are *not* fully valued in our culture and caregivers are pushed beyond all human limits for years on end by systems that are not responsive to their needs.

The human family needs to come together to support parents and children. Kind words, a willingness to actively listen with your heart, and kind offerings can go a long way toward altering an irrevocable act and replacing it with circumstances that transform everyone for the better. Even if circumstances for one of these families is beyond your understanding, remember the words of sixteenth-century holy man John Bradford: "There but for the grace of God go I."

Mark and I could easily have crossed the line, becoming the subject of a media story and I the recipient of countless judgmental, sanctimonious comments by people who had never walked in my shoes. I was *wrongly* convinced that every possible avenue had been thwarted. I also believed that one additional stressor, within a brief window of time, was going to be too much for me to carry and I knew that it was only a matter of time until that one additional stressor appeared. Because I fervently believed that the deck of life was so unfairly stacked against us, I felt completely cut off and disowned by God. I couldn't comprehend how a loving God would allow us to suffer so terribly, and for so long.

Fortunately, I had a shred of rationality left and decided to implement a three-day pause on my plan to terminate our lives (yes, I was that close). If my level of suffering didn't ease even one degree during that time, I would follow through with my "ultimate solution."

Now, I absolutely know that my angels intervened to assuage my pain! While the human family (most recently, those part of a legal system that was oblivious to my plight) had seemed to abandon us, my guides and angels were working overtime.

This would later be confirmed in 2007, during my first reading with an intuitive named Amy. She looked at me with loving compassion and said, "You didn't tell me that you wanted to take your life. Your angels are saying that they mitigated your pain down to a level that was tolerable so that you could survive."

Her words described exactly the grace Mark and I were offered at the time. On day two, my despair began to lift, albeit ever so slightly, and by day three, I experienced a bit more relief.

Given the level of Mark's emotional instability during the winter and spring of first grade, I understandably discouraged peers from coming to my home. However, his friend, Katie, repeatedly came by looking for a snack or some emotional first aid. Though it was difficult, I worked at striking a balance between having her at my house and sending her home.

Much of the time, her influence on Mark was a positive one, but the week following the loss of his preferred staff member, he flew into a rage when Katie insisted on carrying her art project home. I was able to safely extricate her from the interaction, only to witness another a few days later when Katie borrowed a bucket of chalk to draw figures in my driveway. Mark perceived these attempts to borrow or remove objects from the house as interference with his hoarding.

I will never forget my shock and horror as he sprang forward and wrapped his hands around Katie's throat. It took every ounce of strength to pull them apart and drag Mark into the garage, where I found myself embroiled in another battle on the dirty entry steps of my home. Even in the immediate aftermath of the attack, Katie continued to express concern for Mark's welfare – and mine – as I struggled to restrain him. Although she appeared to be in shock and was clearly confused as to what was taking place, she seemed to know his actions were beyond his control, and she was exceedingly reluctant to leave us. I firmly ordered her to do so.

I was experiencing a full adrenaline/cortisol rush as I contained Mark on those steps; even still, tears trickled down my face and my body was flooded with his wounded screams. This incident was the final straw for me. What more needed to happen to finally get Mark the help he so desperately required? Surely, the restraint bruises up and down my body would provide adequate evidence?

I called Dr. F. again and demanded that Mark be placed in the psychiatric hospital. I was not going to take no for an answer this time. Dr. F. reluctantly agreed that I could drive him to the psychiatric hospital for a scheduled evaluation, but he insisted that I wait until Monday, as the weekend would not be an advisable time to have him admitted. Once again, I was subjected to the wait-and-see game.

That Saturday, I was so blessed to have Mary, one of my closest friends, arrive at my home accompanied by her second-grade son. Another mom would have shielded her child from Mark's potential unpredictability, but not Mary. She stayed the night, knowing that Mark needed to be distracted by a compassionate peer and I needed to be uplifted by the loving words and touch of a friend. There were some very dicey moments that evening but we thankfully came through them unscathed. However, my gratitude did not prevent the clock from ticking ever so slowly toward Monday morning, with the guillotine perched precariously over our necks.

WHAT I KNOW NOW THAT I DIDN'T KNOW THEN: BY SURRENDERING TO THE LAW OF LEAST EFFORT, WE CAN LET GO OF DEFENSIVENESS AND STRUGGLE.

I know now that I was addicted to struggle in the midst of adversity. During childhood, I was programmed to believe that struggle was inescapable and even noble. I did not recognize that *creating an identity around struggle* was not in harmony with my Divine nature. I was unconscious to the ways in which I compounded my struggles by adhering to rigid ideas about how my life *should* unfold. As Japanese novelist and essayist Haruki Murakami said, "Pain is inevitable. Suffering is optional." I had not yet recognized that I was safe and protected from an eternal perspective, no matter the arduous temporary realities that confronted me.

I struggled incessantly to control my outer reality. I struggled to be heard and validated by others. I waited in expectancy for the health care professionals, the psychologists, the educators, the paraprofessionals, the lawyers, the judge, members of my own inner circle, and even Mark to "attack me," which engendered the very energy I feared the most. After all, I had lived through a childhood where adults attacked in unpredictable ways so that unchecked virus continued to replicate in my life. At a deep unconscious level, I accepted the notion that I deserved to struggle by having to defend my parenting choices.

I added so many layers of struggle that I even created an incapacitating illness. I struggled because my life was out of balance. I struggled because I didn't say yes on my own behalf, nor did I say no to *unnecessary tasks* that robbed me of my precious life force energy. I allowed (imagined) obstacles to consume me with constant worry and thus I frittered away my vitality. I fixated on temporary realities, the circumstances that I didn't want to experience, instead of laser-focusing on a higher vision for my life.

I struggled because I set unattainable and unrealistic goals – also known as perfectionism. I did not apply the *Law of Least Effort,* as coined by Dr. Deepak Chopra in *The Seven Spiritual Laws of Success: A Practical Guide To The Fulfillment of Your Desires* [30] because my childlike ego was caught up in making insatiable demands for specific results; controlling the uncontrollable; and obsessively trying to garner the approval of withholding professionals. Practicing the *Law of Least Effort* would have allowed me to **DO** so much less (by no longer applying my will), and instead potentially manifest so much more.

By applying the *Law of Least Effort,* I would have learned to unconditionally surrender to each one of my circumstances, recognizing that in every so-called problem lies an opportunity for growth. Things would certainly have been quite different had I believed that a home therapist quitting on the spot was in fact a blessing in disguise.

I struggled because I did not consistently listen to my inner voice, nor did I *trust* that voice. I struggled because I did not trust the overarching orchestrating powers of the Universe to bring me a measure of solace. I did not see that when my ego drove me to overwork, overdo, and over-identify with my role as a suffering mother, it blocked me from accessing ninety percent of my solutions as a conscious co-creator with a loving Universe.

I did not know how to quiet my mind and harness the power inherent in relaxing while feeling safe, protected, and empowered. I had yet to discover that though my circumstances were daunting, my interconnection with my higher consciousness could offer the guidance to calm the outer storm and, even more importantly, my capacity to materialize my highest desires – if those desires were in the right timing and alignment with Universal wisdom.

Instead, my unconscious mind broadcast the belief that I was struggling alone in the Universe and therefore, that is the experience I recreated. I had yet to learn that if I only opened myself up to Source, another option was permanently available to me. I did not *live* the practice of gratitude in advance, nor did I practice positive expectancy because my ego was addicted to worst-case scenarios and always waiting for them to appear. Unfortunately, without the right mix of healing tools, trauma has a way of hardwiring these ruts into our brains.

I did not live the power inherent in detaching from my earth-plane realities, knowing that this surrendered action could gift me the grace I was seeking. I did not live focused on the present because my ego was too busy projecting future catastrophes or ruminating about the failures from the past.

Eckhart Tolle says, "Accept – then act. Whatever the present moment contains, accept it as if you had chosen it. Always work with it, not against it." I, on the other hand, habitually worked against things. It was second nature while in the grip of my identity as a warrior mother. By practicing the Law of Least Effort, I would have known how to quiet my mind and come into these potentially adversarial circumstances without resistance, while powerfully communicating and owning my truth, irrespective of what anyone else thought or said. I would have known how to bless my so-called adversaries in advance, while *listening to truly hear* their positions, rather than jumping the gun to defend mine.

In those moments, I did not know how to *Be* peaceful while emitting defenselessness. Although it would have been *a very tall order* for any mother, I did not know how to *Be* peaceful in my son's presence. Instead, though I sometimes appeared tranquil on the outside, I absorbed his frenetic energy and carried it as my own.

Nor was I able to give myself permission to truly sit with my painful feelings so that I could accept and release them. Instead, I repressed them. My ego ordered me to "get on with the business at hand." If only I had relinquished these many burdens, I could have potentially lived free from blame, resentment, and bitterness while assuming full and total responsibility as a creator being.

If only I had made different choices, I could have received the gifts of peace, surrender, and freedom. Now, in hindsight, I recognize that while walking on that sure-footed path, where each step represents the Law of Least Effort, Divine intelligence enters with lightning speed and showers us with grace, while potentially bringing our dreams into physical manifestation.

OBSESSIVENESS OVER OUR CHILDREN

"You are confined only by the walls you build yourself."

Andrew Murphy

Mark left the psychiatric hospital twelve days later with disheveled hair and an unsteady gait. His eyes were glazed over and he barely spoke. During his stay in the inpatient unit, he had refused the hospital food, his newly prescribed medications and his liquid nutritional supplement. He barely slept and was subjected to a traumatizing finger stick test administered without forewarning. Fortunately, Dr. F. wrote an order for Mark's snacks to be provided from home, allowing for some measure of sustenance. Dr. F. decided to continue the new mood stabilizer, while slowly titrating the very same antidepressant that had been responsible for wreaking havoc during the weaning process.

One compassionate nurse called several times requesting that I make the forty-mile commute to administer his protocol. I did so on three extra occasions and those were the *only instances* Mark swallowed his meds. The staff explained that Mark had free will and could not be forced to comply with the psychiatrist's orders. Although I had acted with Mark's best interests in mind, seeing him shuffling around like a zombie made me extremely wary of pursuing this avenue again.

Mark was hospitalized, in part, so that a new medication regimen could be safely implemented – a goal that had been completely thwarted. However, we did realize one momentous benefit: hospital records that explicitly documented Mark's dual diagnoses of autism and bipolar disorder. I carefully read and reread every line of the lengthy report, as though it were a masterpiece that rivaled *Gone With The Wind*. I finally had written proof as to the nature of Mark's condition! This written proof likely contributed to another piece of good news: the court's decision to give me a reprieve regarding rejoining the paid workforce.

During Mark's hospital stay, I actively pursued community resources that could assist him following his discharge. After an exhaustive search, I applied to a state program that served chronically mentally ill children with impaired reality testing. With these hospital records, Mark's case could potentially be reviewed for state funding. I was immediately assigned to Amy, a *wonderfully competent* case manager, and Wanda, a *supportive* parent mentor. The cumbersome application process took five months to complete. With the goal of securing state services, Amy recommended that I include a detailed parent statement that documented Mark's complex needs.

By the time Mark saw the evaluating psychologist, his bipolar illness was no longer in question. He raged in the waiting room, required physical intervention to reach the evaluation room, and was almost untestable. The psychologist wrote that he had never seen an eight-year-old child with this severity of depression and despair.

"His responses…were dominated by uncontrollable depression and anxiety and a feeling of hopelessness about the future. His emotional state was extremely labile for his age and he showed severe problems in impulsivity. His reactions were controlled by both depression and anxiety to such a state that his reality testing frequently broke down."

The psychologist also noted obsessive-compulsive features and risk factors for rage outbursts.

By late November of his second-grade year, I learned that Mark would be entitled to community support, including support workers visiting our home to implement goals toward mental health stabilization. Mark's father and I would no longer be responsible for shouldering the monetary costs for staff members because the state had agreed to "pick up the tab." The grant approval couldn't have come at a better time, as Mark's thinking had deteriorated even further in the wake of the September 11, 2001 tragedy.

Although I successfully shielded Mark from the news on the day of the attacks, the following day he was within earshot of his peers talking about suicide bombers, the destruction of the towers, and the death toll. I prayed that Mark wouldn't be able to process the language being used. Unfortunately, my hopes were dashed because Mark was exposed to an unannounced school assembly to honor the deceased.

At that point, he became singularly obsessed with the event and his extreme fears related to it. Mark had been preoccupied with the topic of death and dying for some time and this event provided a focal point to channel his obsession. I quote from a report that I wrote summarizing his second-grade year.

Mark continues to experience significant periods of depression and hypomanic mood swings. He continues to be fixated on any theme related to death and dying. It is an almost daily topic of conversation. Night hours continue to create the highest risk period for Mark to experience hypomanic or manic mood states. He continues to have intermittent delusional thoughts. Most recently, religiosity has become a frequent preoccupation, including the belief that he will be damned to hell. He continues to have delusions related to alien abduction, grandiose ideas and commands by God. At times, beliefs with a paranoid flavor are present. Mark also continues to be plagued by nightmares that are traumatizing and also include many of the themes above.

In light of the above information, I also considered the branch of the state program that paid for residential placement. Shortly after the grant was approved, I visited a number of facilities, only to become immediately disenchanted with the lack of treatment available. During my visits, I found "throw-away" children languishing in deplorable conditions. After months of looking at facilities, I eventually rejected the residential option for Mark.

With residential treatment off the table, Mark continued his Floor-time hours. He was also enrolled with Paul, a psychotherapist who specialized in treating childhood anxiety disorders. I selected Paul after twenty-some psychotherapists refused to accept Mark's case. Mark was immediately resistant to Paul's systematic cognitive restructuring approach. When Paul asked him to complete homework assignments that would help him replace his distorted thoughts with beneficial ones, Mark's response included plenty of tears, as well as raging and shredding of the homework papers.

Over the course of the next several months, things continued to deteriorate between Mark and Paul. I was rarely invited into the sessions but could overhear the unproductive exchanges and Mark's avoidant behaviors from the waiting room. Matters came to a head when Mark "disappeared" from the gym during a session and was missing in a four-floor building. After vanishing for more than an hour, he was finally located in a broom closet.

Paul asserted that he had never "lost a child" during his career tenure. But Mark was not just any child; indeed, at age eight, he was often able to outsmart the professionals assigned to him. Mark was gifted with finely-tuned survival instincts and he resisted anything that encroached on his autonomy and/or exacerbated his feelings of failure.

After the school district boundaries were reconfigured, Mark attended a brand new school for second grade, necessitating another major transition for a child who found change unbearable. Mrs. D, Mark's veteran teacher, made every effort to be emotionally support-ive during reciprocal interactions. She saw Mark's intellectual potential and believed that he could keep pace with the expectations set for typical children – including homework. Some of the assignments were complicated and lengthy home-based projects that would have been challenging for many kids, let alone one with language, execu-tive function, and motor planning deficits. Mark spent two hours on assignments that were typically completed within one hour.

The additional demands to Mark's already overwhelmingly diffi-cult six-hour school day proved to be too much to endure. There were instances where Mark refused to return home from his bus stop and instead ran to a construction zone behind our house. On one occasion, while en route home on the school bus, Mark verbally threatened to kill himself.

Sydney, a neighborhood peer, breathlessly came to my door and told me, "Mark is missing. He was running back and forth in the bus aisle, screaming, 'I want to kill myself. I want to kill myself.' Then he tried to remove the emergency exit door so that he could jump from the back of the bus. I held him back and stopped him but now he has run away and I don't know where he went."

I eventually found him sobbing in the construction zone behind our house. After navigating so many school-based challenges and disappointments all day long, Mark was unable to tolerate hours of homework. The almost nightly assignments would invariably lead to meltdowns. Mark was already so mentally exhausted and unfocused that it would take hours and hours of review with varying modalities for him to retain a simple spelling list.

I spent all schoolyear trying to convince the professionals that the homework burden was detrimental to Mark's mental health. They could not appreciate his level of distress, as Mark tended to hold himself together during the school day and then fell apart in the safety of his home environment. Today this phenomenon is called *after-school restraint collapse,* but back in 2001, no one had identified this syndrome for children with brain-based disorders.

At all costs, Mark wanted to avoid feeling humiliated in front of his classroom peers. The fact that he was still averaging only three hours of sleep, having his medication dose titrated monthly, and living with a chronically ill mother did not sway the professionals to waive their homework policies. Is it any wonder that Mark took Paul's assignments and tore them to shreds? I felt continual pressure to live up to school-related demands and I deeply regret allowing that pressure to be transferred to Mark.

However, there was at least one positive development on the horizon. The state program also decided to cover the expense of a speech and language pathologist on a short-term basis. I asked the new speech therapist to focus on how we might improve Mark's expressive language abilities, thereby reducing the level of frustration that led to meltdowns. As was now the norm, after hearing about Mark's behavioral profile, twenty-four private speech and language therapists refused to be involved.

Fortuitously, even though Melanie was pregnant at the time, she courageously agreed to accept the job. Even though this assignment was out of her realm of experience, she was willing to at least try to make this arrangement work. She came to my home for approximately six months on an every-other-week basis. Melanie took the time to listen to my recommendations and immediately grasped that she needed to go through "the back door," via the use of a play modality.

When asked to perform a skill that triggered feelings of failure, Mark would immediately shut down or exhibit extreme oppositional defiance. Professionals refer to this phenomenon as pathological demand avoidance (PDA). PDA occurs when the surrounding sensory stimuli, the expectations of the environment, and the emotions of neurologically sensitive children become too overwhelming. Mark's propensity toward oppositional defiance/demand avoidance was an ingrained self-protective mechanism, but one that potentially pushed allies away.

Melanie understood these dynamics and was a talented problem-solver. She offered a number of helpful strategies to improve his ease with language. Of course, the work was labor-intensive, and while Mark consistently made progress with skill acquisition throughout his life, when it came to more complex and abstract skills it would often be months or even years before that progress was clearly discernable.

In the meantime, I also focused on nurturing Mark's social life, including making my home inviting to five neighborhood peers – at no small effort. Though not a single family ever invited Mark to their homes, and I knew I was being used as a free childcare center, I felt it was well worth it for Mark to be able to interact with peers in a natural environment.

I organized games for the kids every morning at the bus stop. I fostered structured interactions where Mark could potentially be successful. I supervised the neighborhood kids during time spent in our inflatable pool, running through sprinklers, bike riding through obstacle courses, rollerblading, sledding, building snowmen, et cetera.

I took Sydny and Mark on community shopping sprees and outings. Sydny spent almost every day in my home for two and a half years. Mark's capacity for pragmatic language, motor planning, generating ideas, and sustained interactions all improved because of his exposure to typical peers. They each brought their own dynamic personalities to the fore.

These children were able to motivate Mark in ways that were beyond me. Mark felt more joy and acceptance when neighborhood peers were present. In the middle of second grade, I was even more committed to these natural interactions, as Mark was discharged from intensive Floortime therapy in late February.

Even though Mark had inched forward developmentally, the cumulative effects of the last six-plus years had continued to exact a huge toll on my health. I was living with ongoing chronic fatigue, chronic pain, irritable bowel syndrome and immune deficiency. I fell ill almost every single time Mark came down with a virus and since Mark was still so chronically ill himself, I was living with ongoing viral assaults as an overlay to my daily fatigue.

I still refused to concentrate on my own health and healing and I had no overseeing physician to spearhead my recovery. Instead, I barreled ahead with a single-minded focus on making Mark's improvement my whole *raison d'etre*. In the big game called life, my shadow personas were still calling all the plays.

WHAT I KNOW NOW THAT I DIDN'T KNOW THEN: WE WILL LOSE OURSELVES IN THE EQUATION IF WE DO NOT ENDEAVOR TO SET HEALTHY BOUNDARIES THAT PROTECT OUR TIME, OUR LIFE FORCE ENERGY, AND OUR HEALTH AND WELLNESS.

> The longer we stay in a violating situation, the more traumatized we become. If we don't act on our own behalf, we will lose spirit, resourcefulness, energy, health, perspective and resilience. We must take ourselves out of violating situations for the sake of our own wholeness. Anne Katherine[31]

I subscribed to Forest E. Witcraft's sentiments: "A hundred years from now it will not matter what my bank account was, the sort of house I lived in, or the kind of car I drove…but the world may be different because I was important in the life of a child." Those sentiments were not at issue. What was at issue was the myriad ways that I chose to deny myself – and the fact that my ego kept me blind to them. *I had unwittingly become the woman whose friends dragged her from her home!* In this instance, there was no team available who could facilitate hitting a bottom – and I'm sure that many among my circle tried to do so.

A boundary is nothing more than a limit that promotes integrity – a form of self-protection for the host. At a foundational level, the human body requires nourishment, water, rest, replenishment, relaxation, balanced exercise, intellectual stimulation, pleasurable activities, play, and joy-filled experiences to function optimally. My body was in long-term deficit and deprivation related to almost all of those requirements.

These boundaries were *invisible* to me because I had never established a strong root chakra. The root chakra is the first chakra at the base of the spine that provides a foundation for all the others that follow.[32] If the root chakra is not solid, the foundation for other developmental stages and their accompanying energy systems is also weakened. It's like building a house on a seriously flawed foundation.

The root chakra relates to safety – feeling grounded in the physical realm; knowing that you have a right to be in your body; a right to live out your physical life; feeling secure; adopting primal trust in a benevolent Universe; and *the establishment of boundaries that promote survival*. I had become so disconnected from my own survival needs that I was unaware of all the ways in which my ego was engaged in abusive tactics that needlessly usurped my energy reserves. I was so disengaged from my inner Self that I was oblivious to what *emergency actions were required to immediately modify the disastrous course I had been traversing*.

Without emotional intimacy with our inner Divine Selves, emotional honesty will be sacrificed. I could not admit to myself that I often *resented the life* I was leading, though this resentment continued to seep out in all kinds of unproductive ways. I didn't see how this cape of martyrdom was a cloak of my own choosing and one that I could permanently choose to discard. I did not recognize the merciless bully that lived within, the very same bully who continued to demand more and more from me, without rebalancing or replenishing my spent reserves.

I did not rely upon my power word, NO (as in "No, I am not available). Instead, my ego raced ahead with an obsessive bent to ensure that Mark didn't live through the same manner of abandonment that I had experienced – ironic, considering that I was re-abandoning my own needs, over and over again. My ego had me go unconscious to the fact that *I would not be able to teach my son anything that I was not willing to consistently teach and model for myself!* I also continued to ignore the reality that I would not be able to continue nurturing my son's needs while ignoring my own.

As Eleanor Brown wrote, "Rest and self-care are so important. When you take the time to replenish your spirit, it allows you to serve others from the overflow. You cannot serve from an empty vessel."

My own internal value and worth were as invisible to me as they had been to my parents. Boundary protection begins with emotional intimacy with yourself and connection with your emotional truths. Children require emotional intimacy from their caregivers that is developmentally appropriate and includes supportive nurturing, acts of physical affection, loving words, and emotional validation, most especially during times of distress.

When we have been denied the emotional intimacy that is required to meet our own emotional dependency needs, emotional harm has occurred. Violations of emotional distance (childhood emotional neglect) are wounds characterized by acts that were *not offered* on our behalf. When violations of emotional distance are the norm in childhood, grave damage has been inflicted upon our fragile sense of self-esteem and self-worth.

I had internalized that I was only as valuable as what I could achieve through hard work and sacrifice. I did not know how to step back from my circumstance as the objective "witness-observer" and take full responsibility for the ways in which Mark was going to continue to experience untold emotional damage living with a mother who was chronically in deficit herself.

What I know now is that I *deserved to rebuild my own foundational root chakra,* just as much, if not more, than Mark deserved to have speech and language therapy, math drills, play dates, and cognitive restructuring sessions. I *deserved* to have my own play dates, my own intellectual stimulation, my own escapes from the tasks at hand, and my own foundational practices for caring for my body, et cetera.

Further, my boundaries were blurred because I came into this life as a highly sensitive empath. It was second nature for me to take on Mark's energy, the energy of others, and even the energy of the collective mass consciousness. I took on Mark's pain and suffering as my own, automatically and without conscious awareness or consent. In the rare instances when I became aware that I was doing so, I rationalized my enmeshed boundaries by telling myself that I was contributing to Mark's very survival. *This belief was fundamentally flawed.*

My most ever-present and deep-seated fear involved losing Mark to suicide. As a result of my empathic nature, I was highly attuned to Mark's despondency, placing me at much greater risk of over-identifying with his darkness, especially as I had not yet let go of my own. I had not yet learned to shield and protect myself from these lower vibrational energies so that I could either allow them to pass through my body or be immediately rebuffed.

Similarly, I did not engage in a regular habit of releasing and transmuting these energies back into the light. Christel Broederlow's statement resonates with me: "Empaths have a tendency to openly feel what is outside of them more so than what is inside of them. This can cause empaths to ignore their own needs."[33] Therefore, boundary protection is paramount for those of us who identify as empathic. My pain quotient would ramp up considerably before I would become cognizant of the fact that my jailor and tormentor resided within. The power to grant my own pardon rested fully within my own hands.

DOUBT AND DISCOURAGEMENT

"Stars can't shine without darkness."

D.H. Sidebottom

As Mark's entry into third grade approached, I decided to tell him that he had joined our family through adoption. At the recommendation of the professionals, I had delayed the inevitable, as during the early years Mark did not possess the capacity to process such a complicated abstract idea. More recently, I had hesitated because of the high-risk nature of Mark's chronic mood instability. Now I had come to the realization that there would never be an ideal time to disclose this information.

Initially, Mark's affect was flat and he asked very few questions surrounding his adoption; however, that period of relative calm was not to last. Within two weeks of learning about his adoption, he flew into a rage over a completely unrelated and seemingly trivial issue. I sat outside his bedroom door waiting for the storm to pass. After almost an hour of raging, an eerie quiet descended. Though it was not unusual for Mark to feel sleepy following these episodes, I was immediately gripped by a very ominous feeling. When I opened Mark's bedroom door, I saw, to my horror, that he was using his entire body weight to force a window opening wide enough for him to leap from the second story of the house. I dashed to the window and pulled him to safely.

Mark sobbed in my arms as he repeatedly cried, "I want to die. I want to die. Just let me die."

According to my records from that time, "After Mark learned of his adoption, he experienced a worsening of his depressive symptoms, an increase in suicidal thoughts, greater abandonment fears, an increased propensity for seeing himself as damaged goods and more intensified feelings of grief in relation to the divorce."

Midway through second grade, Mark's mood stabilizer had been titrated to a therapeutic level and therefore he required much less physical management in my home. That changed, however, after the adoption news. Within days of the disclosure, he had an incident of aggression directed toward a neighborhood peer, with the need for physical restraint on the increase.

At the start of third grade, Mark focused on alien abductions, ghosts, the reoccurrence of the "Big Bang," earth starting over, time being reversed, his capacity to be reborn and the ever-present backdrop of death. He witnessed violent images, dead bodies and graveyards during bouts of restless sleep. Mark was exceedingly hypersensitive to sensory stimuli, as well as the emotions and energy signatures of other people. However, was he also receptive to information from the other side of the veil?

When we examine mental illness from a shamanic perspective, we recognize that the energy bodies of children are potentially scrambled. Children with mental illness are unable to properly ground their energy into their lower three chakras (root, sacral and solar plexus) in this dimensional realm, and at the same time, they are potentially bombarded with spiritual information that is scrambled and unbalanced. At the time, I had not been exposed to the shamanic perspective and was only aware of the perspective held by classic psychiatry.

Mark was enrolled with a competent third-grade teacher in mainstream education, where the shamanic perspective was not considered. His teacher also did not go out of her way to make a strong connection with either one of us. Mark would come home utterly exhausted after a long school day, only to face three hours of homework. Adults trying to bear up under a nine-hour day of demands, with little or no sleep for years on end, while living with the effects of multiple hidden disabilities and unprocessed traumas would crash and burn; yet Mark was being asked to pull off the impossible. My notes indicate that Mark was in a confused, lethargic, stupor almost every single morning – barely able to slog through breakfast. After Mark awakened, I dressed him as he lay in an unresponsive heap. Because he found school to be unbearable, he often pleaded to stay home.

He cried, "I can't go back. I can't cope. I can't cope." As the time for school approached, he frequently tried every imaginable tactic to avoid getting on his bus.

I couldn't fathom why the team at school dismissed my pleas to eliminate the excessive homework that proved to be so counterproductive. They kept forcing Mark into the neurotypical child box despite clear indications that he was far from the same. No matter how well-intentioned they were, they lacked any awareness of the momentous harm that was being perpetrated.

Without adequate sleep, mood stabilization continued to be out of reach, and yet there were no professionals willing to see Mark for a sleep assessment. Mark slept in my bed for the few hours that his body offered him a reprieve from his frenzied emotional state. His whole body was often wracked with tremors, as well as continual night awakenings and night terrors. As a mother who felt powerless to end Mark's suffering, I did not know how to detach myself from feelings of impotency, doubt, discouragement, and guilt.

Further, Mark continued to run away at the conclusion of many school days; he longed to be reunited with former staff and he still acutely grieved his parents' separation. He longed to have a vibrant, optimistic, healthy mother. He continued to spew self-hatred, labeling himself as incompetent, stupid, and a failure. He often lived under a cloud of generalized irritability mixed with euphoria that, at a moment's notice, could transform into violent rage attacks. His condition held him hostage to lengthy provoking cycles, characterized by locating my Achilles' heel and spewing a spate of vicious words.

He made the following heartbreaking statements: "I feel one thousand percent sad all of the time, Mom, I can't put my past behind me. I wish I were like Simba in the Lion King because he learned to do it. Because I'm adopted, I don't belong to you or to Dad. I don't belong anywhere in this world. I have no friends. I am nothing. I am completely alone."

During the winter months, Mark fell ill, which always had a deleterious impact on his mood and thinking. Not only was I burned out from caring for a chronically ill child who missed weeks of school at a time and barely slept, but now I was caring for a child whose mental state deteriorated just as he was beginning to recover physically. After Mark endured his fourth viral assault, I found myself physically managing his explosive outbursts on an almost daily basis. Mark felt existentially alone. He preferred to spend his free time obsessively watching a documentary featuring the Hiroshima atomic bomb – something that I did not believe was in his best interests. He was continually feeding his dark thoughts and dark moods with a steady diet of more darkness, and thwarting that craving was a demanding job that often provoked a rage attack.

Mark experienced a revolving door of workers during his enrollment in Floortime. This circumstance was not surprising, given the demands of the job and the inadequate pay that paraprofessionals received. Every time a worker left, Mark personalized the loss and became increasingly afraid to trust the next person in line. He was particularly grief-stricken, however, over the loss of two favored staff members.

Sue was Mark's most preferred home-based therapist. She was a highly creative play therapist who formed a special bond with him and invested her time and energy into building his world of play and socialization. She conscientiously went beyond the typical expectations to arrange peer dates for Mark, enriching community outings, and novel experiences. She brought art projects and enticing materials that engaged his emotions and his intellect.

During third grade, two additional workers had the stamina, emotional stability, and talent to successfully engage Mark. I was fortunate to have Nicole join our ranks. She successfully formed a trusting connection with Mark, was adept at facilitating playful interactions, and also possessed the finesse to manage his behaviors. After a year's tenure, Nicole left and more of the load fell to me.

Another card in the already unstable house of cards was about to fall. Over the past two-plus years I had formed a strong alliance with Amy, our local community mental health center liaison and my bridge to the state program for mentally ill children. Amy possessed the capacity to engage Mark in the therapeutic process and provided weekly home-based therapy. It was a real blow when she resigned. The replacement worker was sincere, but did not possess any of Amy's talents. She rarely corralled Mark into a room and could not interact with him effectively.

Nicole and Amy were not Mark's only losses. I continued to make our home a welcoming haven for neighborhood peers, most of whom were in the fourth or fifth grade, a year or two ahead of Mark academically. In March, Mark had a successful birthday party with a small group of peers. Sydny, Mark's closest friend, was noticeably absent. This circumstance was a foreshadowing of future events.

That spring and without forewarning, Mark's neighborhood peers abruptly began to snub him. Our doorbell fell silent, leaving me scratching my head as to why. Then came the day he encountered his companions on the school playground. As soon as they became aware of his presence, they flew to their bikes and took off as fast as possible with their laughter and taunts ringing in the air. Mark cried hysterically in the aftermath of this incident. Sydny was no longer willing to acknowledge him at the bus stop or while passing him in the school hallways. Devastated over these losses, Mark concluded that he was strikingly different, damaged, and therefore deserving of this treatment.

Mark coped with the loss of Sydny by obsessively pursuing contact with her whenever an opportunity arose, becoming increasingly demanding with each attempt. She reacted by completely freezing him out and treating him as though he were persona non grata. She did the same with me, though I had served as a substitute mother to her for close to three years. Now, when we crossed paths in the neighborhood, she kept an expressionless gaze pasted to her face. Like Mark, Sydny was only a child, and her abandonment of him was the result of peer pressure that threatened her social standing.

It has been my experience that supportive girls pull back from mentoring special needs children midway through the fourth grade. Toward the later elementary years, inclusion in a typical classroom does not necessarily mean that children *are actually included* as part of the social fabric. Amongst an assigned classroom, these children often experience even greater levels of isolation and loneliness as part of the *invisible club*, which has a high emotional cost that they continue paying for years.

In the face of these heartbreaking developments my overriding emotions were doubt, discouragement, and oppressive guilt. I felt extremely angry with myself for what I perceived as my own naiveté. As usual, my ego was my harshest, unbalanced critic, haranguing me with the idea that I should have been able to foresee the disastrous course I had charted by inviting the neighborhood peers to my home. It also insisted that the emotional toll being exacted on Mark was not in any way worth the benefits accrued to him socially. Once again, I was over-identifying with Mark's experience of abandonment, in part because I avoided healing my own.

Moreover, I was still creating my life from a vibration of resistance, thereby drawing more experiences into my life that would mirror resistance and self-condemnation. One day I would realize that each experience was giving me *another opportunity to learn to accept my life and myself, without conditions.* But that day was still out of reach.

In addition, Mark's sleep deprivation contributed to my own. My brain and body were deprived of the deeper stages of sleep required for muscle repair and optimal health. I spent many of my daytime hours bedridden, trying to catch up on hours of lost sleep from the night before. When I wasn't confined to my bedroom, I was confined for months on end to an Aerobed in my living room with incapacitating fatigue.

My body was so debilitated that I required six hours of paid household help weekly, for which, thankfully, I still had the financial resources to afford. The workers assisted me with mundane chores, such as grocery shopping, cooking, laundry, and household organization. It was a godsend at the time. Just walking to the bathroom and showering proved insurmountable on certain days. I conserved my energy for keeping Mark safe, homework wars, nurturing his interests, community outings, play sessions, providing emotional first aid and the frequent school-related and professional meetings.

I shudder to consider all of the mothers who are required to work full-time outside the home while parenting children with disabilities and their siblings. Some mothers carry all of those responsibilities, in conjunction with managing their own incapacitating chronic health conditions, without the adequate financial resources required to recover their own or their children's ill health. Recovering from chronic illness is typically a lengthy undertaking that is exorbitantly expensive.

Finally, after years of suffering, I placed more attention on locating a physician who could potentially offer some relief. In the spring, through an amazing synchronicity,[34] I was referred to Dr. T., a local holistic chiropractor that specialized in treating fibromyalgia. He immediately impressed me with his compassion and his knowledge. On my initial appointment, he spent over two hours taking a thorough medical history and opined that I had progressed through the spectrum of varied fatigue states from fibromyalgia to Chronic Fatigue Immune Deficiency Syndrome (CFIDS), and was now standing on the precipice of full-blown Environmental Illness. If that circumstance were to occur, I might be forced to remain homebound due to my hyper-reactions to chemicals.

Nevertheless, I felt a measure of hope after he proposed an intensive healing regimen to potentially prevent that outcome. Fortunately, I did not have any idea just how intensive or lengthy it would turn out to be! I immediately started on a program to alkalize my body, repopulate my gut with healthy bacteria and kill off some of the underlying infections that were keeping my body ecology in a state of dis-ease. During Mark's time at summer camp, I experienced my own severe Herxheimer reaction, with accompanying joint and muscle pain, body aches, general malaise, weakness, mental confusion, sweating, chills, and nausea.

After I spent weeks in bed, Dr. T. tested for food intolerances and immediately decided to withdraw me from a number of offending foods. Based on the severity of my healing crisis, it appeared that Dr. T's protocol had been too aggressive for my body to manage in such a short window of time. I discovered firsthand what it felt like to co-exist with the very same yeast overgrowth syndrome that Mark's body combatted during his early years. Due to my global weakness, I was barely able to drive Mark back and forth to summer camp, navigate the revolving door of camp aides, or address the myriad of problems that arose there.

WHAT I KNOW NOW THAT I DIDN'T KNOW THEN: OUR EGOS WILL USE ANY AND ALL MANEUVERS NECESSARY TO PRESERVE OUR ILLUSIONS. THROUGH

THE PRACTICE OF MEDITATION, WE GAIN MASTERY OVER OUR EGOS SO THAT WE MAY MORE FULLY EXPRESS OUR DIVINITY. Now, despite what I have been saying about the ego throughout this book, I'd like to clarify that *it is not our enemy.* In fact, our ego has kept us protected in a yoke of anesthesia and will continue to do so until we are ready to awaken to our Divine birthright: the majesty and exultation of a Soul-led life. Without our egos, we would likely not survive on a planet characterized by unsparing dualities, such as brutality and peace, poverty and wealth, danger and safety, illness and wellness, non-disability and disability, et cetera. Our egos filter all of our experiences through the unconscious mind and will draw conclusions that are false, half-true, paranoid, or outright delusional.

During childhood, our egos erected defense mechanisms as a way of keeping us safe and protected from realities that we were not yet equipped to face. The ego behaves as the great diversionary highway, driving us off course onto remote byways that distract us with all kinds of minutia that, in the big picture of life, will never matter. As part of our ego's ill-considered attempt to mask our oppressive pain, we rehearse, rehash, and recreate our tumultuous, victim-scripted, storylines and dramas, while enacting compulsive, self-defeating, and self-destructive behaviors.

Our egos feed us rational lies, in order to keep us unconscious to our higher powers. Our egos prefer to judge, whine, complain, critique, condemn, and scorn; and, on the other hand, they also prefer to overinflate, brag, grandstand, and pontificate. Our egos make us believe that we are living in a separate body, having experiences that isolate us from everyone and everything. Our egos convince us that our answers are found externally – outside of our intuitive hearts. Our egos are obsessed with manipulating and controlling others and outer circumstances so that we can survive or please others or gain that modicum of approval. Our egos drive us to *be more, have more, and do more!*

Our egos are insatiable and can never be appeased, no matter how much frenzied activity and approval we seek. Eckhart Tolle admonished us to "Stop looking outside for scraps of pleasure or fulfillment, for validation, security, or love – you have a treasure within that is infinitely greater than anything the world can offer." However, our egos have convinced us that our self-esteem and self-worth are measured by the quality of our interactions with our special needs children or on behalf of our children. When our egos enmesh our identity and our self-worth to *our roles*, even those as seductive as mothering our beautiful light-bringers, they have led us astray.

When our egos become *attached* to securing our children's recovery from a specific condition, ensuring specific school-related services, stamping out gut parasites, or changing the social strata of our children's peer experience, et cetera, we have looked for any advantage to control the means to an end. Unfortunately, this approach repels the very things we claim we want and risks setting into motion an unnecessary future cost to our children and ourselves. Our mission is *to choose love over fear.*

Why is aligning with love as the master and fear as the servant so vitally important?

Our point of attraction in the Universe is based upon our dominant thoughts and our corresponding emotional resonance. As Abraham-Hicks said:

> Things are coming into your experience in response to your vibration. Your vibration is offered because of the thoughts you are thinking and you can tell by the way you feel what kinds of thoughts you are thinking. Find good feeling thoughts and good feeling manifestations must follow.

But how do we recognize our vibrational resonance when the ego is such a master at disguising the truth? It takes practice to become conscious of *the Source of our energy*. We begin with the premise that our *mind thinks* and our *heart/Spirit feels*. That sounds simple enough in the abstract but it's often far from it when we're engrossed in daily life in this dense, fear-driven matrix. However, when we approach life with our children as an interesting adventure to be curious about, rather than an arduous set of trials to be defeated, life begins to flow a bit easier. The same is true when we adopt detached curiosity and humor while observing our ego's convoluted machinations rather than being caught up in them.

Forming a consistent habit of meditating is a core foundational practice that underpins discernment – or learning to distinguish when the ego or Spirit is taking the wheel. But is it truly realistic for busy moms to form a meditation practice? I believe that when we prioritize ourselves, meditation is an outflow of that choice. Although meditation takes commitment, it can be integrated into our schedules flexibly. That way, the practice doesn't turn into another failed item on our to-do lists. Through the practice of meditation, we signal to the Universe that *we matter* and *we honor ourselves*, knowing that there are untold benefits – spiritually, mentally, physically – to the point that it can even influence our longevity. *We more quickly tap into our higher solutions and save ourselves all kinds of unnecessary and taxing trial and error.*

If you are a new student of meditation, as I was back in 2011, know that you can start with modest objectives. A seated or resting meditation can begin with a few minutes daily and build to fifteen minutes or longer. The simplest meditation is merely closing your eyes and noticing your deep belly breaths. Each time you observe your belly breath, you give your mind a point of focus. There are a myriad of ways to quiet your mind through moving meditations, such as yoga, Qigong, swimming, painting, or mindfully walking outside.

What sensations do you notice outside of yourself and what sensations do you feel inside your body? What unending thoughts do you observe, as though they are rolling by on a screen? These thoughts offer clues to core unconscious programming that potentially limits you. While seated in waiting rooms, try noticing your breath as you place your attention lightly inside your body. See what sensations are calling for release. You may begin at your feet and slowly scan your entire body all the way to the crown or top of the head. Is your energy light and fluid, or is it heavy and constricted? You can visualize sending white light to any areas of constriction as you exhale the tension and stress down through the bottom of your feet. There are thousands of guided, music, or hertz-based meditations of choice online, so experiment until you find a method that works for you.

Your overall objective is to show up in the present moment and notice your breath, your thoughts and body sensations until you can stand back and observe your thoughts, without judging or labeling them as right, wrong, good or bad. As Deepak Chopra wrote, "Meditation is not a way of making your mind quiet. It's a way of entering into the quiet that's already there – buried under the fifty thousand thoughts the average person thinks every day." Chopra also talks about feeling into the gap between your thoughts. With practice, you will be able to rehabilitate your senses and become more attuned to them so you're better able to decode Divine messages of higher wisdom. An outgrowth of your meditative practice is to harness the power of the moment at hand and become conscious of your buried pain. As Pema Chödrön so eloquently said, "We don't sit in meditation to become good meditators. We sit in meditation so that we'll become more awake in our lives."

RESENTMENT AND BLAME

"Nothing ever goes away until it teaches us
what we need to know."

Pema Chödrön

As the summer drew to a close and fourth grade began, Mark's social, academic, and sleep challenges continued unabated. "Homework wars" dominated our life. If that wasn't enough, Mark was required to attend school thirty minutes earlier so that he could complete his dreaded math homework! Due to a pattern of late transitioning from math time, Mark frequently missed the beginning of class – a brief window of time where students socialized. Mark wisely insisted that he needed to be there during this time, that missing this jumping-off point with peers placed him at an even greater social disadvantage.

During this time we both continued to live with the impact of chronic immune deficiencies, with Mark at the mercy of viral assaults that were then passed to me. The dedicated efforts and compassion of Dr. T. had not prevented my body from undergoing a significant healing crisis. Although I continued under Dr. T.'s care, I also contacted a new physician to explore other complementary treatments. This physician referred me to Dr. S, to whom I forwarded my medical records and underwent the battery of lab tests, yet it would be months before I finally got an appointment to see Dr. S. face-to-face. He impressed me with his compassion, his lengthy years of experience, and his vast knowledge of functional medicine.[35] In the future, I would come to know him as a modern-day "Renaissance Man." He was also married to a beautiful woman who was valiantly engaged in healing from her own long-term illness.

Dr. S. agreed to manage my autoimmune thyroid disorder. He ordered further tests, started me on a new regimen of nutritional supplements, and recommended that I begin weekly nutritional IV support. The second IV infusion gave me my first temporary energy boost and left me with greater cognitive clarity.

The timing couldn't have been better, because Mark's upcoming birthday party was scheduled at a local movie theater. Cole, Mark's primary classroom peer, went out of his way to demonstrate kindness and empathy toward Mark and willingly came to the party, seemingly unconcerned about the impact on his social standing. This party was also noteworthy because Mark's father and I came together to celebrate this special occasion. Mark actually looked happy and content and even verbalized feelings of happiness at the close of the party.

That happiness, however, was short-lived, as he continued to live with pronounced anxiety, as well as extreme OCD characterized by hoarding behavior. During the wintertime, Mark fell into a depression, necessitating an increased dose of his antidepressant. During this time period, my dear friend Mary and her son invited Mark to his upcoming ice-skating party. At the time, I carried a certain level of confidence that Mark would successfully regulate himself during the event, as the year before he had managed appropriately while attending a karate party. Had I intuited what was to come, I would certainly have kept Mark home.

During the skating portion of the party, Mark began to obsessively pursue and cling to Mary's son, oblivious to his need to divide his attention amidst a large group of fifth-grade peers. Once things moved to an enclosed party room, Mark's behavior escalated out of control. I spent the majority of my time monitoring him as he raced back and forth among the outer party rooms and hallways of this building, spewing his vitriol. You may wonder why didn't I just escort him to my car? I knew with certainty that Mark was not going to willingly leave the premises. He loudly verbalized threats and his body was *at war*. My own body was drenched in sweat as I attempted to prevent him from entering the primary party room and engaging with the public

It was not always possible to prevent him from charging in and out of various rooms. Those in attendance at the party were not aware of the imminent threat that was lurking just inside and beyond their door. After over two hours of managing his behavior singlehandedly, I was able to surreptitiously alert Mary as to what was happening. She waited until most of the partygoers had left, then she encroached on Mark's right side and I encroached on his left. Mark began screaming incoherently and crying as we exited the building. Once we hit the brisk cool air outside, we both grabbed an arm simultaneously.

At that point, we were forced to manhandle and drag Mark's adrenaline-surged body to my car. My most vivid memory surrounds Mark's awareness that his relationship with this long-term friend had permanently shifted. He had invited Mark to the party out of the kindness of his heart but he too was ready to move on to a new social stratum. Mark sobbed inconsolably all the way home, asserting that his life was no longer worth living. His pain surrounding abandonment had once again become unbearable.

Then, just as spring emerged, this antidepressant dose increase precipitated a mixed bipolar state, one characterized by extreme highs and lows that alternated in rapid succession. Mark's attempt to put his fist through my car window is a standout memory of that time.

During May, Mark lived through a complete breakdown in functioning. In light of his prior stay at the psychiatric hospital – specifically, the interruption of his nutritional and medication regimens – I considered and rejected seeking treatment there. He was now taking therapeutic levels of his mood stabilizer and any immediate stoppage of his medication could be extremely dangerous. Dr. F. increased Mark's dose of mood stabilizer and added an anti-anxiety medication to be used on an as-needed basis. Although this plan was quite reasonable, the dose of mood stabilizer had to be subsequently reduced. His agitation worsened and his lab results were elevated, indicating physical toxicity. Further, the anti-anxiety medication had provided little to no benefit.

Based on Mark's psychiatric emergency, the school wisely reduced his attendance to half-days. However, the academic demands were still coming fast and furious, including a multistep project that demanded he display his newly acquired knowledge on a T-shirt. Mark was expected to show off his academic prowess by wearing his masterpiece and parading through the school hallways!

I could barely stomach the wildly absurd double life we were leading. Mark was expected to perform academic feats by day; then, in his off hours, he morphed into someone else entirely – someone who carried and acted out unbearable pain, his own and what he had absorbed from being forced to participate in the ways of this world. So, when the school refused to waive the project, I completed it for him, careful to imitate his work. Though this went totally against my grain, I was not about to leave my son to be sacrificed on some bureaucratic altar for completely senseless reasons. His life seemed to be on the line, even though Mark and I were the only two people who fully recognized it.

Indeed, jumping through pointless academic hoops as I kept my son on this planet was not the only weighty concern at the time. I was also carrying another heavy burden related to Mark's health.

During the previous five years, Mark had been seeing Dr. Z, an endocrinologist, and more recently, Laura, his physician's assistant, for monitoring of his thyroid disorder. In January of his fourth-grade year, another bomb was detonated. (No matter how many times these bombs exploded, I was never, ever, prepared for them.) Laura showed me that Mark's growth curve had precipitously fallen to the first percentile.

"Mark needs to undergo a complete work-up," she said in a flat, brusque tone, "and an X-ray of his hand to determine his bone age. The first step involves consultation with a pediatric gastroenterologist so that we can rule out celiac disease. More than likely, Mark will need to be admitted to the hospital for outpatient tests. He will need to undergo a brain MRI with contrast dye to rule out a pituitary tumor. If that comes back negative, we will schedule him for a clonidine stimulation test on an outpatient basis in the hospital. That test will tell us if he in fact has a pediatric growth deficiency disorder."

Once again, my brain was trying to speed up to process the rapid-fire succession of words. Notwithstanding my notetaking, shock was setting in. My mind rattled off the following: *Did she just say, pediatric growth disorder? What the hell is that? What kind of stimulation test is she recommending? Did she mention the words "pituitary tumor" as though instructing me on how to make a peanut butter and jelly sandwich? Does she actually think that Mark could have a brain tumor? Focus! Think! Ask a reasonable question!*

Finally, I managed to get out the words, "Is he going to need to undergo an endoscopy under anesthesia?"

Laura responded, "Well, that will be the gastroenterologist's call."

"Do you have someone you can recommend?"

"No, you'll need to call your insurance company."

This can't be happening. This can't be f**king happening right now.

Laura was still speaking, and I paused my inner monologue long enough to catch the phrase, "You'll want to call the Magic Foundation. They can walk you through the lengthy process of qualifying for the medication with your insurance company. This medication potentially costs up to forty thousand dollars per year."

I had been standing during her entire diatribe and suddenly I felt dizzy, weak and lightheaded. *Maybe,* I thought, *I can collapse right here and never have to be revived.*

But I heard myself say, "What kind of medication could possibly cost forty thousand dollars?"

She coldly sidestepped that question and answered another I hadn't thought to ask: "Oh, you will need to deliver the medication through a nightly subcutaneous injection. Synthetic growth hormone is actually recombinant DNA, and fortunately the methods have greatly improved through the years. The older protocol used to put children at risk for leukemia."

"Are you saying that if he has this condition, I will need to give Mark a daily shot?"

"Yes."

My mind raced ahead. It took four people to hold Mark down for a blood draw and this woman, with her objective professional demeanor, was saying I would be expected to singlehandedly give him a daily shot! *This can't be real. This can't be f**king real.*

Later I would come to understand that growth hormone does so much more than promote growth in children. Growth hormone is released in the body during stage three of the nightly sleep cycle. It helps in the regulation of body composition, body fluids, muscle and bone growth, sugar and fat metabolism and contributes to healthy heart function. Growth hormone also supports cognitive function and the regulation of mood. The diagnostic clonidine test would stimulate the pituitary gland to begin secreting growth hormone in bursts that are measured at spaced intervals, via a blood draw during a three-hour window in the hospital. The peak growth hormone level determines whether a child's parameters fall within expected levels of hormone production.

I didn't know what bits and pieces of the conversation Mark overheard at the endocrinologist's office, nor what information he had unwittingly absorbed. He didn't raise any questions on the way back to school, but that didn't necessarily mean that he wasn't acutely aware of my abrupt mood shift. I tried to hold myself together and present a façade of normalcy, but my muteness during the car ride was a clear indicator that something was gravely wrong. I felt like my world had just collapsed without any forewarning.

After dropping Mark at school, I went to my bedroom, crawled into bed, and sobbed uncontrollably. Laura had written, "Rule out pituitary dwarfism" on the medical paperwork, which led me down a terrifying rabbit hole. Mark's shoe size hadn't increased in close to four years. He had not lost a single baby tooth since first grade, and he was approximately a foot shorter than his peers of the same age.

The testing alone sent panic coursing through my veins and set my mind on fire with catastrophic thoughts. I fixated on the contrast dye that was going to be injected into Mark's brain during the upcoming MRI, fearing he would either have a systemic allergic reaction in his body or an inflammatory response. Once the dye was injected, it could not be removed!

Of course, "normal" life did not stop just because of this new development. In my normal, Mr. Rogers didn't appear, dressed in his comfy sweater and tennis shoes, to good-naturedly guide his compatriots through an idyllic, make-believe neighborhood. In my normal, Mark came in the door and exploded. Indeed, my normal was a soap opera that had aired more episodes than *General Hospital,* with me serving as executive producer and lead cast member – my role, a panicked, overwhelmed, chronically ill, middle-aged woman who had dealt with one too many life-changing crises. All I wanted was for this long-running series to be canceled.

I wanted to abdicate my responsibility and turn it over to someone else – someone who would be more emotionally equipped to handle this news, someone who wouldn't fall into the ego's trap of assigning blame and finger-pointing at so-called adversaries while carrying a weighty catalog of resentments. I wanted to turn it over to someone who combined the optimism of FDR, the problem-solving abilities of Henry Ford, the perseverance of Thomas Edison, and the physical prowess of Michael Jordon. Michael could easily have held Mark down and whipped the needle in with one sweeping gesture.

On this particular day, as Mark was in the midst of his massive rage attack, Neil, his worker, casually walked through the front door. *Thank God,* I thought, as I did not have the emotional reserves to cope with another one -or two-hour cataclysmic episode. I had never left a worker alone to manage Mark's rage attacks before, but if there was any time I needed to do this, it was now.

Mark was already in hot pursuit, targeting me with his venom. As I ran to the garage to escape, six-foot-three-inch Neil enclosed Mark in a standing basket hold as Mark flailed and struggled by kicking his feet full-force. With Mark's animalistic screams ringing in my ears, I slid into the car and immediately shut the door, then pushed the garage door opener, clicked my seatbelt in place, turned on the ignition, put the car in reverse, and depressed the gas pedal.

The next thing I heard was the sound of metal on metal as I side-swiped Neil's van. In my haste to get away, I had neglected to take into account that another vehicle sat in my driveway. The damaged side mirror and gouged side might not have been a big deal, if only the van had been registered to Neil. Instead, the van was the property of a therapeutic day school that employed him and permitted his personal use.

At that point, I was so overwrought I could do nothing but sit there, staring aimlessly ahead, hoping against hope that I would awaken from this cosmic nightmare. My tears had dissipated; however, I now felt an uncomfortable and forceful pounding of my heart. At least it was thankfully still beating in a familiar rhythm – possibly the one thing in my life that hadn't changed.

After a moment, I tried to gingerly dislodge my car from Neil's van, only to freeze again when I heard the awful now-familiar scraping sound reverberating through the air. Neil must have heard it too because he appeared in the driveway. He briefly surveyed the damage, then entered the van from the passenger's side and masterfully backed up, disentangling our vehicles.

He then took one look at me and said in a commanding voice, "Just go. Just leave. We'll figure this out later."

I spent much of Neil's shift driving around aimlessly or parked in a lot, trying to decompress. However, this did not prevent panic from setting in during the wee hours of the night. My pulse was pounding in my ears. I experienced hours desperate for ample oxygen as I struggled to inhale deeply as my palms sweat and my mind raced. Without warning, tears streamed down my face. After my interminable, tumultuous night ended, I immediately initiated the same action I had taken following Mark's alleged poisoning by a contaminated well: I made an emergency call to Kelly, Mark's consulting nutritionist.

Kelly wholeheartedly agreed that injecting the dye into Mark's brain during the MRI could set him up for an inflammatory response and advised me not to allow it. When we hung up, I took a moment to get my emotions in check, then placed a call to Laura. I was still extremely angry that a physician's assistant, and one I barely knew, had delivered the suspected diagnosis. Although I respected her capabilities, I believed that information of this magnitude, with such life-altering consequences, should have come directly from the doctor.

After weeks of phone outreach, I finally spoke to Dr. Z, who was not at all patient with my line of questioning. He did not believe that Mark could forego the dye during his brain MRI. My frustration turned to shock, however, when he announced that unless I chose to acquiesce to his recommendations he would allege medical neglect on my part with the State Department of Child and Family Services. I couldn't believe that a physician with whom I'd had such a long-standing relationship was bullying me. I felt betrayed, disillusioned, and forced into capitulating.

The appointment with the gastroenterologist devolved into an exceedingly frustrating experience. He ordered a blood test to rule out celiac disease, which seemed pointless as Mark's diet had been gluten-free for eight years, making it highly unlikely that an antibody to gluten would be found.[36] In addition, Dr. N. saw no indication to test for anything else, and while I was enormously relieved that he was not going to scope Mark, I was exasperated by the fact that he also didn't see a reason for an office examination. Through the years, it had been all too common for Mark's physicians to be so intimidated by his behavior that they refused to even listen to his heart and lungs.

Eight months slipped by before all the required diagnostic steps were completed. (Mark would be a fifth grader before we received a definitive answer concerning growth hormone supplementation.) The health care system and insurance bureaucracies consumed my life. I spent endless hours researching the latest non-needle delivery methods, only to be told by Dr. Z. that his practice would not support such a plan. His rationale: "We've never used those methods before," which for an out-of-the-box problem-solver like me was infuriating.

To say the brain MRI was a traumatic experience would be an understatement. Mark's father was present, and my most vivid memory was of him prying Mark's hands from the grasp bar in the bathroom as Mark fought with all his strength to escape the insertion of the IV needle. Finally, my former spouse was able to carry our son, then exhausted from the struggle and drenched with sweat, to his hospital bed, however, Mark continued to whimper as they restrained his body and inserted the IV needle. We then waited for the sedatives to take effect. Later, I peered through a glass panel door as they prepared Mark's semiconscious body to be slid into the MRI machine.

If only I could have received advance knowledge that Mark would come through this testing unscathed, the wait for them to complete it would have been less excruciating. Instead, it felt like time stood still as I sat in the waiting room with a blaring TV mounted in the corner and made silent petitions to God on Mark's behalf. During this unending wait, I was seated amidst strangers and away from my former spouse. This physical separation foreshadowed the future.

As Mark's fourth-grade school year came to a close, his dad announced that he was relocating to another state for an advantageous career opportunity. By July, he was a five-hour drive away and planned to see Mark every third weekend for one and a half days.

At the same time, Mark was still undergoing intrusive medical tests for a suspected growth disorder; he was in the process of recovering from a severe mood episode in the spring; he was weathering the abrupt abandonment of Neil, who had walked off the job without explanation; and he was adjusting to the loss of his secondary home and a more consistent schedule with his father.

And in the midst of these transitions, I was still cleaning up the debris from another surreal experience with Mark's home-based mentor, Terence. Against my better judgment, I couldn't bring myself to strip away another meaningful presence from Mark, particularly a male influence. Terence had been assigned to Mark for several months when I began to suspect that he was using "creative" accounting methods with Mark's spending money. When I insisted upon receipts so that I could carefully monitor Mark's expenditures, circumstances appeared to temporarily improve.

Then, while accompanying Mark to the local library, Terence decided to appropriate Mark's library card and abscond with CDs from the music collection – two thousand dollars' worth. Apparently the plan was to copy them for sale and then return them without discovery, and when this did not happen the library demanded that I pay the exorbitant fines and replacement costs as well.

When I reported Terence's behavior to the hiring agency, they demanded that I make an immediate police report. I greatly resented adding another burden to my burgeoning to-do list. Why was it my job to report his crime to the authorities? I had more important matters at hand.

Since I couldn't very well ignore the matter, I went to the local police department only to discover that Terence had a lengthy criminal record of theft and drug-related charges. I was shocked to discover that my son's mentors were never screened for lower-level crimes, meaning that anyone without a history of sexual or violent crimes could easily pass the state fingerprinting system – and end up in my home!

Just as egregious, in my opinion, was the insistence by the hiring agency that I terminate Terence's job during his upcoming shift. I brought my most commanding presence to this interaction, however, for quite some time after, I lived with the fear that Terence, or someone he knew, would find a way to retaliate against us. Fortunately, he decided to cut his losses, while I lost a lot of precious time trying to convince library officials that my fourth-grader did not pose a future threat to their merchandise!

All of these machinations I classified as the cost of doing business with the state. There had been a cast of characters sent by the contractual agency that I wouldn't trust to tend a garden, let alone mentor my son. Tony showed up to work after all-night binges, hung-over and reeking of alcohol. He was asked to leave after his second infraction. Then there was Frank, who waltzed into work in open-toed sandals in the midst of blizzard-like conditions with mounds of snow outside. During a trip to a local science museum, he decided to take possession of Mark's handheld Game Boy. On the car ride back home in the car, I found myself arbitrating between Frank and Mark, both of whom grabbed for the device simultaneously. Childlike Frank had to go. Then there was Angela, who left Mark unsupervised for a lengthy period of time at a birthday party at the local Chuck E. Cheese.

Turmoil was the ever-present backdrop of our lives. That summer, Mark returned to camp, where the physical bullying and taunts from peers escalated. I rushed Mark to the pediatrician for bouts of unrelenting chronic eczema; a severe allergic reaction to something he ate; and a sprained ankle that came about after his fellow campers pushed him into the pool.

Once, after yet another urgent call, I rushed to the camp and was infuriated to discover Mark alone in a bathroom, wracked by sobs, with angry, raised, red welts covering almost every inch of his body. After days of investigation, I never determined the cause of Mark's hive attack. However, from that point forward, Mark's pediatrician insisted that an EpiPen Jr. Auto-Injector be in his possession at all times.

During Mark's time at camp, he re-enrolled in weekly psychotherapy with Amy, our former home-based mental health worker. The local mental health center had finally stopped the merry-go-round of less-than-stellar home-based mental health professionals. After a bit of legwork I located Amy's new psychotherapy practice and gladly made the forty-mile drive knowing she had the talent to assist Mark.

As Amy got up to speed with Mark's current challenges, his three-year re-evaluation with the school team was moved to July and August. As a result of Mark's emotional collapse at the end of the schoolyear, the multidisciplinary team agreed that his current educational and clinical data could be re-assessed and reviewed prior to Mark's placement in fifth grade.

With that circumstance in mind, I hired an educational advocate, Guy. Guy spent considerable time gathering the pertinent information and reviewing all of Mark's records. He fully agreed that Mark would benefit from a therapeutic day school,[37] but he did not believe that I had adequate ammunition to force the district's hands. For the first time ever, Mark pleaded with me to locate a *stress school:* a setting that would reduce his school-related stress and help manage academic demands. He was acutely aware that the *game of keeping up* had cost him his mental health and wanted to attend a school where he was on the same playing field as his peers.

School districts are notoriously reluctant to place students in private segregated schools, firstly, based upon the intent of the law, which states that students shall reside in the "least restrictive educational setting possible" and secondly, because the tuition for private schools is exorbitantly expensive. Without a referral from the school district for a planned visit, I couldn't even step foot through the door for a fact-gathering mission.

The district completely thwarted my repeated attempts to visit two local therapeutic day schools. Then, after hours seated at the re-evaluation meeting with Guy by my side, they gave me the option of re-enrolling Mark in full inclusion for fifth grade at his home school (in other words, more of the same) or placement in a district-wide self-contained classroom for children with more extreme behavioral and emotional challenges. Of course the district invited me to visit said program – one that didn't cost them substantially more to educate Mark.

WHAT I KNOW NOW THAT I DIDN'T KNOW THEN: PERFECTIONISM IS A FORM OF EGOIC SELF-ABUSE THAT FORGES AN ILLUSION OF SAFETY. When the ego relentlessly chases standards on behalf of our children that, irrespective of effort and energy expended, can never be achieved, we are lost in a form of self-abuse. Perfectionism is worlds apart from healthy striving for excellence. Healthy strivers are inwardly focused on self-improvement, whereas perfectionists are hostage to the tyranny of *needing* external acceptance and approval.

Perfectionists are addicted to outside approval and acceptance as a way to prop up their sagging self-esteem. Their entire sense of worth is *based upon performance,* which they obsessively critique while also obsessively monitoring the responses of others in their environments – especially the authority figures. I agree with Anne Lamott's view that "Perfectionism is the voice of the oppressor."

Childhood is typically the breeding ground for perfectionism. *Children erroneously internalize the belief that they are responsible for controlling other people's perceptions of their behavior.* They ceaselessly monitor their own behavior as a barometer for whether they can ensure their physical and emotional well-being. They have learned to adopt a pattern of hyper-compliance and pleasing as a means of self-protection.

Perfectionism is characterized by errors in thinking. The biggest error of all is adopting the belief that we are required to live perfectly; present an image of perfection; and do everything perfectly in order to avoid or minimize the painful feelings that come from experiences attached to the sting of shame, blame and/or judgment. *Perfectionists come to believe that they are their accomplishments and thus, they adopt an identity around neurotic over-achieving.* The ego convinces us that it is never safe to step off the treadmill of chasing the unattainable. As perfectionists, we are caught in the trap of black-and-white thinking, concluding that our end results either approached the mark or were deeply flawed.

The ego will repeatedly reinforce that mistakes are unacceptable while driving us to gain that modicum of outside validation. In the event that we've actually encountered shame, blame, or judgment, the ego will insist that we double-down on our efforts. Rather than questioning the faulty premise of earning others' support through performance, we work even harder the next time around to stamp out our so-called deficiencies or to gain our desired outcomes. Thus, an addiction is fueled. None of this faulty thinking serves anyone. Although our society offers us external rewards, they come at an exorbitantly high price. Our rigid thinking and fear of failure rob us of happiness, dreams fulfilled, resiliency and, potentially, even our optimal health.

Although I was aware of my need to appear perfect during childhood, in the wake of the trauma surrounding Mark's needs I did not fully appreciate the repercussions of my addictive perfectionism. I did not yet understand that my unrealistic, unreachable, standards could never be met, consigning me to live in a state of chronic dissatisfaction. As a perfectionist mother, I unconsciously placed myself at high risk for anxiety, depression, chronic procrastination, risk-aversion, and strained relationships.

As focused as I was on eradicating my own faults, I could also at times turn that laser-pointed focus on eliminating the faults of others. Doing so is a boundary violation of the highest order, and one that clearly does not promote emotional safety in relationships. Not only was my ego caught up in the faultfinding and blaming brigade, but I also found myself perpetually doing more than was reasonable, and consequently, I burned myself out physically, emotionally and spiritually. As EFT Master and abundance coach Carol Look said:

> Being a perfectionist cuts you off spiritually. Regardless of your beliefs, you tend to not feel 'plugged in' to your spiritual source --not present–you are always looking for positive feedback based *on* your performance rather than who you really are. You often feel a deep emptiness because values and meaning are based on the wrong ideal.

I was never able to recognize when enough was enough. I researched ad infinitum, looking for that one more scrap of information that might lend itself to improving my own or my son's circumstances. I was blind to the inherent limits that were strikingly obvious to others. My home life was inseparable from my "work life" as a special needs parent. I unconsciously used my addiction to work and my need for perfect appearances, as a way to mask and escape from my painful feelings and low self-image.

Dumping the perfectionism mom habit goes a long way toward healing our lives. I have learned to manage my perfectionism by setting healthy boundaries; ensuring that the work and recharging/renewing parts of my life are in more optimal balance; and prioritizing essential tasks from arbitrary ones. I now recognize that *not every task requires the same level of commitment.* I now consider that my body has a finite amount of energy that should not be squandered; thus, I give myself permission to complete menial tasks or tasks of less importance in an "acceptably average" manner. I also now embody the freedom attached to those two words.

In order to short-circuit aspects of my perfectionism, I have integrated the "Observe and Correct" technique into my daily life.[38] Via Observe and Correct, I have learned to validate, with kindness and compassion, that it is safe for me to display less-than-perfect behavior. I now accept that it is safe to make a misstep, because missteps are integral to the learning process. As an empowered mom, I choose to "respond with ability" by observing my gutter balls, taking responsibility for them, and when possible, correcting them and pivoting at the soonest point in time.

I have learned to focus on the correction, rather than participating in the ego's survival cycle of *observe, complain, blame, and explain.* By investing my energy in the *correction,* I avoid rehearsing my ego's old tired storyline related to the fear of being rejected, criticized, humiliated, or abandoned. Authentic and lasting approval can only come from within. Seeking external validation is an ego trap that keeps us from thriving. As Wayne Dyer so eloquently put it, "What other people think of me is none of my business. One of the highest places you can get to is being independent of the good opinions of other people."

WORRY AND OVERWHELM

"Ego says, 'Once everything falls into place,
I'll feel peace.' Spirit says, 'Find your peace
and then everything will fall into place.'"

Marianne Williamson

Another school year commenced. Mark moved to the new self-contained classroom with four other fourth-grade peers. Before the start of the schoolyear, a pre-visit was arranged so that Mark could meet his new staff members and gain comfort with the physical surroundings. While there, I was immediately dismayed by the social worker's comments, which I perceived as condescending. Although Rachel had never met either one of us, it seemed to me that she believed she had all the easy answers for Mark. She also seemed to conclude that Mark's issues were in large measure due to a lack of discipline in the home. To put it mildly, Rachel and I did not get off to a winning start.

Unfortunately, over the course of the next two years, our relationship did not improve. Throughout much of Mark's life, I had struggled to impress upon the professionals the nature of Mark's condition: *an invisible disability that is brain-based in nature.* Dr. Ross Greene, Ph.D., a psychologist formerly of Harvard Medical School, has written a number of influential books on the subject: *The Explosive Child; Lost at School; Lost & Found;* and *Raising Human Beings;* he is also the originator of the Collaborative and Proactive Solutions (CPS) approach. Dr. Greene recognized that children with brain-based disorders lack essential skills, which interferes with their mastery both at home and at school. He believed that *these children would do well if they could!*[39]

Children with brain-based disabilities are often deficient in planning ahead, reasoning, anticipating consequences, delaying gratification, reading social cues, thinking flexibly, generating good solutions, making inferences, multitasking, and expressing themselves verbally, just to name some examples. Dr. Greene purports that a family or educational system that is bent toward punitive and adversarial actions will lead only to further alienation and disenfranchisement for children who already feel misunderstood, criticized, and condemned by the key adults in their lives!

Moreover, our school systems continue to remain entrenched in an overly simplistic theoretical model, with antecedent-behavior-consequence the overarching, established mode of intervention. With the wrong characterization of the problem comes the wrong prescriptive solution. I learned from Dr. Greene that we can best support children in advance of circumstances that will likely push them beyond their capabilities by forming a close partnership with them to help them solve issues that *they deem important.* Our efforts need to be proactive and preventative, rather than reactive, ineffective, and potentially harmful. No matter how much time I spent trying to educate the professionals as to what could best serve Mark, many professionals could not let go of their antiquated ways of looking at problem behaviors.

On the other hand, I appreciated the demeanor of the speech language pathologist. She was immediately on board with Mark's needs and she approached challenges with creative and collaborative solutions. Fortuitously, I also found Mark's teacher, Mrs. A., to be competent, compassionate and, open-minded. Off the record (*way off*), she wholeheartedly agreed that Mark belonged in a therapeutic day school. Unfortunately, Mrs. A. had no power to sway the district to move Mark out of her self-contained classroom. However, she did hold the power to immediately modify homework assignments to infrequently or none at all, which reduced Mark's stress level immeasurably – and my own!

Because most of Mark's peers were assigned to mainstream classes for the majority of the day, Mark was afforded more one-to-one instruction with Mrs. A. He also benefitted from the relaxed pace and the positive social and emotional connection with a caring adult. Mark left the classroom for three inclusion subjects and, midway through the year, a fourth class was added. I wasn't concerned about the self-contained curriculum being "dumbed down" because my pressing priority was reducing Mark's stress and stabilizing his mental health.

Mark did continue to struggle during unstructured periods of time. Lunch in the mainstream cafeteria left him ostracized and isolated. The phone never rang for Mark nor were there any invites from school peers. For the first time in Mark's life, he did not commemorate his birthday with a party. His world narrowed down to intermittent contact with Forrest, his best friend from pre-school days. Mark complained incessantly of abject loneliness.

It was heartbreaking to hear him characterize his experience in fifth grade with the following sentiment; "The kids in social studies treat me as though I am a piece of furniture, hidden in the corner."

Mark's new home-based mentor, Kelly, provided some balm to his wounds. Kelly not only had experience parenting her own teenage children, but she also possessed the sensitivity, upbeat nature, and finesse to work effectively with Mark. She was reliable and she did whatever she could to successfully engage Mark. Kelly even invited Mark to her home so that he could socialize with her entire family.

Mark enjoyed baking in Kelly's kitchen, playing with her dog, jumping on her outdoor trampoline and watching movies with her

entire family. Finally, Mark had a second home where he felt unconditionally accepted. Blessedly, this arrangement continued for some
time until the mental health center decided that Mark could no longer
be included there, as it was considered a boundary violation and posed
a liability for the agency. I understood the rationale for such, even
though this decision compromised Mark's sense of stability.

While Kelly and Mrs. A. certainly made a positive difference, there
was nothing they could do to prevent Mark's ongoing acute illnesses.
Throughout December, the whooping cough compromised Mark's
body. I prayed that I wouldn't come down with the bacterium and,
for once, I was spared. I was also under considerable stress, anticipating the start of Mark's nightly growth hormone injection. The tests
had definitively confirmed that Mark indeed had pituitary dwarfism. The
inordinately expensive monthly medication and accompanying supplies
had already arrived in their square cardboard shipping box.

I took one look in the package and nearly fainted after viewing
a set of needles that were approximately one inch in length. I would
have slept better at night with the advance knowledge that these needles
were *only* used for reconstituting (mixing) the sterile water solution
with the powered medication to generate liquid human growth hormone. The medication would then be delivered via a much smaller
needle directly under Mark's skin.

I also wish I had known that the human growth hormone would
rather quickly eradicate Mark's lifelong pattern of falling ill with
chronic viral assaults. The Universe had truly delivered a miracle to
us! None of the health care professionals had predicted this advantage
when presenting the upside to the injection. Another miracle arrived
in the form of The Magic Foundation,[40] which put me on the right
path to ensure that the exorbitant cost of the medication would be
covered by insurance and educated me, via their newsletter, about rare
childhood endocrine disorders.

Before I became aware of the significant and life-enhancing advantages of human growth hormone, I first had to undergo training at the

endocrinologist's office to administer it. I was offered *one lesson* to master three steps; reconstituting the medication; drawing the medication into a syringe; and finally, injecting Mark. I was very grateful that my lovely friend Mary accompanied us to the appointment.

Mark was so terrorized it took three people in the doctor's office to restrain him so that he could receive the shot. How in the world was I going to singlehandedly accomplish this task at home? I spent untold hours on the phone trying to enlist a home-based nursing service to establish a nightly routine of injections – and dealing with Mark's health insurance company, which finally agreed to pay for three home visits by a nursing service. Yet twenty nursing agencies later, not a single nurse was willing to accept the assignment!

Eventually, a nursing supervisor told me that though she had stopped making home visits years ago, she would come in the evenings to assist me. I considered Nurse Sheila to be an earthbound angel! Although I met with her on only three occasions, she immensely changed our lives for the better, showing me strategies that immediately solved some of the problems I encountered. She also spent a great deal of time listening compassionately, and in fact she was the first person who acknowledged the enormity of my challenge.

Knowing our success depended on it, I tried to plan out a routine. I decided it would be best to seat Mark in front of the TV, with one of his most preferred videos as a distraction, while I gave him the shot, followed by his most preferred food reward. On day one, Mark ran away and hid in the furthest corner of the second story of our house. I had the highly stressful task of dragging him down the stairs and to the dreaded chair, while he fought with all his strength to avoid what he saw as an assault. Then Nurse Sheila restrained him in the chair while I, with my hands visibly shaking, stuck the needle in and depressed the plunger.

Sheila noted that my pace for medication delivery through the needle was too slow. She advised me to practice using a water-loaded syringe and apple as a stand-in for Mark so I could master the mechanics.

Amazingly, by the third day of dosing, Mark had become a bit more desensitized to the new routine and I was able to manage the circumstance going forward.

Within the first ten days of dosing, Mark experienced an atypical side effect – excessive weight gain – and I immediately made a doctor's appointment. When Mark stepped upon the scale, the incredulous nurses were able to see the results for themselves and Dr. Z. halved the dose. From that time forward, things progressed in a smooth fashion. While there was no observable improvement in Mark's depression, his cognitive profile or his sleep disruption, the injection did result in an immediate boost to his immune deficiency! The angels had blessed us with an enhanced quality to our lives! Additionally, Mark grew four inches during the first year on the injectable, rather than his yearly average of three-fourths of an inch. Although he had a long way to go, progress was steadily being made.

With the winter months upon us, Mark was besieged with his expected escalation of depressive symptoms. In early February, I found him seated on the floor of the living room with the barrel of a toy gun resting inside his mouth as he mimicked pulling the trigger. Mark was at the mercy of ongoing suicidal thoughts and in his despair repeatedly begged me to complete a suicide pact with him.

Terrified, I tried desperately to find a competent local child therapist who would willingly accept Mark's case and his insurance. After yet another exhaustive search, I located two potential candidates who could see us on an emergency basis. Things did not go at all well with therapist one; however, therapist two, Dr. Jane Houghtaling Walker, was a complete breath of fresh air! My life was about to dramatically transform for the better, and that change arrived not a moment too soon.

For the next sixteen years, Dr. Walker would be a steadfast, shining beacon in our lives. She quickly comprehended Mark's complex needs, was able to anticipate his struggles, and competently and proactively managed the challenges he presented. Her professional demeanor, coupled with her calm, grounded, statements moved his needle forward. She also fully supported my parenting strategies and showed up for me in a myriad of ways that no other professional had done to date. She did so, in part, because she was living through a personal experience as a reference point. Jane passionately advocated for our needs during our most crucial periods of darkness.

The arrival of spring did not alleviate Mark's suffering. According to my records, he was "irritable, hostile, self-denigrating, depressed, experiencing crying jags, provoking cycles, and worsening hypomania, most especially at night." Prior to the start of school, Mark underwent panic attacks, characterized by retching and gagging. Once again, Dr. F. added an antianxiety medication to the regimen and, once again, it did not lessen his symptoms. Additionally, Mark was at the mercy of intermittent delusional thoughts, the most disturbing of which centered around aliens kidnapping him for the purpose of manipulating his brain.

Mark regularly came home from school reporting that he had been taunted, hit, and kicked in a covert manner during lunchtime, while begging to be removed from the cafeteria. By May, Mrs. A. appeared to spend more and more time out of the classroom and was increasingly detached from Mark's emotional pain. She did not share my sense of urgency related to the lunchroom circumstances. I went over her head to the District's Director of Special Education. She referred the matter to a behavioral specialist, who went to the school to conduct observation and data collection.

I was stunned to learn that the problem was much, much worse than I had initially feared. She observed Mark dumping his lunch into the trashcan so he could avoid his seat at the table, which provided a cover for male peers to physically abuse him away from the watchful eyes of staff members. He would then spend his lunchtime curled in a fetal position on the grass, sobbing and alone, without support from anyone.

To say I was outraged when I heard the report – and from the district's own behaviorist – would be a gross understatement. The bright

side was that I finally had the leverage to remove Mark from the cafeteria, as his physical state and mental health were in jeopardy. For two
weeks, Mark ate alone in his classroom. Then, without notifying me,
Mrs. A. transitioned Mark right back to the cafeteria.

Neither Mark's brand-new Bichon Maltese, nor his enrollment in
therapeutic horseback riding lessons, was enough to mitigate the damage
being done in the school environment. I was so relieved when the schoolyear finally came to a close and full-time summer camp commenced. Mercifully, Mark's depressive fog began to lift as his longed-for growth spurt
continued; however, he was now facing another challenge: puberty, with
a flood of hormonal changes that exacerbated his symptoms of OCD. Not
only was hoarding an ongoing feature of Mark's condition, but he now
ruminated over *dangerous* insects, germs, and skin-related obsessions.

He continually checked the bottom of his shoes for contaminants.
At times, he could barely walk because he had to do so after every step.
He was also hostage to the compulsion to examine his arms for suspected contaminants, and in the evenings he avoided walking our dog
outside for fear of contact with insects. The smallest gnat would trigger
panic. Quirkiness related to OCD symptomatology did not help Mark
fit into the social groupings at camp.

Despite all of the upheaval surrounding Mark's summertime functioning, camp personnel reported an improvement in his overall capacity
to conform to programming expectations. Given the fact that Mark
found change unbearable, it was significant that he was able to adapt
to two newly assigned aides. His improved capacity to cope was one
indicator of his forward momentum.

Between summer camp and the start of middle school, Mark and
I took a brief three-day vacation to Kings Island Amusement Park.
Typically, Mark displayed optimal levels of functioning during vaca-
tions that featured his most preferred activities. For years, he had been
obsessed with roller coasters and seemed to better regulate his body
by engaging in thrill-seeking rides. For the most part, things went as
planned during this vacation – with two notable exceptions.

The first event took place at a water park, when Mark consumed French fries that, unbeknownst to us, had been cooked in a vat of oil with cross-contaminant food sources. Shortly thereafter he walked nonchalantly out of the pool with his facial features swelling to an enormous size. His eyes were almost swollen shut and his lips were getting bigger by the minute and had a scary blue cast.

With shock setting in, I exclaimed, "I'm so sorry, Mark, but we have to leave the park right now because you are having an allergic reaction to the French fries and your medication is back at the hotel. None of this is your fault, but to make sure that you are safe, we have to pick everything up right now and go!"

Mark instantaneously burst into wracking sobs as I quickly rushed him from the park. As we raced toward the car a mile away, my mind was racing about what to do. To halt the reaction, I could either use the Epi-pen injector or give him Benadryl. On the one hand, I knew how Mark would react to the Benadryl – not so with the massive dose of adrenaline. On the other hand, I had the Epi-pen on me, while the Benadryl was safe and sound in a hotel room drawer, fifteen minutes away. As Mark did not appear to be struggling for breath and he insisted that his throat was not swelling shut, I chose the more conservative option; still, the car ride to the hotel was the longest of my life.

Mark was incapable of swallowing pills, so once we got to the hotel I quickly broke the capsule and added the powder to a liquid we kept in the minifridge and then waited for it to take effect. Thankfully, he was fine, but this traumatic experience was forever burned into my psyche and convinced me that it would be unsafe for Mark to eat in public restaurants for the foreseeable future.

The second incident happened when we were headed home. During long car trips, Mark watched DVDs on a portable player. Approximately one hour into the car ride, Mark discovered that he misplaced two DVDs and a highly preferred DVD case and immediately *demanded* that I turn the car around to retrieve his prized items. When I was not willing to do so, Mark exploded. Promising him replacement items did not deter his eruption.

I pulled the car to the berm. After thirty minutes on the side of the road, a state highway patrol officer pulled in front of my car, parked, exited his vehicle, and walked back to my window. Naturally, he wanted to know what I was doing stopped on the side of the road. His entry into our life made no impact whatsoever on Mark's incoherent screams, cries, and body slams emanating from the backseat.

I quickly told him about the circumstances, feeling *very* apprehensive as to whether the officer would believe me. After all, Mark did not appear physically different from any other child. The patrolman asked if there was anything he could do to assist me, and I explained that there was nothing to be done other than wait for the episode to run its course, which, judging from experience would be at least thirty minutes. I assured him that I would not start driving my vehicle until peace descended. To my immense relief, he reluctantly returned to his car and, eventually, drove away.

I sat in the car, my mind racing with angry thoughts. *Is this the kind of thing other people do on vacation? Am I having any fun? No, I'm not. This ride home is not fun at all. In fact, this experience is not worth it to me.* Though, blessedly, the raging finally subsided, it was replaced with a different kind of torture: four hours of Mark's continual demands that I turn the car around to retrieve his missing items. While I listened to his verbal diarrhea, I continued my retreat inside my mind.

Two can play at this game, Mark. While you repeat your incessant demands, I will silently think my incessant refrain: "Karen, this is not worth it. It's not worth it. It's not worth it." This would *not* be the last time that I would need my silent mantras. Fortunately for me, I was oblivious to all the ways that middle school would bring even more sweeping, unanticipated, and cataclysmic change to both our lives.

WHAT I KNOW NOW THAT I DIDN'T KNOW THEN: THE PRACTICE OF DETACHED INVOLVEMENT IS AN ESSENTIAL INGREDIENT IN THE FULFILLMENT OF

OUR DESIRES. While mastering detachment, we find ourselves grappling with a central paradox that is fundamental to parenting. Detachment affords us the opportunity to be passionate about our parenting journey, while remaining dispassionate about any outcomes achieved during childhood. *Detached involvement* does not imply that we give up or take a defeatist stance related to our children's optimal potential in life. True holistic parenting is based upon the following premise, as explained by Deepak Chopra: we serve our highest good as creator-beings by placing a single-pointed focus on what we want to realize, while practicing the Law of Least Effort, combined with detached involvement. Through the practice of detachment, we begin to feel safe and secure with the uncertainties inherent in physical life.

According to author David Richo in his book, *The Five Things We Cannot Change…and the Happiness We Find by Embracing Them,*[41] there are five immutable facts inherent within life's uncertainties: 1) Every single element of life is changing or heading toward an ending; 2) Life does not always go according to plan; 3) Life is not always fair; 4) Pain is an inescapable fact of life; and 5) Everyone is subject to fallibility. Humans do not necessarily behave in a loving and loyal manner all of the time!

As we accept those five irrefutable guideposts, we are more available to step into what Deepak Chopra labels the "Field of Pure Potentiality," where magic, mystery, excitement, adventure, dream realization, synchronicities, and miracles are born. As we release our attachment to preconceived notions around what *should* occur for our children, we embrace the unknown; embody the wisdom embedded in uncertainty; and access our freedom from the egoic conditioning that springs from the traps our wounded inner children found themselves in during our troubled childhoods. An elevated life is stymied when we recreate from old templates that are rooted in a worldview of deprivation, fear, and scarcity – and a view of ourselves as less-than-stellar beings.

Deepak Chopra taught in *The Seven Spiritual Laws of Success* about the Law of Allowing, a subset of the Law of Detachment. The Law of Allowing presupposes that our children are in fact already fulfilling their Divine life purposes. As we detach, we unconditionally accept that our children are in charge of *co-creating their own experiences.* As Wayne Dyer so eloquently stated, "Peace is the result of retraining the mind to *process life as it is,* rather than as you think it should be." Unless a child's physical life or safety is in grave jeopardy, *we can choose to observe their creations, without judging them, rescuing them, fixing them or trying to control them*!

By doing so, we allow our children the freedom to find their highest potential, without us interfering in unnecessary and potentially harmful ways. We release them to learn from throwing their own gutter balls, *even when their learning trajectory appears dramatically different and/or is paced much more slowly than the learning curve of others.* We release them to co-create for themselves, which is different than merely enduring their "less-than-ideal" behaviors.

We afford them the autonomy to do so because we've certainly benefitted from the space to throw our series of gutter balls. As we detach, we modify our ego's rigid and preconceived ideas around how things should proceed. Per Deepak Chopra, we are not served when our egos *force* solutions on problems, thereby creating even more problems for everyone in our orbit. Detachment affords us the blessings inherent in *choosing happiness over righteousness.* As Master Hu Dalconzo writes in *The HuMan Handbook: A Guide Book For the Inner You*:

> Detaching is a lifelong process of making peace with the fact that you are exactly where you are supposed to be, doing exactly what you are supposed to be doing for your highest spiritual good, even if it doesn't feel good. Because in a perfectly evolving Universe, it cannot be any other way. [42]

Detached involvement is based upon our unquestioning belief in our inherent power to manifest all desires that are in harmony with the Divine. If we choose to *deny and limit* our true co-creative powers as mothers, we find ourselves at the mercy of the ego's search for security. Instead of engaging in an ongoing chase for the illusion of security, we can relax knowing that our tiny little ego-minds no longer need to maneuver and micromanage the details of how transformation will occur. We can release our ego's need to know exactly *HOW* Source will orchestrate the time-space continuum of events to bring about the highest good for our children and ourselves. We can release the ego trap of a fixed, controlled, perfectly timed end result for our children, *so that we may feel happy, fulfilled, successful or safe.*

While Mark was undergoing testing for a growth hormone deficiency, imagine how much easier my life would have been if I had been able to trust in an overarching Divine plan for his well-being? What if I had believed deep within my Soul that Mark's needs were indeed being handled? What if I could have stood apart and relaxed as I observed the experience Mark was creating, without adding layers of terror to his continuously swirling vortex of emotions?

A favorite mantra of mine that I eventually came to rely upon was the following: *I release Mark to the Love of the Universe.* Now, when my ego wanted to box with Mark's, I was able to implement a number of boundary scripts – or phrases I repeated inside my mind: "I am safe, even when my mind doesn't agree with you. I have dissolved all FEAR (False Evidence Appearing Real), knowing that we are ONE in Spirit. I am fully awake because *I SEE and FEEL the presence of Spirit* within each one of us. I release all struggle, knowing that Mark is a *Perfect Being of Light And Love.* In the face of Mark's escalations, these grounding statements helped me embody more neutrality.

Other scripts I came to rely upon during heated interactions included:

- *I can be present with you as long as you lower your voice and respect my boundaries;*
- *I can be present with you as long as you breathe deeply first and then continue speaking to me using a calm tone of voice;*

- *I will begin driving the car again when you have lowered your voice and it is safe for me to do so;*
- *I will be more than willing to continue communicating with you as long as you can breathe deeply first before you continue speaking because I need you to respect my boundaries* (I often paired these statements with a gentle hand gesture that signified lowering the voice volume);

And my phrase of last resort:

- *I will no longer participate in this conversation, as this interaction is not producing a helpful outcome.*

Clearly these scripts are far from appropriate for many children living with special needs, as they presuppose that they have the language processing and intellectual capacity to benefit. That said, irrespective of how children present in their physical bodies, we can all embrace the following eloquent goal of detachment by Sri Chinmoy: "Your heart must become a sea of love. Your mind must become a river of detachment."

SELF-RIGHTEOUSNESS

"The problem with righteous indignation is that even
when
you're right, you're still left feeling indignant."

Bill Crawford

Another schoolyear commenced. Mark was now a sixth-grade middle school student assigned to a self-contained classroom for children with emotional and behavioral challenges, with opportunities for inclusion in two mainstream classes. After hearing that Mark's new teacher, Mrs. P., was not only a very experienced teacher but also a reading special-ist who had a knack for helping special needs students improve their reading comprehension, I was feeling optimistic. Little did I know that I was in for what Queen Elizabeth would have called an *annus horrib-lis* – and that despite all I had already been through I was completely unprepared for it.

Within the first two weeks of school, Mark suffered from daily retching and gagging attacks over the toilet and begged to be kept home from school. I learned that on the third day, he had seen one of the special needs students being wheeled out of the building on a gurney, in need of emergency medical/psychiatric care. While I felt bad that Mark had to witness this, my greater concern was related to the alleged statements made in response to the emergency.

Mark asserted that he had been told by Mrs. P. in an authoritarian manner, "You will be the next student wheeled to the psychiatric hospital if you do not stop crying and arguing with teachers during the school day."

Mark had never been a *completely* reliable reporter of conversations due to his tendency to misinterpret social cues and his auditory processing and language challenges, heightened by his anxiety disorder. At the same time, I felt extremely concerned because Mark was adamant that this threat had been made. I could not fathom that Mrs. P. would actually make such a statement because it would be both unethical and illegal to call an ambulance for non-compliance/crying by a child with autism.

That weekend, while I waited for clarification, Mark experienced a complete breakdown in confidence. The alleged remarks had been particularly triggering for him, given his past trauma in the psychiatric hospital and his fear of history repeating itself. He did not sleep, had ongoing sobbing spells, experienced bouts of dry heaves and felt completely incapable of resuming school. Mark also reported that peers were tormenting him during the bus ride home. When Monday came, I chose to physically drag him to the bus – a decision I regret to this day.

As soon as he was launched, I called Mrs. P. and was beyond stunned to learn that she had indeed made those statements. She had a very cavalier attitude when I described the impact of this approach on Mark. I asked her to assure Mark that she would not be calling an ambulance to take him away. When our conversation closed, I felt confident that she would immediately follow through with my request; however, that afternoon, when I asked Mark, he insisted that no such conversation had occurred. He also continued to insist that he should be kept at home.

The next day, when I again contacted Mrs. P. to hear her side of things, she immediately confirmed what Mark had told me.

"I had no intention of discussing the matter with Mark," she said. "At this point, he is fine. There is only one problem presently, and that problem is *you*. You are attempting to undermine my authority as the classroom teacher and I'm not going to allow your behavior to interfere with Mark's best interests. I'm not going to allow it at all."

All the color drained from my face and my heart dropped to my feet. Had I been standing, I would have been forced to sit down. I fell mute, as though I had been physically slapped across the face.

Had this been a physical assault, I would have had grounds to have Mrs. P. terminated. But something worse had occurred. She had bullied me with the exact style of emotional blackmail that she had used to bully Mark. Even though I was a highly competent, middle-aged woman with above-average intellectual and social skills, I felt utter shock settle in. I fell silent for several long seconds as I scrambled to think of an apt response.

Finally I said, "This conversation has reached an impasse. We clearly see things very differently. I need to think about what needs to happen next."

I then quickly got off the phone and burst into tears. Those tears, which I would continue to shed for hours, were not related to her opinion of me. They came from a place of fear and desperation because I did not see how I was going to protect my son from someone whose behavior I perceived as incredibly damaging. She posed a huge threat to everything I had worked to achieve surrounding the stabilization of Mark's emotional life. In my view, she also posed a threat to his self-image, his self-esteem, his capacity to feel emotionally safe and his capacity to have balanced mental health.

I had to quickly pull myself together, as I was scheduled to visit the classroom for curriculum night the following evening. The thought of sitting at a small intimate table with three other parents and Mrs. P. made my stomach lurch. I felt so much animosity toward her that I did not see how I was going to put up a convincing façade as her collaborative partner. In the end, I managed to white-knuckle through the evening, only to return home and begin composing my complaint letter to the principal and key administrators of the school. A conference with the principal, Mrs. P, and the social worker, Rachel, was set for early October.

Bob would also accompany me, an experienced school advocate. Bob had also been diagnosed with Asperger's Syndrome and understood the condition from an insider's view and was the perfect individual to assist me. After two lengthy and costly preparatory meetings, I looked forward to having him by my side at the conference, only to be very disappointed when at the last minute he told me that due to a scheduling conflict he would be unable to attend.

Fortunately, I could count on Wanda, my parent mentor from the local community mental health center. Wanda had been a godsend. She knew firsthand what it was like to parent a son with a brain-based disorder and was there at every turn to offer expert guidance and emotional support; in fact, she had regularly assisted me in preparing for Mark's upcoming IEP meetings.[43] Over the years, she had also recommended a number of books[44] that were invaluable in preparing a more optimal educational plan for Mark. Indeed, despite the former psychologist's allegations, I had not been dissuaded from reading lots of books!

I came to the school meeting well-prepared to iron out our differences. My objective was to paint a picture of the type of environment that would be a match for Mark's needs. Instead, Rachel, with whom I was not simpatico, and Mrs. P opened the meeting by insisting that it was completely unacceptable for Mark to cry at school.

Mrs. P. asserted, "Mark is a middle school student and it is now time for him to *behave* like a middle school student. We will no longer permit him to be babied and coddled. If he cries, he is going to be segregated from the classroom."

I rebutted by citing the research that states that children on the spectrum function emotionally at approximately two-thirds of their chronological age. Based upon the known findings, Mark was functioning emotionally as an eight-year-old.

"Legislating that Mark no longer cry in school is completely ineffective," I continued. "Just because you insist that an elephant should fly, that doesn't mean he has the ability to lift off from the ground. Based upon Mark's developmental level and the extraordinary stress he is facing during this transition to middle school – and because he clearly cannot meet the developmental expectations in this environment – it is unrealistic to assume that he won't exhibit a stress reaction of crying during the school day. Attending middle school for the first time is a *major life transition* for Mark. The primary premise of his placement in this self-contained classroom is based entirely upon his *significant* emotional and social needs. Mark, like anyone else, will either respond to stress by acting in or by acting out. Setting an expectation that crying is unacceptable does not in and of itself move Mark forward developmentally. Isolating him to a detention room for hours does not move him forward developmentally. He is crying because he does not have access to any other coping methods. He is arguing over expectations due to his heightened level of anxiety, his limited confidence in his ability to succeed, his inflexibility and his need to control his environment in order to manage his stress. Every one of these behaviors is directly related to his disability and by law he should not be penalized for displaying behaviors that are beyond his mastery at this time. The first order of business needs to be looking at adaptations in the environment to lower Mark's stress and to boost his feelings of mastery."

Though I presented what I believed was a strong case based on my personal experiences and well-established research around Mark's challenges, the school staff insisted that his behaviors were attention-seeking in nature. We continued for ninety minutes to hash out the issues, yet were no closer to resolving them. They still ascribed the wrong motivations to Mark's behavior, therefore, the wrong prescriptions logically followed. The principal backed up his staff's positions in their entirety, saying he did believe that any new accommodations were necessary. At the conclusion of this meeting, Mark continued to despise school and he continued to spend long stretches of time in the detention room – a closet-sized room with a small desk inside. The only concession made was an offer for me to observe the classroom so that I could be further reassured or placated (depending upon your perspective) that all was working for Mark's benefit.

During the observation, I became *even more* disheartened than ever. I anticipated that Mrs. P. would "clean up her act" until I left the building, only to revert to her punitive methods. What I saw that day shocked and disturbed me. With her over-confident manner, she seemingly saw nothing untoward about her teaching tactics. She began by referring to the students' calculators as the "devil's tool," with only one student out of four understanding said reference. This student had been in Mrs. P's class the prior year and was familiar with her methods.

Using idiosyncratic jargon is extremely confusing for students who have trouble comprehending non-literal language; furthermore, though the teaching segment was rich with academic content, it was geared to the three students who held the capacity to comprehend it, without modifications for a student with a more profound case of autism. I was even more appalled, however, by Mrs. P's response when one of the three students was off-task.

"What did you do Michael," she asked, her voice dripping with sarcasm, "leave your brain at home over the long weekend?"

Michael never responded to that inquiry. Instead, he was ordered to the tiny, adjacent "segregation/detention" room while the aide remained seated at the back of the classroom. For the next forty minutes, Michael alternated between opening the door to taunt his classmates with off-color comments and stepping back into the classroom, only to return to his lair with a flourish of a door slam. At one point, he found *a hammer* inside the teacher's desk and was swinging it provocatively as he twirled in circles in the middle of the room. I couldn't comprehend why the aide didn't speak with him privately, or have him take a walk so that she could uncover his unmet needs, potentially preventing this high-risk behavior. Deescalating a conflict by temporarily removing a child from an over-stimulating or problematic environment is called an "antiseptic bounce."

Children's maladaptive behaviors are not haphazard. There are underlying reasons for them and in this case none of these reasons were being addressed. As Ross W. Greene, explains:

> When there's a good fit between skills and expectations, that's called compatibility, and we would expect a good outcome. When there's a poor fit between expectations and the capacity of the kid, there is incompatibility, and that's when we see people exhibit challenging behavior.

Another "lost" student, Noah, ended up withdrawing into a bean-bag chair on the floor for most of the lesson. Mark and one other classmate were the only two students following the assignment.

Once the teaching segment ended, Mark was asked to type a hand-written paper on the computer. He had struggled with fine motor challenges since toddlerhood, and at age twelve still found typing – which required visual scanning abilities, optimal motor planning, and fine motor dexterity – to be very frustrating and laborious. There were no adaptations offered to lessen the related stress. Mark fell into defeatist talk and displayed high levels of frustration. Because his distress signals were ignored, I decided to approach Mark and created a makeshift stand so that his paper was at least in an upright position. Because there were no simple adaptations for keyboarding offered, Mark's frustration continued unabated. I could see his exhaustion setting in, and it was only the beginning of his school day.

After my classroom observation, I solidified my decision to hire a special needs attorney to assist me in getting Mark moved to a therapeutic day school. Mark's therapist, Jane Walker, was in complete agreement that the teaching environment was having a very deleterious impact on Mark. After spending weeks screening attorneys, I retained Michael K., who recommended an assessment at a Center for Pediatric Mood Disorders. He hoped that an independent evaluation could sway the school district to accede to my wishes.

Spending the day dragging Mark to another hospital setting in the inner city was not on our preferred list of activities. Mark exploded in the car; sobbed uncontrollably once we arrived; spent considerable time refusing to walk to the building; and was completely resistant to being evaluated by the lead psychiatrist, Dr. M. The waiting room of such centers feels like a little den in hell. Underserved children from the lower socioeconomic groups are warehoused there. Helping Mark into the building at the beginning of the appointment was no easier than helping him transition back home.

On our last trip there, Mark ran away to the top of a dirt mound, refusing to return to the car. He had noted that a large cross, previously implanted in the mound, was now absent, and he was unable to adapt. Mark demanded a visit to the nearby church so that we could uncover the mystery behind its disappearance. At the time, getting answers to this conundrum was the last thing I had in mind and yet I decided that following Mark's lead was easier than forcing the issue.

During the month-long process, I provided Dr. M. with extensive information so he could make an appropriate finding on Mark's behalf; however, I was not permitted to accompany Mark to the evaluating room during the three individual appointments. As a result, Dr. M. was completely unsuccessful at getting Mark to enter his interview room or to remain there. Mark spent the first two appointments fleeing from Dr. M, and during the third they spent approximately fifteen minutes together, ten of which were spent playing a simple card game.

Dr. M. eventually wrote a report stating that Mark's educational placement was quite appropriate to meet his needs. In fact, he told me in person that Mark's IEP was the "Cadillac of IEPs." While I could see why he held this view, from his vantage point in the middle of "Dante's inferno," I believed that Mark's "Cadillac IEP" was meaningless because the people in charge were driving the car over the cliff. Planning for the upcoming showdown with the school district consumed my days. Most of my energy felt wasted. I was rooted in place, shouting into a windstorm with no one there to hear my pleas.

The school staff did not acknowledge that a problem even existed. Mark wasn't capable of participating in a solution. Dr. M. wasn't invested in assisting us. Added to all of those factors, my body was breaking down in new and unexpected ways. During my morning hours, I found myself hostage to my bathroom as I lived with the symptoms of unrelenting lymphocytic colitis.

During this phase with Mark, my ego had run amok and was in complete resistance to the circumstances at hand. Once again, I was blinded by my full-blown addiction to struggle. My vibration emanated from a blaming stance; entering into combat with so-called adversaries; and leading with my ego's need to win while obsessively investing in the illusion of being able to control outcomes. My energy was feeding the extremes as I went into unwarranted emotional, physical, and spiritual deficit. My ego had me put the pedal to the metal as I barreled at high speeds down the long and convoluted road. So far, the Universe had mirrored my lowered vibration by putting up one insurmountable wall after another. But my ego wouldn't allow me to observe these dynamics, detach from the drama, and course-correct before an even higher price was paid.

When the IEP meeting convened, I had four professionals accompanying me: Jane Walker, Wanda, Michael K., and Dr. M., who participated by phone. At the conclusion of the lengthy meeting, the school district agreed to reword some statements in the IEP document at my behest; however, they made only one helpful modification. They agreed to transport Mark by a private cab to and from school so his safely could be ensured.

I vividly recall standing on the front steps of the school after the meeting as my attorney espoused the following position: "Maybe you can begin implementing the same behavioral methods at home that the middle school is using during Mark's school day? That way, everyone involved will be on the same page and with a consistent approach, Mark's behavior will start to improve."

Hearing his words, I was outraged by what I perceived as a betrayal. It seemed to me that he could have at least said, "I'm sorry that we didn't achieve the outcome you had hoped for today." Instead, I was being told to alter my parenting approach. The school staff repeatedly reinforced the message that Mark's problems at school and at home were rooted in a lack of discipline on my part. The implication was that his chronically ill, burned-out mother, refused to "put the screws down" and back up the tough love approach that was fundamental for Mark conforming to age-appropriate expectations. After spending thousands of dollars in legal fees, I believed that my attorney had joined ranks with the enemy camp!

I can't recall if I even bothered to refute what I considered to be Michael K's uncalled-for statements, however, I know that as we parted ways I was determined to never communicate with him again. Gratefully, I still had Wanda and Jane in my corner. They both understood the stakes for Mark, as well as my feelings in the aftermath of the meeting, and validated my efforts.

Following the debacle at the school, I raised the flag of surrender and made a decision I had hoped I would never have to make. I called Mark's case manager, Micki B., and informed her that the time had come to initiate placing Mark in a residential treatment center. Micki was newly assigned to Mark's case and felt it was imperative that I reconsider my decision and alternatively accept short-term, home-based family therapy, but I refused and instead reiterated Mark's urgent need for placement. I had forcefully hit the wall one too many times. I knew that another round of family therapy wasn't going to alter my life with Mark. I was down on my knees, finally choosing my own self-preservation, irrespective of the potential detrimental consequences for him. I quote from an official report that I compiled summarizing my life at that time:

Mark has been staying up until midnight most nights and getting up an hour earlier for school this year. Mark's ultra-rapid mood swings were in evidence with regular explosive outbursts at home. Mark fell into verbally abusing me for hours almost every day. I have had to physically restrain him twice during November and am now greatly limiting his community outings. At 100 pounds, physical intervention is becoming untenable for me. Mark not only exhibited severe mood instability, but he also came home from school in a cognitive daze. He was frequently unresponsive when spoken to, had significant "stim bursts" and was displaying primitive self-stimulatory behavior that I had not observed in approximately five years. His eyes would glaze over and he essentially was not in contact with his surroundings. In November, Mark mentioned hearing a voice whispering inside his head, which he could not decipher. This voice was upsetting to Mark.

As a consequence of the above profile, in conjunction with low medication levels in Mark's bloodstream, the dose of the mood stabilizer designed to combat rapid-cycling symptoms was increased in October. By December, Dr. F. informed me that Mark's lab work demonstrated elevated liver enzymes. This elevation was likely due to the dose increase, in conjunction with the long-term use of the medication.

Although Dr. F. immediately lowered Mark's dose of medication, he also recommended that I consult with a gastroenterologist to get an opinion as to how to proceed. Elevated enzymes could potentially damage Mark's liver, an organ that performed hundreds of vital functions. Because pediatric gastroenterologists are few and far between, I returned to abrasive Dr. N., hoping that I could show him Mark's lab work, have a short conversation regarding the matter and relay his findings to Dr. F. Things did not go according to plan.

Dr. N. insisted on seeing Mark in the office and rerunning his own lab findings. Managing Mark's behaviors during medical appointments had become increasing impossible. He sobbed uncontrollably, shouted incoherently and typically tried to flee the premises, often requiring physical restraint. During the initial appointment, Dr. N., made no effort to examine Mark. I felt the strain, trying to talk and listen to Dr. N., while Mark spewed his hostile commentary in the office. Bringing his preferred technological device did not prevent Mark from decompensating. Gone were the days when medical professionals delivered bad news as toddler Mark repeatedly crashed his stroller into the furniture. Mark was now a sixth-grader and no longer easy to place in a "basket hold." As mentioned above in the excerpt from my report, I had discovered firsthand that my five- foot three-inch body was no match for one hundred pounds of Mark's adrenaline-fueled rages.

Dr. N. insisted that I make a future follow-up appointment to discuss the test results, but when I appeared for the second appointment he had no recollection as to why I was there. He then quickly became hyper-focused on the fact that I did not bring Mark to the office. Because Dr. N. had consistently refused to examine Mark or interact with him, what was the point of dragging him along, only to retraumatize him and escalate my own stress levels?

Dr. N. did not see it that way. He felt justified to verbally unleash his contempt. After his tirade passed, Dr. N. finally gave me "the numbers," which unbeknownst to him, indicated that Mark's enzymes were now even more elevated than on previous tests. I wanted to make a quick exit with a copy of the labs in hand. After this entire charade, Dr. N. refused to discuss his medical recommendations with me, instead haughtily insisting that he would speak with Dr. F. himself.

I checked out, swiftly went to my car, and burst into tears. My mind floated back to the memory of a horrible meeting with Attorney S., with whom I had gone for Mark's special needs trust. As that prior movie began to replay, it was as if I was back in that cramped, dark office, with him towering over me as he screamed.

"You dare to show up in my God★★n office almost a year late from the time the court set a date for this trust to be completed. What the hell have you been doing in the meantime? Do you think it's f★★king acceptable to defy a court order? You have a college education and yet you behave like a stupid imbecile, without a brain in your head. You dare to ask questions about the legal language, wasting my time. I am not going to answer these ridiculous questions. Do you hear me? Do you understand that this is a f★★king serious matter? This is not a game. Answer me, then!"

This man, who a moment prior had appeared to be a friendly, grey-haired grandfather type, underwent a complete Dr. Jekyll/Mr. Hyde transformation. This *so-called professional* dared to, in abusive language, challenge me on what I had been doing with my time? Gee, allow me to ponder. I had escorted my zombie-shuffling son from a psychiatric hospital; I had spearheaded a five-month application to the state so that Mark could have access to mental health services; I had continued to hire, train and coordinate Mark's twenty-five hours a week of play therapy; I had implemented speech therapy in my home; I had driven Mark to weekly psychotherapy appointments; I had spent long hours engaged in homework battles; I had attended twice-monthly team meetings at the school; and I had slowly titrated psychotropic medications – all of which were done on barely any sleep while combating one virus after the next and with little to no personal energy reserves.

I need to point out that the money earmarked for the trust had been left untouched during the yearlong interim. All of Mark's funds were protected. Yet I was being berated and abused for my so-called negligence. In my former life, I would have immediately walked out and never gone back. I would have told this man he was no better than a bully. I would have put him on notice that I planned to report him for unethical conduct. But my traumatized *little girl* sat cowed, frozen into silence, immobilized and passive. At the time, my ego asserted that I lacked the energy to begin anew with another competent special needs trust attorney.

Now, though my relationship with Attorney S. was long over, I was experiencing mental anguish over the fact that other authority figures felt free to demean and humiliate me. However, there was no time to wallow in these lower emotions because I still had other more pressing concerns to address. After my abysmal experience with Dr. N., Dr. F. decided to wean Mark – very, very, slowly – off his mood stabilizer. One of the initial challenges was determining what replacement medication Dr. F. could safely prescribe.

After I gathered extensive information from the pharmacist, Dr. F. started Mark on a trial of a new anti-seizure medication that was commonly used in the treatment of bipolar disorder. This particular medication posed less risk to Mark's liver. In February, I began titrating Mark's newly prescribed medication ever so slowly. Mark did not complete his weaning from his anti-seizure medication until June. However, during December of this schoolyear, there were more signs that things were heading in a disastrous direction.

Mark and I were invited to a small Christmas gathering at the home of Mark's childhood friend, Forrest. Because Forrest's mother chose to host the event, I believed that Mark would be in an emotionally supportive environment. I knew that he would be amongst a handful of other special needs families. Even though I had never met three of the participating families before, the evening began on a pleasant enough note. During dinnertime, all the children congregated in the basement. In my view, the adult supervision was inadequate. I took it upon myself to continually leave the dinner table so that I could monitor Mark's emotional regulation. Once dinner ended, the children became increasingly hyperactive, chasing one another through the three floors of this massive home.

As the chasing escalated, with barely a notice from the parents in attendance, I felt increasingly anxious in response to observable signs that Mark was becoming more and more overstimulated. Mark's overstimulation had been set into motion by one of the children whose behavior was mercilessly provocative toward him. To protect the safety of the other children, I was forced into a very long physical restraint on the cold hard floor of the upstairs bathroom. I felt quite fearful that the hard surfaces in the bathroom would result in one of us getting injured. During this interminably long restraint, Mark's animalistic screams went unheeded. My plan was to physically steer Mark from the home as soon as he was calm enough to leave the bathroom.

That plan did not come to pass, as Mark wrenched free from my grip while I was attempting to physically escort him down the staircase. Unfortunately, Mark's manic episode required a second restraint shortly thereafter in the safety of the quiet basement. However, I discovered that Mark's provocateur had followed us there with the intention of continuing his relentless verbal taunts. As I struggled to safely contain Mark, I ordered his agitator upstairs. He refused to comply with my directives and instead fled to a closet, which served as his base for repeatedly opening the door to discharge his verbal missiles. In response to the demeaning commentary, Mark flew out of control and I was seemingly the only adult cognizant of the circumstance.

I repeatedly yelled for assistance but with the noise factor in the house, no one heard my cries for help. I waited for a considerable period of time, trying singlehandedly to diffuse Mark's explosiveness. My hellacious evening continued uninterrupted, as the barrage of below-the-belt put-downs were directed to Mark. All of the parents chatted amiably in the dining room with barely a notice as to the unsafe and uninterrupted game of chase, as well as Mark's and my absence from the "festivities." Finally, after sweating profusely in the basement, I made the decision to drag Mark from the home. This decision was not made lightly, as my car sat a block away from the house.

I was not at all confident that I could wrangle Mark across the basement floor, up a flight of stairs, through the first floor of the house and out to my car. I decided that I truly had no choice. As I drug Mark through the first floor of the house, while demanding that my purse and coat be brought to my car, I fleetingly glanced at the shocked look on Forrest's mother's face. She uttered some words of advice as I manhandled a screaming, incoherent Mark from the house. I did not have the luxury to focus on what was being said, as my immediate objective was to get Mark to the safety of our home without an even worse scenario unfolding.

Around this time period, the local movie theater became the setting for a second traumatizing incident. Going to the movies was typically a safe proposition. At the conclusion of the film, I recall holding Mark back, while bracing his arms over his head and forcing his entire body against a wall. Mark spewed his paranoid and incomprehensible ideas while the theatergoers emptied out of the screening room, many of them shooting glares in my direction. After this second frightening interaction, I determined that it was no longer safe for me to accompany Mark in the community. I again quote from my documentation at the time.

> Mark has also continued to be quite depressed with fairly frequent suicidal threats in evidence (approximately every six weeks), in conjunction with ongoing statements indicating hopelessness and self-loathing. Mark verbalizes remorse and guilt following rage attacks but truly does not seem able to contain his emotional intensity.

My application to various residential treatment centers had been repeatedly denied. Seventeen facilities on the state list had rejected Mark because of his complex, multi-faceted needs. Most facilities excluded Mark on the basis of his autism; most were unable to provide for his specialized diet; almost all stated that they could not administer his daily growth hormone injection; and none of them wanted the legal liability that came with Mark's risk of anaphylaxis.

Blessedly, there were a few bright spots that lightened my load during Mark's first year in middle school. One positive in Mark's life continued to be his relationship with his mentor, Kelly, who was consistently available for his emotional and social needs. Mark also formed a friendship with Jeff, a peer from his classroom. From time to time, Mark socialized with both Jeff and Forrest. A third positive was Mark's response to the growth hormone injection. The observable difference between Mark's short stature and the normative height of his peers was less obvious over time. Additionally, instead of continually being felled by one virus after the next, Mark was now affected by a number comparable to his peers.

During routine appointments with the endocrinologist, Mark's test results indicated stable progress, with one notable exception. Dr. Z. was quite concerned that Mark had not lost a single baby tooth for five long years! In light of the fact that adult tooth eruption is sometimes significantly delayed in children with growth deficiency disorder, Dr. Z. asked me to consult with Mark's dentist. Mark's dentist opined that his adult teeth were not going to erupt without surgically removing his twelve remaining baby teeth. Next, she recommended their removal in a hospital setting under general anesthesia. I spent weeks addressing the all-consuming insurance hurdles that stood in the way of medical coverage for Mark's same-day-surgery.

Fortunately, Mark's dentist waved the lab work and other required pre-operative testing. Although Mark was present during the pre-operative interviews, he did not grasp the circumstance that awaited him. I knew that it would be in Mark's best interests to delay the inevitable.

Thus, I woke him at 3:00 a.m. to give him advance notice about his upcoming surgery. As expected, during the next two hours, he fluctuated from hysterical tears to extreme agitation and racing thoughts related to absconding from his home. He required continual supervision to prevent him from escaping from the house or harming himself. During the brief respites from his hysteria, I tried to help him process his fears with limited success. He eventually whimpered beside me.

Kelly arrived at 5:30 a.m. to accompany us to the hospital. I knew that it would be impossible for me to singlehandedly manage the one-hour commute. Kelly served as an earthbound angel throughout the entire ordeal. As expected, once admitted to the hospital, Mark required physical restraint to insert the IV.

He repeatedly cried out in a small, helpless voice, "This is the end, Mom. Goodbye. They're killing me. I'll never see you again. I'm sorry for everything I ever did. Goodbye, Mom."

I stood there with tears trickling down my cheeks, feeling as powerless and despondent as he did.

When Mark finally awoke in the recovery room, I was shocked to observe his level of agitation, his extreme confusion, and the guttural screams that reverberated around me. The nurse reassured me that pre-adolescent males under the influence of anesthesia often behaved in this manner post-surgery. Mark left the hospital with a mouth full of blood-soaked gauze pads.

An extensive period of recovery followed, during which he subsisted on water, tiny remnants of plain rice cakes, and unsalted French Fries. It took over an hour for him to eat each meal, and he rapidly dropped ten pounds. Fortunately, his adult teeth began to erupt over the next month, which helped to slow the weight loss.

Mark was not the only one who had a miserable experience while undergoing same-day surgery in 2006. That summer I had to undergo a D & C[45] at a local surgical center, after which my attending nurse not only repeatedly ignored my complaints of extreme nausea but also spoke to me in a dehumanizing way. Blessedly, Kelly came through for me again by supervising Mark from the time summer camp let out until my return home. At least my post-surgical recovery instructions didn't require me to eat like a baby bird!

Being flat on my back seemed to be my only respite from caregiving duties. Although Mark's dad supervised him during one week in August, I had other responsibilities to fulfill. During my so-called "vacation week," I flew to Kansas to evaluate Heartspring School, a well-established and well-regarded residential treatment center for children with autism. The Illinois director of the state program for mentally ill children was willing to consider approval of this out-of-state facility for Mark.

During my visit, I was extremely impressed with the quality of care, the richness of the programming, and their flexibility, as well as the professionalism of the staff. They demonstrated a willingness to provide for Mark's complex needs, and even had a nurse onsite who could deliver Mark's daily growth hormone injection. I also liked the fact that Heartspring was affiliated with a nearby medical center.

The one potential drawback for Mark was the type of children in residence there. Many, if not most, were intellectually impaired, at least on paper, and had quite limited speaking abilities. It appeared that Mark would have little to no social companionship of a comparable nature; however, the staff eased my fear about this by assuring me that they had previously worked with a teen with a profile similar to Mark's. During his stay there, this young man had held a part-time job in the community and after several years of treatment was discharged to study in college.

The staff felt very confident that they could meet Mark's needs and were more than willing to accept parental input. Though Heartspring seemed to check all the boxes, my feelings around sending Mark there were complicated, to say the least. They also turned out to be moot. My plane had barely touched down on Illinois soil when I learned the state director had abruptly resigned to spearhead another state department. The new top dog, Dr. H., immediately pulled the plug on the Kansas facility. There was nowhere for Mark to go, except back to his assigned substandard junior high school program.

Before Mark resumed seventh grade, there was one additional change in the offing. My former spouse informed Mark that he and his wife were now expecting twins.

Mark verbalized his immediate concern. "Dad, are the twins conjoined twins?"

Mark was reassured that the twins were healthy in every known way. However, as the news of the pregnancy sunk in, he became increasingly anxious about his place in his dad's life and whether his importance would diminish following the birth of the twins.

WHAT I KNOW NOW THAT I DIDN'T KNOW THEN: THE UNIVERSAL LANGUAGE OF FEELINGS IS THE LANGUAGE OF OUR INTUITIVE SELVES. THIS LANGUAGE POTENTIALLY GUIDES US IN THE RIGHT SPIRITUAL DIRECTION. Surprisingly, as a practicing psychotherapist for sixteen years, I did not fully understand the language of feelings and their connection to the somatic body. As a survival mechanism, I had learned to disassociate from my body. Without a foundation for fully embodying my physical form, I was often disconnected from or out of sync with my bodily sensations. Bodily sensations are a feedback system allowing us to access life's wisdom. When we flow with life, we feel good. When we resist Universal flow, we drop into a lower vibrational state.

As previously stated, anything we resist in life will persist and may persist in a heightened form. The Divine asks us to notice our state of being via our feelings. Our feelings are messages that reinforce whether we are either *in harmony or out of harmony with some aspect of our authentic Selves, the present moment and/or our Divine purpose for living.* Because our Western culture rewards us for resisting, repressing, minimizing, denying or avoiding our emotional pain, we often struggle with speaking the language of feelings. Even women, who historically have had more permission to access feelings than men, have grown up with the understanding that it was neither acceptable nor safe to show anger or fear, or to shed tears in front of authority figures.

We've been offered a badge of honor for adopting stoicism or cynicism in the face of our family dysfunction. We've been taught to push past or push down our uncomfortable feelings, to discount slowing down enough to actually *honor our feelings.* Adopting a courageous stance, while taking the emotional risk to be vulnerable enough to *feel* our *uncomfortable feelings,* underpins our capacity for healing. It underpins our capacity to prevent chronic and long-term states of dis-ease from manifesting in our bodies as incapacitating illness, autoimmune disease, or a life-threatening crisis.

Michael A. Singer, in *The Untethered Soul: The Journey Beyond Yourself*,[46] used an apt metaphor. He asked his readers to imagine having a thorn lodged in one arm. Take a moment to imagine this scenario in your life. Imagine that a thorn is touching a major nerve, protruding from your arm, and triggering pain, even with air lightly circulating around it. Because of the position of your thorn, you aren't able to roll over, sleep comfortably, engage effectively in your activities of daily living or easily approach other people. This thorn prevents other people from getting close to you.

By ensuring that nothing contacts or disturbs your thorn, your ego believes that you have adopted a creative solution. You shield your thorn by building and maintaining a protective device that provides a protective cover. This device is complex and heavy and is permanently adhered to your arm. Unfortunately, your device is too large to comfortably gain entry into your home; therefore, it is necessary for you to erect a larger set of front doors to accommodate it. The truth is that protecting your thorn has now invaded every single aspect of your life and is *dictating everything you do*. While you've been distracted with safeguarding your thorn, you've never had the opportunity to discover the root cause of your thorn's existence.

Because you have never uncovered why the thorn became lodged there in the first place, your solution is contaminating your relationships, your emotional life, your career, your finances, your spirituality, your recreational time, your sex life, and even your health. Of significance, your emotional thorns are not protruding from your arm but are instead buried deep inside, invisible to the naked eye and therefore easy to deny.

The true purpose of feeling your uncomfortable sensations is *to release the negatively charged energy from your body and to engage in psycho-spiritual surgery, for the removal of your thorns*. As Doc Lew Childre, Founder of the HeartMath Institute asserts, "Physiologically, it simply doesn't matter whether your anger [or substitute any feeling here] is justified or not. The body doesn't make moral judgments about feelings...it just responds." Everything in life has an energetic footprint. Feelings are no different. Sometimes that energetic signature is a higher vibe state. We more readily release our ecstasy, our tears of joy, our uproarious laughter, and our passionate enthusiasm, as those energies more easily pass through our bodies.

It is our uncomfortable energies that potentially become trapped inside our cells for a prolonged period of time. Many of us have developed a pattern of intellectualizing our feelings, instead of processing and releasing them. "The challenge that most people have with processing their feelings is that they are trying to process them through their 'thinking mind.' You can't THINK your FEELINGS. You either *feel* them or you *repress* them with THOUGHTS."[47]

Author John Gray[48] developed a *"Feel To Release Chart"*[49] that characterizes the intellectualization of feelings as emotional blocks. Dr. Grey makes a distinction between these emotional blocks and what he terms "healing feelings." Following a stressor, we experience a healing feeling when we experience a constriction in our throats, a tightness in our shoulder blades, nausea in our stomachs, flushing in our face, sweating in our palms, et cetera. These energies surface in our bodies in present time, irrespective of whether the triggering circumstance is currently happening or is a memory of a prior event. If a bodily sensation isn't present, we are lost in either intellectualization or an emotional block.

We have learned to label these body signals with arbitrary cognitive words such as sorrow, anger, disappointment, sadness, or shame, et cetera. When we give ourselves permission to *feel these energies* so that we may release them from our cellular memory, we gain a holistic benefit. Dr. Grey designed his chart with the intention that it would be used flexibly with poetic license. It has twelve healing feelings and is divided into four horizontal categories: Emotional Blocks; Global/General Feelings; Healing Feelings; and Holistic Benefits.

Global feelings arise when your ego has created a defensive worldview – a pattern of suppressed pain, deemed an emotional block of resistance. For example, the first category on the far left of the chart begins with the healing feeling of *anger*, moving to the holistic benefit of *boundary defense*, moving to *betrayal* [the global/general feeling] and, lastly, *blame* [the emotional block]. In this example, if your ego has used blame as one of your default defense mechanisms, you have likely solidified a worldview that says that other people can't be relied upon, thereby creating a self-fulfilling prophesy that your trust will indeed be betrayed. It may be listed under emotional block or general feeling, but either way it represents the mind's half-truths and delusions. In order to heal, your intention must be to release the toxic energy out of your body, rather than attaching to the labels or the ego's storyline.

During Mark's time in sixth grade, my ego blamed his teacher for his regression in functioning. My ego felt betrayed because I viewed her actions as unconscionable. My healing feeling was anger. By processing and releasing my anger, I would have then been able to take the guided actions necessary to set appropriate boundaries without getting enmeshed in the drama. But here's where the poetic license comes in. When my ego blocked my healing feeling with blame, what I primarily needed to release was not anger, but fear and sadness. I was fearful of the influence this teacher wielded in Mark's life and sad as I stood by helplessly watching my son struggle with the classroom dynamics. By processing my fear and sadness, I would then have been able to release feeling powerless and discouraged. By doing so, I could have better detached from the circumstances at hand. Essentially, the chart is to be used as a map, while allowing our spiritual sight to lead the way.

As we release our unprocessed feelings, we are able to open our hearts and no longer choose to carry indifference and callousness toward our own or other people's emotional pain. When we feel and release our sorrow, we are able to grieve our losses attached to the decimation of our parenting dreams. When we feel and release our frustration attached to all the ways that the systems aren't responsive to our children's needs, we are then able to persist in the face of obstacles that last longer than we could ever have imagined. Or, when we validate and release our anger, we are then in a position to set healthy, appropriate, boundaries in response to a professional's bullying.

Your feelings are not only integral to the healing process but are also there to assist you in choosing an aligned action with a holistic benefit. Per Dr. Grey's chart, when you release sadness, you are able to receive closure when something ends. When you release fear, you stimulate your adrenals to become engaged so that you can avoid the emotional block of anxiety. When you release disappointment, you are able to detach and move on from an unexpected event that crushed your expectations. When you release worry, you are able to prepare to take the optimal actions that support your success.

When you release embarrassment, you are able to accept yourself unconditionally, even when you display less-than-ideal behaviors. Releasing envy helps you to take steps toward improving your own and your family's circumstances. By releasing hurt, you are able to identify the source of your pain, rather than slipping into the emotional block of self-pity. Feeling and releasing the vibration attached to being scared helps you embrace a new beginning so that you can learn from a fresh opportunity. Releasing shame helps you avoid repeating actions that will result in feelings of remorse. *In summary, irrespective of the triggering event or the healing feeling that has been evoked, none of us can heal what we are unwilling to feel and release.*

> All negativity is caused by an accumulation of psychological time, and denial of the present. Unease, anxiety, tension, stress, worry, and all forms of fear are caused by too much future, and *not enough presence.* Guilt, regret, resentment, grievances, sadness, bitterness, and all forms of nonforgiveness are caused by too much past, and *not enough presence.* ~ Eckhart Tolle

Once you recognize that you have allowed yourself to become enmeshed in a painful story, a replication of the past or an unconscious projection of future doom, you are able to recognize that your ego is the source of your energy. With awareness, you have the opportunity to course-correct so that your energy aligns with trust in your Higher Power.

Once a triggering event has transpired, the key question is the following: where do I feel this uncomfortable body sensation? Without any connection to your body, it means that you have repressed your pain with thoughts, leaving you with the energy of righteousness, blame, depression, judgment, procrastination, self-pity, confusion, discouragement, powerlessness, hopelessness, indecision, or toxic guilt, et cetera. All is not lost, even when you identify with your ego, your emotional blocks and the victim archetype. This cycle takes effect, not as a form of punishment, but rather as an opportunity to awaken to your healing powers and your capacity for psychospiritual growth!

Unfortunately, I had not yet passed the intermediate course in the school for growth and development. I kept auditing the same class again and again. My self-righteous ego was bound and determined to control the course of the tempestuous waters. I found myself at war with an entire cast of characters who my ego frequently judged as deficient in some significant way, including Mark's teacher, a school social worker, school administrators, an advocate, an attorney, a gastroenterologist, state administrators of the program for mentally ill children, hospital personnel, a head psychiatrist of a leading clinic for mentally ill children, strangers at movie theaters, and even Mark, plus a fourth-grader who wouldn't leave us alone at a party!

My ego had appointed me as the ringleader of a three-ring circus filled with down-on-their-luck clowns; elephants that circled in a haphazard direction; rare white tigers that slept in the ring; dancing bears who no longer danced; and jugglers, acrobats, and trapeze artists who missed every one of their stunts. And yet, my ego refused to let me see that I held the power to just step outside the ring. After all my impassioned words were uttered and all my earnest actions were concluded, Mark began and ended his sixth-grade year in the exact same location where all the pandemonium had commenced.

The Universe didn't budge on that point, no matter how much my ego pushed for a different reality. For nine long months, Mark and I remained in a fixed pattern of stagnation or regression, as the earth easily made its way around much of the circumference of the sun. Mark would be at home for another summer, only to return to the exact same middle school program for seventh grade.

PESSIMISM AND FRUSTRATION

"Life always waits for some crisis to occur before revealing itself at its most brilliant."

Paul Coelho

November 21, 2006 will forever be etched in my memory. Almost exactly twelve years to the date of Mark's original autism diagnosis, one of my most catastrophic imaginings came to pass. After sixty facilities rejected Mark, I agreed to have my seventh grader admitted on a thirty-day provisional basis to a residential treatment center (RTC). It was, aside from deciding to divorce, the most heart-wrenching decision of my life. Looking back, it's easy to see how it marked a colossal turning point in both of our lives; at the time, however, I questioned whether my resolve was precipitating disastrous and irreversible repercussions.

Dr. J., the medical director of the RTC told me that if Mark tolerated the environment without risk of anaphylaxis, his stay there would be extended beyond the month. For the immediate future,

Mark would no longer reside in my home. At the time, my ego broadcast the following lie: because this eventuality had come to pass, all of the passion and commitment I previously put forth had been in vain. Mark was accepted into a newly created housing cottage that was designed to serve children and teens with Asperger's syndrome. In 2006, Asperger's included children who were of average to superior intellectual development. These children exhibited restricted interests; had difficulty comprehending abstract language, including inferences and non-verbal cues; displayed significant social impairments and were generally considered to represent the "high functioning" end of the autism spectrum. [50]

Arranging for Mark to begin treatment at the facility was fraught with all kinds of impediments. On two different occasions, Mark's placement had fallen through – or rather derailed – due to the medical director's ambivalence. As a result of the second delay, Mark was forced to undergo two weeks of intensive, full-time, home-based monitoring. Once the reality of life in an RTC began to settle in, Mark's emotional state fluctuated between massive denial and complete despair, with intermittent suicidal thoughts. Finally, as a result of the political pressure applied by the organization's overseeing corporate body, combined with the facility's financial need to operate the brand-new unit at full capacity, Mark's placement was secured.

Thanks to case manager Micki B.'s presence, Mark was safely ensconced in the back seat of the car, en route to his new locale. Mark's face was pasty white and he appeared to be in a state of terror that mimicked shellshock. Upon arrival, he required physical assistance into the building because his legs buckled. While I completed over three hours of intake paperwork, Mark's body was frozen in a fetal position under a nearby table, as he emitted intermittent whimpering, moaning, and crying.

Because Mark had been incapable of altering his maladaptive behavior, he ferociously clung to denial in order to protect himself from facing the reality at hand. When children are unable to learn from prior experiences and cannot fully benefit from a world shaped by natural consequences, it's inherent upon the key adults to recognize that these symptoms are the hallmarks of brain-based disorders. No matter what factors had contributed to this eventuality, I clung to a fragile acceptance that this day had finally arrived.

After three surreal hours at the intake table, a photo of Mark resembling a mugshot was snapped, and then we were separated from one another. Mark was taken to his living quarters, while I was escorted to the nursing station for another round of meetings. I spent hours educating the nurses about Mark's medical history, his medication regimen, and the best methods for delivering his growth hormone injection.

At the conclusion of the nursing consultation, I was taken to Mark's private bedroom, where I found him lying prostrate on the bed. The room itself was quite small and narrow, with the bed, a tiny side table, and a desk placed against one wall and a small dresser on the opposite wall. A small window faced out to the access driveway. A staff member, Kim, had already begun to unpack Mark's belongings. She exhibited a pleasant, kind demeanor and seemed willing to help organize everything. All of this quickly faded to the background as my ears rang with Mark's repetitive comments expressing despondency and anguish. As I had anticipated, it was quite clear that my decision to bring Mark here had completely shattered his spirit.

As I listened to his desperate commentary, I broke down sobbing, followed quickly by Kim, who also found it unbearable to listen to. After another couple of hours arranging his belongings, it was time to leave. Mark sobbed uncontrollably while imploring me to take him home. I was forced to wrench his arms from around my neck so that I could begin exiting the unit.

As I turned and began walking away, I heard his piercing screams and entreaties from inside the room and, later, from the small bedroom window, "Mom, come back. Mom, come back. Mom, come back. Mom, please come back."

I continued walking; got in my car; immediately started the engine; and robotically drove down the driveway. I felt numb, empty, and completely dejected. In order to quiet my racing mind, I hyper-focused on every aspect of my long drive home. When I entered my home, I plopped down on my sofa still wearing my winter coat and holding my purse. I immediately took note of Mark's empty chair. It was in that very moment that my body was flooded with overwhelming loss. It seemed the entire house was permeated with it.

Mark's intense and overwhelming energy had suddenly dissipated. The atmosphere felt dead. I felt my own deep sense of depersonalization – as though only part of me had been present during the intake process. I forced myself to go through a few self-care measures, then, later, as I climbed the stairs to go to bed, a thought struck me: What am I going to do now with the overflowing love that I still feel in my heart for Mark? Where am I going to direct that love now?

And in that very moment, my biggest fear set in and fired off a series of questions. Would I ever have the chance to see Mark alive again? Would he live through his first night away from home? Would Mark be alive to attend our first therapy appointment, two days away?

Fortunately for me, it would be months before Mark disclosed that he had been up that whole first night ruminating on ways in which to end his life. For the next three days he refused to leave his room for meals, to shower, interact, or attend school. He emerged only to shuffle robotically to the bathroom and back again. I was unaware that Mark was exhibiting this level of shutdown and discovered much, much later that the first time he left his room was to attend our therapy appointment.

When Mark entered the room, he flung his arms around me and held on as if for dear life. (He would also tell me months later that during his first night away from home, he experienced grave doubts that I would ever return to see him.) When, after several minutes, he let go of my neck, I noted that his clothing and hair appeared quite disheveled. He had prominent purplish half-circles under his eyes. Although I expressed immense concern for his well-being, I was never apprised of Mark's level of despair; nor, as mentioned, was I made aware that he should have received an emergency assessment during his initial days in the unit. This would not be the only instance of negligence that I observed during his first month at the center.

By Christmas, I discovered – and thankfully so – that Mark's dose of mood stabilizer had been halved by mistake. Apparently, Dr. J. had written it down incorrectly when Mark was admitted. As a consequence of this drastic, "cold turkey" drop in the dosage, he had not only been processing the shock and trauma of being left in the facility, but he had also been doing so without the full therapeutic support he was used to. The discovery of the error brought an end to Dr. J.'s tenure as medical director, but this did little to assuage my outrage or concern for Mark's welfare.

Indeed, throughout Mark's stay at the RTC, which was extended past the initial thirty-day assessment, there would be a litany of mishaps, including mistakes related to the delivery of the growth hormone injections. Another example was the guarantee, made to me before Mark's admission, that the staff were well trained in the therapeutic tenets of Stanley Greenspan's foundational work and that every child would be offered an individualized sensory diet.[51] It would be months before Mark had access to a sensory room, and even then there were no occupational therapists on staff to prescribe or facilitate an individualized set of appropriate sensory activities. Instead, a group of children was turned loose in the sensory room with "cottage" staff (the facility was organized into cottages) supervising to ensure their safety.

A few of the cottage staff members were lovely, kind-hearted women who treated the children compassionately. Others were "old-school," having worked in facilities for decades, and took a very rigid, simplistic view of problem behaviors. Still others, notably some temporary weekend staff, barely rose from the sofa. They watched TV or sat around gossiping and were not at all invested in helping children. Unfortunately, a tiny minority of the staff appeared to be "thugs." They presented as street criminals and operated with violence and intimidation toward their wards. Right before Mark's eyes, Jimmy, his closest friend on the unit, became a victim of this aggression, leaving him with significant bruising all around his neck after being thrown to the floor and choked. Yes, the administrators fired physically abusive staff members, but it was always after the fact.

Over time – and given the constant staff turnover, in conjunction with the paucity of professionalism and programming content – any illusions that I held about the potential therapeutic benefits for Mark at the RTC were stripped away. He had, for all intents and purposes, been warehoused. During his stay there were two executive directors, three assigned psychiatrists, two clinical directors, two assigned therapists, four Asperger Cottage Supervisors, and three assigned teachers in Mark's classroom. Unfortunately, six weeks into his stay, Mark's first highly seasoned psychotherapist left.

The next therapist, Katherine, was a novice who appeared to know little to nothing about autism. She labeled Mark's unclear expressive speech patterns as "gibberish" on his written goal sheets. Given the fact that Mark had spent years in painstaking and intensive speech and language therapy and was clearly doing the best he could to express himself, I found that pejorative label unprofessional, not to mention insulting. From my vantage point, Katherine did not possess the confidence, therapeutic knowledge, or flexibility to engage Mark in a meaningful process. She also made it clear that she wanted little to no input from me.

She believed that Mark's issues were in large measure due to a lack of parental hierarchy in the family. In other words, Mark had taken advantage of my weakness and had essentially bullied me to get what he wanted.

"You've allowed yourself to become a doormat," she stated, "You're behaving like a battered woman. Mark is the tyrant and you have become his slave."

There may have been some truth to that viewpoint, but I viewed her perspective as a gross oversimplification of the situation.

Interestingly, she appeared to have no more control than I did. The state grant that paid for Mark's time at this institution stipulated weekly family therapy sessions. During those sessions, Mark spent the entire time avoiding any semblance of participation. He repeatedly drew on Katherine's dry-erase board without permission. Week after week, he flung her deck of cards around the room. He blew bubbles in her face. He stood behind her and tousled her hair. He sheepishly hid behind an open children's book. He wandered around the room, seeking comfort from every object he could find. He interacted with and commented on these objects, derailing any focus on his struggles.

Katherine spent most of the session engaged in a power struggle with Mark over her requirement to have him seated on the sofa with his feet on the floor. For close to a year, while observing these dynamics, I managed to remain silent.

During our private time together, Mark asserted, "Katherine is an actual alien who wants to blow my head off with a gun."

These statements were indicative of Mark's unchecked mental illness, characterized by extreme paranoid thinking. There was clearly no level of trust or therapeutic alliance between them.

Indeed, Mark spent his initial months there using massive denial to anesthetize himself. He asserted that he would no longer reside on the unit by the new year; then, when January came and went, he said he would be discharged by his birthday in late February. When no such release date occurred, he shifted his focus to the end of the school year as his moment of liberation.

"I'm not concerned," he told me. "I'm going to bide my time. They'll be forced to release me at some point. They have to let me out before I turn twenty-two."

In the meantime, Mark displayed little to no motivation to meet objectives that would be rewarded with a home visit. Nor was he interested in visiting with our dog on the grounds. His position was one of abject defeat and resignation – one that shocked even me. I never imagined that he would dig his heels in to such a degree and demonstrate such little desire toward securing his arrival back home.

Maybe deep in the recesses of his psyche, Mark possessed not a shred of confidence in his capacity to meet any of his objectives. Ten months into his stay, the administrators took matters into their own hands and warned me that Mark would be discharged before his one-year anniversary date arrived. I was horrified by the thought that Mark would be back on my doorstep with negligible progress having been achieved, and frightened of the backlash I would certainly face.

I believed that the real reason behind the threats of discharge was the administrators' exasperation with my ongoing advocacy efforts. I was in the habit of writing regular complaint letters that were occasionally forwarded to the overseeing director of the entire state program for chronically mentally ill children. Although I tried to wisely pick my battles and exercise restraint, my efforts were deeply resented. Fortuitously, Micki B., who was still overseeing Mark's case on the local level, stepped in and ardently joined my efforts to forcefully advocate for a six-month delay in Mark's discharge. Thankfully, the treatment team reluctantly conceded.

Although this delay was granted, my overwhelming frustration unexpectedly boiled over during a therapy session. I felt infuriated over Mark's avoidance tactics but I was even more incensed with Katherine's complete inability to establish any semblance of a working alliance with him, in tandem with her ongoing statements related to my "ineffectiveness." I knew that I didn't have any power to influence Katherine's behavior, so when my frustration reached its peak Mark became my target. Though I was well aware that I was mandated to attend weekly family therapy as a condition of Mark's continued placement, my white-hot emotions overruled my logic.

I shouted, "Mark, I'm done. I've had it. I am sick and tired of spending hours and hours of my precious time commuting here for these appointments with you. I am not coming back again. I refuse to watch you engage in these ridiculous and self-defeating power struggles with Katherine. *This entire experience has been a complete waste of my time.* (Note to self: this is not a good statement to make when trying to win over the gatekeeping therapist!) I refuse to allow this yearlong pattern of completely unproductive behavior to drain me of the small energy reserves I have left. I will continue to visit you here on the weekends but I will **not** be attending any other therapy sessions unless and until you can give me your word that you will wholeheartedly commit to working on your issues – the very issues that landed you here in the first place. I'm no longer willing to continue to give more to this process than you do. You need to be all in! *You need to get serious* and actually *take a seat on this sofa*, listen to the feedback you're being given, and buckle down and start working to meet your goals so that you can get yourself discharged. Only *you* can be responsible for your own life. I am not coming back again. This is my last family session, unless something drastically changes and those changes are seen immediately and consistently."

At that point, Mark did what Mark typically did when the circumstance exceeded his coping abilities. He bolted from the office without permission and exited the building. He then chose to sit alone on a picnic table on the grounds of the property. After verifying where he was, Katherine and I waited fifteen minutes for him to return to the office. I sat silently hoping against hope that a contrite Mark would walk back in with his head hung low and a renewed commitment to change in evidence. No such thing occurred. Instead, I escorted a quiet Mark back to his living quarters and once again I drove away with deep sorrow and heightened fear in my heart.

Mark's ongoing resistance was not the only weighty concern on my mind. Tandem to Mark's first year at the RTC, I lived through my father's drastic physical and mental decline. Dad had stopped drinking alcohol in his sixties and in the aftermath of Mark's diagnosis became one of my biggest supporters. Thirteen years later, he was a shell of his former self, having lost his eyesight and experiencing extreme digestive challenges, along with total weakness and body wasting that left him bedbound and with compromised thinking capacities. His calm, reasoned demeanor had been replaced with global fear and bouts of irrational thinking and, eventually, delirium. Even though I resided three hundred and seventy-five miles from my childhood home, I spent an inordinate amount of time on the phone solving problems and coordinating his care.

Shortly after the delay in Mark's discharge was granted, I learned that my father's passing was imminent. Although Mark had yet to earn a scheduled home visit, I made a request for him to accompany me to Ohio for the funeral. I felt it was important that he be present to process the loss of his grandfather. Katherine and the rest of Mark's team members were against this, save one: his school speech therapist, Susan C.

Susan was a lovely person who went far beyond the call of duty to assist Mark. She created speech exercises that were designed to appeal to his interests and allowed him extra computer time to pursue his fixation with horror films. Susan even capitalized on this interest to teach him a series of language inferences.

Upon meeting Susan, Mark had flatly refused to enter through her office door, which perplexed her and prompted a consultation with me. Once she understood the depth of his fear of failure and rejection, she immediately course-corrected and instead spent the initial months clearly outlining her flexible expectations, listening to Mark's perspective, honoring his fixations, addressing his concerns, and establishing a trusting relationship with him. She did not force him to enter her office until he felt ready to do so.

After investing several months of her time with Mark, Susan informed me that he had become one of her favorite clients. As for Mark, *his trust and confidence in the assigned professionals meant everything.* Though such a foundation is a prerequisite for success for *everyone,* it holds even greater significance for children who have felt the sting of being misunderstood and rejected. By the end of my father's life, Mark and Susan's relationship had solidified, and she vigorously defended his right to attend the funeral. As a result, the rest of the team reluctantly granted my request to take Mark out of state for the upcoming week.

The day of the trip we got a late start, as I first spent hours driving to the RTC and more time packing Mark's things, and didn't check into our hotel in Northwestern Ohio until approximately four a.m. When I awoke several hours later, I had a raging sore throat. Mark and I didn't arrive at my parents' home until the early afternoon. After carting all our possessions inside, my fever felled me. I collapsed in a bed adjacent to my father's hospice bed.

By 5:30 p.m., my body was crying for sleep in a quiet upstairs bedroom. As soon as my head hit the pillow, my sister informed me that I was needed downstairs for final goodbyes. My father had lingered for days awaiting my presence. I stood beside his body as his soul left the physical world. The gift of being present for my father's final moments will forever be engraved in my heart. One of the most poignant moments in the entire week occurred when Mark stood with his back to the wall in the narrow hallway and saluted as my father's body was wheeled by.

With one small exception, Mark handled all of the family dynamics beautifully. Later in the evening, his panic took hold, as he became gripped with overwhelming terror that I would fall apart emotionally. With reassurance and time, Mark came to realize that he was safe, even while witnessing a normal grief process.

Mark even handled my mother's challenging behaviors. My mother was in the throes of Alzheimer's disease, and the accompanying stress and change in her routine exacerbated her symptoms. Mark patiently answered her repetitive questions and followed my advice by physically steering clear when she became highly agitated and confused. Though a lot more work would need to be done, that memorable week in Ohio marked the fragile beginnings of a turning point in my relationship with Mark.

In the meantime, he was also dealing with the kinds of challenges that often exist in institutional settings. I had seen for myself how peers on the unit had brutalized Mark physically; he had been repeatedly struck, kicked, and even choked. I had also been made aware that Mark's property, including two DVD players, had been stolen and damaged beyond repair.

Further, I learned that an older, streetwise, and mentally ill cottage mate had been excessively lecturing Mark on the topic of sex. Immediately sensing that he was grooming Mark in order to sexually exploit him, I managed to get him quickly transferred from Mark's cottage and into a unit where he would allegedly receive closer supervision. To protect Mark, I had often enlisted the aid of Mark's psychiatrist so that he could immediately be reassigned to different roommates. At one point, Mark mentioned that one of his cottage mates had recently absconded through the bedroom window. Mark told me that he was planning to follow suit and leave in the same manner.

As I dropped Mark back at his living quarters after an outing, he made the following statements: "Look at the cottage. It looks like a scary evil face that is whispering to me. It is telling me that I don't belong here. It is telling me to get out. It is telling me to run away and that I am better off dead. I'm going to run to the railroad tracks, lie down there and end my life. I'm sorry, Mom. I have to say goodbye to you. Thanks for all you tried to do for me but it's just too late for anything to be any different."

Knowing that Mark's destiny was not within my control, I felt panicked and heartsick. Nevertheless, I immediately called the top administrator insisting that Mark's psychiatrist immediately evaluate him and that locks and alarms promptly be placed on the cottage bedroom windows. Mercifully, before my next visit, locks had actually been installed.

Since Mark's admission to the unit, I was made aware that his life had repeatedly been spared. Looking back, I truly don't know whether Mark would have survived without the support of his most preferred cottage mate, Jimmy, who had arrived six weeks after Mark. Approximately three years Mark's senior, Jimmy had also been quite demoralized over the circumstances that landed him at the facility. His long-term foster mother was no longer able to care for him, and since he was seventeen and possessed the Asperger's label he was not considered a viable candidate for another placement. That's when the Virginia social service system sent him to Illinois.

Jimmy and Mark clicked immediately and spent most of their time talking about favorite subjects, pursuing their mutual hobbies, and fantasizing about all the myriad of ways that they could escape their circumstances or retaliate against those who they perceived to be their persecutors.

Almost immediately, Jimmy impressed me as a very thoughtful young man who did not require the *supposed* intensive therapeutic rehabilitation provided in a residential treatment facility. Jimmy cared deeply for Mark and encouraged him to keep putting one foot in front of the other. He was also deeply religious and supported the notion that there was a Divine plan for Mark's life. Without the exceptionally close brotherhood between Mark and Jimmy, I'm not convinced that Mark would have had any respite from his ongoing despair. Their camaraderie and dark humor were reminiscent of combat veterans who shared an experience from the inside that others would never be privy to or fully comprehend.

Then, weeks before my father's funeral and with little notice, Jimmy was unexpectedly discharged from the facility. Due to Jimmy's swift exit out of state, I was never given the chance to say goodbye and wish him well. Mark was devastated in the wake of Jimmy's departure; however, that loss, coupled with the unexpected ultimatum I had delivered in Katherine's office and the experiences surrounding the aftermath of my father's death, sparked a shift. It was as if Mark suddenly realized that only he could pick up the pieces of his life.

He actually began to show up in therapy with a renewed commitment, sitting in his assigned seat and actively participating. Although much of the content was not geared toward someone with autism, Mark attempted to benefit in whatever way he could. Indeed, at the start of 2008, Mark was granted a four-hour pass, then, finally, week-end visits home.

As for me, I had finally committed to my own healing, and connected with some of my personal answers. During Mark's first six months at the facility, I underwent weekly intensive colon hydrotherapy treatments[52] as well as regular lymphatic massage, gall bladder and liver cleansing. I also incorporated juicing into my daily regimen. Basically, I overhauled my lifestyle. Although the process proved to be quite taxing for my body, I incrementally felt more energized, dropped weight, improved the tone and look of my skin, and replenished lost nutrients.

Because I was no longer solely responsible for Mark's daily care, I had the time, space, and mental wherewithal to attend classes and events at a local metaphysical healing center. I studied and voraciously read on a number of subjects pertaining to the "nature of reality." This material reignited my childhood search for answers to many of life's "bigger questions." I began participating in a prayer circle and a metaphysical book club, embarked on a vision quest, and took classes in chakra healing and mystical traditions. I immersed myself in the teachings of various thought leaders and spiritual healing methods. I consulted with a medical intuitive and enrolled in training to master the basics of the Emotional Freedom Technique. [53]

My passion for these subjects was ignited after I received a DVD of *The Secret*[54] from my dear childhood friend, Jane B. Even during my darkest days, Jane B.'s friendship had never wavered. After Mark's autism diagnosis, Jane faithfully shared self-help methods that were geared to support my physical, emotional, and spiritual recovery.

Watching *The Secret* started a massive chain reaction that upleveled my life. I felt that intuitive click that instantly alchemized a miracle. In describing my experience, I borrow from the words of Marianne Williamson: "A miracle is a shift in perception from fear to love – from a belief in what is not real to faith in that which is. That shift in perception changes everything."

I printed the top one hundred quotes from *The Secret* and began to internalize their wisdom. I had come home to truths that my ego had let me forget during this incarnation. I excitedly shared these affirmations with Jane Walker and discovered that she too was integrating these tools.

"You're like the overnight singing sensation that has been at her career for twenty years," she said of my efforts - a statement that profoundly and succinctly summed up my journey!

When I began exploring life coaching as a potential career, I wondered whether my work with the Law of Attraction had inspired it, or was it actually something I had been called to do for some time. I recalled how years earlier, from 2003 to 2006, I had spent time glued to the one hundred and fifty episodes of *Starting Over,* a reality series that featured six women living together at the *Starting Over House* for the purpose of personal transformation. I remember being fascinated by the combination of practicality and spirituality modeled by Iyanla Vanzant and Rhonda Britten's empowerment exercises.

Rather than being consumed almost every waking moment by Mark's needs, I had begun to earnestly consider the scope and shape of my own life; I was charting my path forward. However, my time of solitude would soon come to a halt.

During Mark's last months at the RTC he was transferred to a brand-new "transition" cottage that prepared residents for discharge. This cottage was highly structured and the caliber of staff seemed to be a cut above the staff on the Asperger's Unit. Mark was no longer allowed unlimited access to his DVD player at his leisure. The emphasis was now on structured activities, peer socialization, and the completion of assigned tasks. I wasn't a fan of discipline that entailed long stretches at the table in silence with folded hands, but I did appreciate the fact that more structure had been added to his day.

At the behest of Katherine, I was asked to schedule a sleep study for Mark. The staff finally concurred that Mark was at the mercy of a severe and unrelenting sleep disorder. During the spring, Mark was so sleep-deprived that he sometimes fell asleep during school hours. After an exhaustive search to schedule Mark's sleep study, I continued to run into the same level of prejudice that I had previously undergone. I eventually was forced to take Mark to a center's gatekeeper – a pulmonologist.

During the office visit, the nurse asserted that Mark's need for a sleep evaluation was a "no-brainer," however, it was clear from the moment Dr. A. entered the room that she did not concur.

After posing a number of questions, she haughtily asserted, "Mark does not need a sleep study. The problem is obvious. He has anxiety – a hallmark of autism."

At that moment, I quickly interrupted, "I do not believe that anxiety is the explanation for his sleep disorder. Mark exhibits mania. There is a clear difference. But how can we ensure that there is not more than meets the eye going on here? I'd like to rule out whether there is any other reason for his eleven years without sleep."

Dr. A. adamantly refused to order the evaluation, instead recommending a nightly sleep hygiene program, the results of which would be documented on data sheets. She prescribed a sleeping pill – a benzodiazepine hypnotic agent that had typically been prescribed to treat insomnia on a short-term basis. Because I was well aware that this medication had the potential to be habit-forming, I felt quite concerned about the prospect of Mark ingesting it. However, at that point, I truly didn't believe that I had much of a choice, given Mark's upcoming discharge. Something had to be done to improve his sleeping patterns – and it had to be done quickly.

I agreed to go along with the plan for a thirty-day trial period. Six months earlier, I had also conceded to adding another medication to Mark's pharmaceutical cocktail. Mark had been prescribed a medication that was not in standard use by psychiatry but one that did have some efficacy for generalized anxiety disorders. In my estimation, the benefits of that medication were subtle but I had been prepared to continue to cooperate with Mark's psychiatrist. Graduation from eighth grade was in the very near offing, and shortly thereafter, Mark had been slated to leave the facility.

In anticipation of Mark's return home, I consulted with Dr. F., who agreed to accept him as a returning patient. Dr. F. decided to substitute an extremely low dose of an anti-psychotic medication as a replacement for the sleeping medication that would soon be discontinued. Amazingly, the hypnotic agent did actually help Mark to restore a normal sleep cycle! Although I was encouraged by the results of the medication, I also felt extremely unsettled about the effects of an anti-psychotic medication on Mark.

Making plans for Mark's future medical care, his medication regimen and his sleep hygiene program were not the only irons in the fire. After a massive amount of legwork, I felt ecstatic when the school district agreed to continue Mark's enrollment in a therapeutic day school. This time, the administrators were completely on board with placing Mark there! And wonder of wonders, Mark had been accepted into a school that emphasized the performing/expressive arts! Mark was slated to begin high school during the upcoming summer term.

These were not the only changes afoot. Micki B., who had been our champion and a huge support before and during Mark's stay at the RTC, was no longer assigned to our family. Micki's employer was no longer overseeing services to chronically mentally ill children with impaired reality testing. I had my ear to the ground as the parent grapevine buzzed with negative commentary about the newly assigned agency. However, once I became acquainted with Alison, Mark's newly assigned case manager, I was pleasantly surprised! I wondered… could the Universe actually be aligning all of the supports necessary for Mark to succeed in the community?

There was more encouraging news as well. During weekends home from the unit, Mark had been assigned to a brand-new community mentor. Rosemary, a woman in her early sixties, had spent years working with mentally ill and developmentally disabled clients. She had also reared four children of her own. The positive chemistry between

Mark and Rosemary was immediate. But never in my wildest imaginings could I have envisioned the next enormous positive step in Mark's journey. Seemingly, *out of nowhere*, an email that would *forever change everything*, dropped right into my inbox. An acting troupe for special needs students had recently been created right in my hometown!

After seeing Mark perform in plays and talent shows at the residential school, Susan, his speech therapist, had strongly advocated for him to participate in a special needs acting troupe; however, the only opportunity to do so was hours from my home. Now, Mark was accepted into this local performing troupe and he would have the opportunity to attend acting classes on Saturday mornings, right in our backyard!

Before all these new pieces of the puzzle could be arranged, I had attended Mark's eighth-grade graduation ceremony. I felt heartbroken watching Mark struggle during what should have marked a happy milestone in his life. Instead, he had sobbed uncontrollably as he entered the stage and remained inconsolable during the long ceremony. At the conclusion of the formal proceedings, Mark ran from the auditorium and disappeared. I felt on edge as Mark was missing for over an hour. Eventually, the school principal discovered his whereabouts. In line with Mark's talent for outwitting staff members and locating great places to hide, he was eventually found in the fetal position in a basement kitchen cabinet! Irrespective of this disturbing episode, nothing was going to derail Mark's anticipated return to his childhood home.

At the time, knowing that Mark was anticipating such a momentous transition back home, I tried to convince myself that Mark was caught up in his weighty fear of failure and thus I shouldn't be too quick to judge his suitability for a return home. It was essential that I keep an open mind and give him every opportunity to start anew. Despite any trepidation that we were feeling, on June 6, 2008, with my car fully loaded, Mark and I drove past the welcoming sign of the RTC for the last time. As I momentarily stopped the car before turning onto a major roadway, we both glanced behind at the familiar motto underneath, "Believe, Trust, Achieve."

WHAT I KNOW NOW THAT I DIDN'T KNOW THEN: VALIDATION IS AN ANTIDOTE TO EGO RESISTANCE. WHEN WE VALIDATE THE TRUTH IN ITS ENTIRETY, OUR EGOS WILL HAVE NOTHING FURTHER TO MIN-IMIZE, DENY, REPRESS, OR UNCONSCIOUSLY REEN-ACT WITH OTHERS. At a time when we were traumatized and pushed beyond our coping abilities, our egos stepped in to help us survive. The ego is forced to offer us one of two strategies: either it persuades us to discount and ignore our pain, or over-identify with that pain by wearing it as a badge of honor. Without validation, we may find ourselves swinging back and forth from pole to pole. We might overreact to trivial events because there is a very small, needy, wounded tyrant inside of us who demands to be seen and noticed. This little tyrant is carrying a lifetime of pain that requires emotional release. Via the practice of validation, we potentially choose to actively attend to the little tyrant and the small, voiceless invisible ones inside ourselves who are illuminating the path to our healing. When we are triggered emotionally, our earlier conditioning propels the ego to either act against ourselves, react negatively to people and situations, or both.

Our objective is to locate the *true source* of our pain and heal by dissolving all limiting aspects of us, rather than replaying the trauma or violation over and over again in our energy field. We have the power to address the source of our pain and we can also *decide to value ourselves enough to give ourselves permission to feel our uncomfortable feelings, because feelings are never right, wrong, good or bad.* When we validate our feelings, we take all the time we need to honor our authentic vulnerability so that we may move through the *release* process in a safe private space. We speak to ourselves as we would speak to a favored child, with a loving, soothing, and compassionate voice. After all, we are speaking to our inner children – the parts of ourselves who were ignored, abandoned, rejected, or betrayed during our turbulent childhoods. Iyanla Vanzant had it right when she wrote, "Nothing destroys self-worth and self-love faster than denying what you feel...Honor your feelings. Allow yourself to feel them."

By validating our feelings, we avoid slipping into a state of premature positive thinking, also known as "toxic positivity." Premature positive thinking is a form of magical thinking that permits us to notice and overemphasize the positive aspects of people, events, and experiences while blinding ourselves consciously or unconsciously to the harmful impact of what we have endured. Premature positive thinking is our ego's way of distorting reality, all done under the guise of having us avoid facing and releasing our pain. It's a form of spiritual bypass. In contrast, validation is an action step that allows us to courageously acknowledge the true impact of events, as well as our attendant feelings. Validation supports us in *unconditionally accepting events as they actually happened*.

Through the validation process, we speak the truth about whatever slight, injury or trauma transpired, knowing that the truth will invariably set us free. Validation does not mean that we are condoning or excusing our own – or anyone else's – unbalanced behaviors. Validation supports us in speaking from the heart, by taking full responsibility for our part in our co-creations and, simultaneously, giving ourselves the benefit of the doubt in a non-judgmental way.

When validating, it's helpful to remember the *"three N's,"* which stand for *normal, natural and necessary*. Validation is founded on the principle that painful feelings are *normal*, although it is not highly functional to keep active in our energy fields. It is *natural* for uncomfortable feelings to show up in our bodies as messages from Spirit, nudging us to perform psycho-spiritual first aid at the soonest point in time. In order to move forward in a healthy way, it's *necessary* for us to learn to digest, process, and release our feelings so that we may assuredly gain the accompanying holistic benefits. [55]

Validation also prevents us from slipping into the defense mechanism of intellectualization, where we *rationalize or try to explain away our pain with a storyline.* Instead of intellectualization, we give our bodies permission to relax, confident in our capacity to surface our healing feelings, without any pressure to justify or defend them. This process helps us refrain from recycling the same painful storylines again and again. Via validation, we avoid slipping into the ego trap of wallowing in self-pity, guilt, shame, depression, or other lower vibrational states. Further, validation allows us to completely let go of the pain we have already wisely processed so that we may receive compassion, freedom, and joy. Validation is one of the most important gifts we grant ourselves, because doing so aligns us with the truth of our own magnificence and, by extension, allows our children to experience the grandest expression of us.

Validation potentially begins by consulting John Gray's "Feel To Release Chart," or you can skip "the so-called diagnostics" and simply tune into the uncomfortable blocked energy or dis-ease within your body, such as the tightness in your throat, the nausea in your stomach, the aching in your shoulder blades, et cetera. You then rate the temporary discomfort from a one to a ten, with one being barely noticeable discomfort and ten being unbearable discomfort. You begin with the present circumstance that has triggered you emotionally and *I recommend the use of energy psychology, particularly the Emotional Freedom Technique (EFT), as the quickest and most effective way to validate so that you may discharge trapped electro-magnetic energy from the body.*

EFT helps you rebalance the mind/body/spirit connection. While tapping on specific acupressure points, you process and remove toxic energy from your energy field, while improving the flow of chi or life force energy. Tapping begins with validating the blocks that hinder you from accessing your full powers. From there, you are able to move into reprogramming your unconscious mind so that you can achieve a more empowered state.

You might wonder whether addressing your blocks out loud is a way of reinforcing your limitations. Actually, it's the reverse. You must be willing to courageously look at and acknowledge the unvarnished truth of your experiences (validation) in order to unconditionally surrender and forgive yourself and anyone else who has potentially harmed you. Anyone else's "good intentions" are irrelevant, because if real harm took place the cells in your body remember the toll enacted. It is up to you to respond with ability by shining the light of consciousness into your darkness.

You start with a three-part set-up phrase that is spoken out loud while you're tapping on the karate chop point of the non-dominant hand. The karate chop point is located on the fleshy skin on the outer edge of the hand, between the base of the baby finger and your wrist. You use your four fingers on your dominant hand to tap against the karate chop point. Here is an example of a set-up sequence, "Even though I feel anger toward Dr. A., I deeply and completely love, honor, and accept myself. Even though I am sick and tired of the professionals not listening to me, I deeply and profoundly love and accept myself. Even though my whole body feels tired in this moment, I deeply and completely honor, love, forgive and accept myself."

If your ego is objecting to you using the set-up phrase, "I deeply and completely love and accept myself," you can begin by softening this phrase to "I'm willing to relax and see what comes up for me"; or "I'm open to seeing this circumstance a bit differently now"; or "I'm willing to explore how I can begin to love, accept and forgive myself completely." If possible, irrespective of any mind objections, it's important to emphasize the second part of the set-up sequence when speaking out loud.

During phase two, you tap firmly but gently about seven times in a row on each acupressure point, using the index and middle finger, before moving onto successive energy meridians in the body, beginning with the inside corner of the *eyebrow* (EB) (it doesn't matter which side you choose or whether you choose both sides), and moving to the bone bordering the *outside* of the *eye* (SE), then the bone *under* the *eye* (UE) *near the slant of the nose*, then the valley *under* the *nose* (UN) and above the upper lip, then the *chin* point (CH), which falls in the crevice between the lower lip and the chin and next, using the flat of your hand you tap on top of both beginning points of your inner *collarbone* (CB), and then you tap about three inches *under the arm* (UA) *where the side panel of the bra resides, using all four fingers* and lastly, you use all four fingers to tap on the *top of the head* (TH).

During this basic tapping, you begin with a chosen reminder phrase or your list of ego objections. The short reminder phrase identifies the challenge. For example, "this anger toward Dr. A." repeated on each tapping point or "this knot at the top of my stomach" or "my helplessness," et cetera. When tapping with ego objections, you can include your fear-based thoughts, your fear-based bodily sensations, your self-recriminations, the blame directed at others, and all the ego-based reasons why something can't work in your favor.

I recommend closing your eyes and listening to your self-defeating voice, as you add other statements such as, "feeling dismissed; feeling discounted; not being seen; feeling helpless again; feeling powerless; not having my voice recognized; not having my wisdom heard; Dr. A's arrogance; feeling invisible; I'm so tired of feeling invisible," et cetera.

You don't need to be rigid or perfectionistic about what phrases you use. Just relax into the process, trusting that the right validation phrases and your attendant feelings will arise. Once you have gone through a number of tapping rounds on objections and the discomfort in your body has dissolved, you move into replacing those objections with positive affirmations.

It isn't necessary to *fully* believe the affirmations when you utter them, but it is helpful to say them with as much conviction as possible. Once you have cleared one layer of fear, you may need to explore another aspect of your fear-based experience as you validate and release the truth in its entirety. For example, after clearing my anger toward

Dr. A., I may need to release the toxic guilt tied to all the years that Mark struggled with sleeplessness. Even when it doesn't satisfy your rational mind, toxic guilt needs to be addressed.

Once you begin to feel a measure of relief in your body, you can transition into tapping accompanied by affirmation phrases. I find it helpful to start my affirmative phrases with the word *maybe*, as in, "Maybe there's a way to find peace with this experience after all; maybe there's a way to focus on the positive outcome, in spite of Dr. A's approach; maybe I'm more powerful than what my mind is telling me; maybe I AM safe; maybe I can advocate effectively for Mark; maybe I'm not responsible for anyone else's reaction; maybe I can let go so that I can move forward," et cetera. Using *maybe* helps you move more gradually into embracing positive statements without your ego so strenuously objecting.

From there, you can embrace positive affirmative statements such as, "I choose peace over righteousness every time; I respond with ability in any circumstance; I surrender to any outcome trusting the wisdom of the Universe to guide me; I choose to let go of this experience; I AM safe; I AM strong; I AM capable; I AM effective; I AM powerful; I AM protected; I accept myself exactly as I am in this moment; I enter the flow of the Universe with ease," et cetera. At the conclusion of tapping, the ranking of discomfort in the body should be down to a one or zero. If the ranking does not drop to this level, more rounds of tapping need to be done, or there are other aspects of the experience that need to be validated and released.

Once you have addressed the present triggering event, it's helpful to ask yourself, "When was the first time that I experienced something similar to this event? It's helpful to go back in time to the earliest *specific* childhood memory that mirrors the current experience. If you are unable to surface a *specific* childhood memory, you can trace backward a decade at a time to a companion memory. Record that memory in a journal for your next round of tapping. Then you can introduce EFT's "movie technique," whereby your memory plays silently in your mind's eye, allowing you to witness it. The movie technique captures a specific moment in time that has a definite beginning, middle and ending point. *(If your movie is extremely traumatic, it's wise to have an EFT practitioner walk you through the process.)*

You close your eyes and begin to observe the plotline *a few steps before* the triggering event happened, then allow yourself to start the movie. You freeze the movie at the point where your body holds the emotional hook and the accompanying sensations. Do your palms sweat? Do tears spring to your eyes? Do you clench your jaw? Do you carry weight on top of your chest? Once the uncomfortable energy is witnessed, you can freeze the triggering action and give the movie a name. The name signifies or reflects the core-wounding scenario. In my example with Dr. A., I would ask myself, "When was the first time that I felt the important people in my life discounted my message?" Next, I allow my subconscious mind to bring up an experience and what surfaced for me was an event that took place in kindergarten.

I named my film *Mrs. W. Grabbed the Scissors.* In this example, my teacher forcefully demanded that as a left-handed student, I cut paper using left-handed scissors, even though I politely explained that I used right-handed scissors for cutting. I rated the intensity of the feeling at a seven. At this point, I begin with the set-up phrase repeated three times, "Even though I have this movie, *Mrs. W. Grabbed the Scissors,* I deeply and completely love and accept myself. Next, I run through the tapping points while silently repeating the name of the movie. When I am able to reduce the intensity to a one or zero, I then begin tapping on the start of the movie and gradually advance the film forward. At any point in time, when the emotional crescendo kicks in, it's important to freeze that part of the movie and use the basic tapping recipe to reduce the accompanying feelings in the body until the intensity vanishes.

Once you have cleared the emotional peaks at each significant portion of the story, you can re-run the entire movie in your mind's eye to make sure that you are neutral about every single aspect of your experience. If necessary, you can then go through the movie again, narrating the story out loud while exaggerating all of the sights, sounds, smells, and sensations of touch to confirm that you remain in neutral territory.

If by any chance you still have lingering emotional energy, you can return to the karate chop point and say, "Even though I have this remaining energy around XX movie, I deeply and completely accept myself and all of my emotions." You can then carry out another round of tapping. There are additional tapping points on the wrist and the non-dominant hand that can be added to your tapping session. These hand points are part of the "9 Gamut Procedure." [56]

Research has demonstrated that the 9 Gamut Procedure has been particularly effective for chronic health conditions. Dr. Dawson Church, PhD., [57] has been at the forefront of organizing the dearth of empirical studies related to the more complete version of EFT. Over time and with consistency, even short ten-minute tapping sessions can produce a transformational impact. Follow your intuition and make the process manageable for yourself.[58] Remember, "It's better to feel your blocked feelings for ten minutes…then to keep blocking them, which causes you to relive them again and again for the next ten to twenty years." [59]

RUNG THIRTEEN

STILLNESS AND CALM

"You know great things are coming when everything
seems to be going wrong.
Old energy is clearing out for new energy
to enter. Be patient."

~Idil Ahmed

Mark returned home and immediately began attending the summer session at the new therapeutic high school for the expressive arts. Though it was doubtful that Mark would ever morph into someone who enjoyed attending school, I felt grateful that he willingly entered the school van. For the first time in eleven years, Mark went to bed at a reasonable hour and consistently slept through each night! He also exhibited greatly improved behavior. I quote from an email that I forwarded to Katherine shortly after his return home: "Mark has been home for a little over a month and he is adjusting beautifully. He hasn't threatened me once, slammed doors, thrown property, or verbally abused me. He does not perseverate for hours anymore. In fact, he has been cooperative, helpful and pleasant most of the time."

Given the events that were to follow, those dramatic changes were a complete gift.

The year ahead turned into one filled with unanticipated doctor visits for both of us. In October, Mark was diagnosed with a nineteen-degree lumbar scoliosis or curvature of the lower spine. The endocrinologist referred him to an orthopedic surgeon; however, rather than explore a surgical or a bracing option,[60] I decided to take Mark to two holistic physicians. Eventually, I reduced Mark's home exercises by having him work exclusively with just one physician. This physician had a record of getting great results on behalf of patients with scoliosis. He also had a wonderful bedside manner and was an expert in osteopathic healing and cranial osteopathy.[61] He built Mark a customized heel lift to decrease the uneven level of the sacral base.

During October, in the midst of Mark's weekly therapy, I underwent a brain MRI and was stunned to learn that I had a benign pituitary tumor that was secreting high levels of growth hormone. The recommended course of action was brain surgery to remove "a micro-adenoma."[62] Four physicians endorsed the surgical option, including the lead endocrinologist at the University of Illinois Hospital. Leaving the tumor intact was not a viable option because it posed a risk to my vision and to my overall health. I was advised to avoid the progression of Acromegaly[63] and the disfigurement associated with that condition.

Two days before Christmas, and while Mark was visiting his father, I underwent a transsphenoidal pituitary surgery, performed by a neurosurgeon and an ear, nose, and throat surgeon. The surgical instruments were guided through my nasal opening into my sphenoid sinus and ultimately into the pituitary itself. At the conclusion of the procedure, I was told that my surgery had been a complete success! My surgeon found the tumor in a liquefied state and insisted that he had easily vacuumed it into his surgical instrument.

As soon as the surgical anesthesia wore off, I experienced an ongoing night of misery due to the pain associated with the nasal packing. Following the trauma and sleep deprivation that my body endured in such a short window of time, I felt that I was nowhere near stabile enough to return home to independent living. That circumstance did not prevent my health insurance company from discharging me thirty hours post-surgery. My friend Carolyn picked me up from the hospital and, after observing my fragile condition, graciously invited me to stay overnight at her home.

Carolyn's assistance was not the only support I received. The founder of the metaphysical center also arrived in the midst of atrocious winter weather conditions and spent considerable time praying on my behalf. She not only provided extensive emotional support immediately following the surgery but she also helped locate a part-time caregiver to assist me during my recovery process. I could never have anticipated that this caregiver's two-week stay would ultimately turn into a three-month sojourn!

Unfortunately, I went on to develop serious and long-standing post-surgical complications. On December 31, Mark returned home and felt dismayed to see me collapsed on the sofa undergoing another health-related crisis. Within the next few hours, my condition rapidly deteriorated. Fortunately, Mary stepped in and accompanied me to the hospital, while Carolyn came back to my home to temporarily supervise Mark. By the time I reached the emergency room, I realized that my life hung in the balance. My brain felt like a battery drained of all its electrical charge, while my body felt like its quota of vitality was rapidly being siphoned away.

My body was undergoing a life-threatening adrenal crisis, in part because my unhealed pituitary gland was no longer efficiently communicating with my adrenal glands.[64] I was at risk for such a complication because of a chronic pre-existing health condition – adrenal insufficiency. After admittance to the hospital, the attending physician ordered powerful IV steroids, which gradually stabilized my condition. These IV steroids were the start of other future emergency measures. Over the next several months, Dr. S. was forced to up my dose of medication significantly. On two separate occasions, he found it necessary to prescribe more potent steroid treatments in order to prevent life-threatening adrenal crashes and subsequent hospitalizations.

All of these emergency steps were required following my second emergency hospitalization on January 11, when I acquired food poisoning from a restaurant and fell violently ill. My adrenals were completely overpowered by the contaminants in my body. My body had previously undergone severe food poisoning on a number of occasions but never anything close to the magnitude of this illness. Concurrent with my food poisoning, Mark was suffering from a severe respiratory flu. Even though Mark was not well, he rushed to the bathroom in the middle of the night and after witnessing the shocking sites, he immediately placed an urgent call to Mary.

Later in the evening, at Mary's request, Mark called for emergency assistance. The paramedics arrived and struggled to carry my dead weight downstairs in a transport chair.

With my few reserves of strength remaining, I whispered, "Mark, it's going to be okay."

Once inside the ambulance, the paramedic made a number of unsuccessful attempts to insert an IV while venting about Mark's angry demeanor.

He stated, "What in the hell is wrong with your son? Why is he demanding to ride in the ambulance with you? Why is he screaming and crying in the driveway? What is going on?"

I mumbled weakly, "Mark has high-functioning autism."

Even during one of my lowest moments, I was not given a reprieve on having to explain my life to others.

The paramedic's response was predictable. "He doesn't look autistic." [65]

In that moment, I had no reserves for righteous anger.

Mary accompanied the ambulance to the hospital and was saddled with the duel tasks of soothing Mark's panic and advocating for my best interests. Mark arrived in his pajamas and still weakened from the flu, but that didn't prevent him from gifting me a stuffed bear that sang the Jackson 5 anthem, "I'll Be There." I spent the next several days in the hospital while they stabilized my adrenals and tried to bring my chronic diarrhea under control. During my absence, my part-time caregiver became Mark's full-time caregiver.

I returned home, only to spend the next nine months predominantly bedridden. It would be October of 2009 before an explanation could be found for my severe muscle weakness and debilitation. Unbeknownst to everyone involved, my thyroid gland had gone haywire, sending my hormones into overdrive. After twenty years of living with Hashimoto's Disease, a chronically underactive thyroid, my hormones had instead revved up into full-scale, over-activity. My endocrinologist diagnosed me with Graves' disease (autoimmune hyperthyroidism) and immediately prescribed a medication to suppress the thyroid gland. Fortunately, this medication began to work optimally and almost immediately. I would stay on it for close to a year until the Graves' disease went into remission.

I had placed Mark at the RTC after answering an urgent inner call to attend to my health. Now Mark was back at home and diligently working to put his life back on track, while I found myself lurching from health crisis to health crisis and no longer fulfilling my parenting role as I had envisioned. In the aftermath of my so-called successful surgery, my ego had bypassed discouragement and depression and sent me down into an epic case of despair. Even after the start of the new medication, I was temporarily left unable to drive independently or stand or walk without assistance.

Carolyn recommended that I call on Patrick, a Reiki master,[66] who offered home-based sessions for a two-week interval. After working on my body twice, he believed that there was *only one healer* who possessed the *gravitas* to help me and he was adamant that I see her immediately. However, my ego refused to stand down long enough to entertain that option.

Neither would Patrick, however, and he continued to call, urging me to make an appointment with Kaaren Thomas, a medical intuitive with shamanic abilities.[67] He even insisted on providing transportation and mobility assistance. At that point, my ego capitulated. Patrick and I had been complete strangers, and yet he selflessly chose to extend himself, without receiving any financial compensation.

When the ego relents, there are earthbound angels who assist us during our darkest times.

During my second session with Patrick, I was shown a vision that sustained me. I saw a massive phoenix flying low to the ground in a valley, only to rise above everything as it soared in its full glory, no longer encumbered by anything below. I believed that this mental vision proclaimed my ultimate triumph over my circumstances and encouraged me to be steadfast in my faith, despite my ego's attempt to keep my expectations at rock bottom.

Still, I entered Kaaren's door a hardened skeptic. After eleven years of trying almost every possible intervention to heal my debilitating illness, I now found myself at one of my lowest points physically. Fortunately for me, Kaaren had experience with hardened skeptics and treated me with gentle compassion. At the end of the session, she showed me a thank-you card written by one of her clients, another woman labeled a "lost cause" who was now in recovery.

It would be years into the future before Kaaren informed me that her electrodermal screening device had initially measured my life force energy at a mere twelve percent! An optimally healthy person's reading would approach one hundred percent. The electrodermal device measures the skin's electrical resistance and helps identify energy imbalances along Chinese energy meridians. This device potentially identifies underlying reasons for illness such as allergies, organ weaknesses, food intolerances, and nutritional deficiencies, as well as traumas, trapped emotions, and familial patterns that predispose one toward disease. The device also ascertained specific natural healing remedies that would ameliorate my specific body burdens and potentially improve my overall physical constitution. I continued to partner with Kaaren as she addressed layer upon layer of toxic influences, while also seeking the support of a holistic chiropractor, who I saw twice weekly for the next year.

During this same time period, Mark's synthetic growth hormone was discontinued for thirty days as part of a retesting protocol to determine his body's natural capacity to produce it on its own. Mark entered the hospital and underwent a traumatic insulin tolerance test,[68] administered with an IV. This test is routinely done at age sixteen to determine if growth hormone supplementation is still required. Mark went on to be diagnosed with adult growth hormone deficiency and his endocrinologist recommended that he resume his daily growth hormone injection for the foreseeable future.

I was able to come to terms with the endocrinologist's recommendations for Mark. However, I felt totally unprepared for the phone call placed by the wife of Mark's osteopath during the evening hours of May 1. As a partnering physician, Dr. A. M. specialized in treating adult patients with chronic fatigue syndrome. With almost no preamble, she informed me that infectious Bartonella had overrun Mark's body.

I sat on the floor in my bedroom and I immediately grabbed a sheet of paper. "I'm sorry but can you repeat that and can you spell it please."

She did so. "Mark urgently needs to be seen by a Dr. James Schaller in Florida, that's S-C-H-A-L-L-E-R. Dr. Schaller is the foremost expert on Bartonella in the country. I think you need to call him, order his classic books on Bartonella, and get Mark there immediately. After seeing the striations on his back,[69] I am convinced that he needs a work-up for Bartonella. He also needs to be tested for Lyme disease, as Bartonella rarely exists in isolation from chronic Lyme disease."

I queried, "After seeing what on his back?"

"The striations look like angry red stretch marks and are running horizontally across Mark's back."

After asking her to spell striations, I asked, "Did you just say that Mark might have Lyme disease? As far as I know, he hasn't been in contact with a tick. How could he possibly have Lyme Disease?" My mind drifted back to Mark's time on the Asperger's Unit. Could he have encountered a tick on the grounds of the facility?

She abruptly asserted, "Mark doesn't need to have come into contact with a tick in order to contract Lyme disease."

"Isn't there someone local who can assist Mark? Can't *you* do something to assist him?"

At that point, she reiterated that Dr. Schaller was the only physician who could help Mark and after reinforcing that final point, she suddenly ended the call.

Mirroring Mark's original diagnosis, I was seated alone on the floor, the only difference being that this time the lights were on in my room. That detail didn't prevent my body from slipping into shock. I had never noticed these "striations." I felt disoriented, confused, and completely overwhelmed. Who was this Dr. Schaller and how in the world was I going to make the emotional and financial expenditures to get Mark to Florida? Even if I could pull that off, how was I going to do so given the debilitated state of my body? Nevertheless, as was my predilection, I immediately ordered Dr. Schaller's books and made contact with his office.

Dr. Schaller believed that bipolar illness was a common mimicking condition of atypical Bartonella, a condition where the Bartonella bacteria fused with Mark's red blood cells, invaded his brain's vascular system and weakened those structures. The striations were another example of how this infection abnormally impacted blood vessels in the skin. My heart sank when I noted that the pictured striations featured in Dr. Schaller's books matched Mark's back striations to an exact tee. As soon as I discovered that Bartonella had the capacity to disrupt Mark's heart rhythm, fear overwhelmed me.

After lengthy conversations with Dr. Schaller's receptionist, I felt that the recommended protocols were overly aggressive for Mark and were exorbitantly expensive. I also knew that I was in no position to travel to Florida monthly for Mark's follow-up care. While I gave further consideration to working with Dr. Schaller, I took Mark to a local MAPS (Medical Academy of Pediatric Special Needs) practice. This practice had recently hired a psychiatrist who trained under Dr. Lee Cowden, a well-known Lyme Literate practitioner who espoused the use of herbal protocols.

Dr. Cowden was quite familiar with the two camps of practitioners in the Lyme Community.

> The ramp-up camp believes in slowly increasing antibiotic doses and the number of medications that patients take over time, so that they can avoid horrendous Herxheimer reactions... Conversely, [the "blast 'em hard" camp, espoused] the advantage of hitting the bugs hard right off the bat, so that they are caught by surprise. The downside of the "blast 'em" approach is that patients get stronger Herxheimer reactions... Others herx so badly that they think they are going to die.
> ~ Ginger Savely [70]

Dr. Cowden didn't see the wisdom in either of those approaches because there was considerable evidence to show that in either scenario, following the discontinuation of antibiotic use, ninety percent of Lyme patients relapsed back into chronic illness. In light of the fact that Mark's lab test came back confirming the Bartonella diagnosis, I felt it was imperative that Mark commence treatment at the soonest point in time.

An infectious disease specialist at a major Chicago hospital believed that Mark did not require treatment of any kind. Unfortunately, *chronic* Lyme disease and atypical Bartonella were not recognized conditions in the world of infectious disease. Had Mark contracted acute Bartonella or been infected by what's termed, "cat scratch fever," his condition would have fallen into the parameters of what infectious disease physicians address. Additionally, if Mark had walked into the doctor's office with the classic bulls-eye rash seen in acute Lyme Disease, he could have been prescribed a six-week course of antibiotic treatment. Here's what Dr. Robert Bransfield, Psychiatrist at the Rutgers Medical School and past President of the International Lyme and Associated Diseases Educational Foundation had to say in a transcript from an interview published in ContagionLive in April of 2017:

> Now, there are seven hundred articles documenting the validity of chronic Lyme disease. There are about three hundred looking at psychiatric symptoms associated with chronic Lyme... There's a large amount of peer-reviewed evidence supporting the validity [of chronic Lyme]...Without a doubt, chronic Lyme disease does exist.[71]

Neither the medical body of infectious disease specialists nor the FDA recognized the existence of chronic Lyme disease. As a result, health insurance companies did not cover the cost of treatment for chronic Lyme disease and Bartonella. I quote from a report that I wrote at the time.

> I currently face decisions related to the Bartonella infection and all its ugly repercussions. This condition presents itself one year after Mark's discharge from residential treatment. This period is also a time when I have observed Mark demonstrate his highest level of emotional stability since age three. This event comes about when Mark has begun to consistently sleep through the night, in contrast to the chronic sleep deprivation seen during the past eleven years. This circumstance takes hold when Mark has actually begun to comply with household expectations and boundaries being placed on his behavior. Additionally, with reminders, Mark has been able to take his medications without fail. This circumstance also occurs during a time when Mark has started to develop a fragile relationship with special needs

peers and has begun to invest himself in a special needs acting troupe.

Mark was seen by Dr. Cowden's protégé for a few months. The psychiatrist completed extensive testing and started Mark on a protocol that was designed to improve his nutritional status but unfortunately created unintended side effects. She also recommended that Mark undergo treatment using the Zyto technology. The Zyto, like Kaaren's electrodermal device, measured galvanic skin response via a computer, delineating body burdens, such as environmental allergies, organs weighed down by too much toxicity, mineral and vitamin deficiencies, as well as acute viral, parasitic and bacterial exposures. The Zyto also measured the compatibility of specific nutritional supplements and medications that might bolster Mark's health.

The Zyto could potentially direct energetic frequencies that would gradually rid Mark's body of the opportunistic infections that were responsible for his striations, altered vascular system, night sweats, fatigue, chronic nose bleeds, and likely even his mood swings. However, remembering that less had always been more for Mark, my inclination was to proceed very cautiously. Ultimately, I decided to forego the targeted Zyto frequencies and instead chose to have Kaaren work with Mark using her more conservative approach. I believed that her intuitive gifts, combined with the electrodermal device, could best serve as a foundation that would support Mark's healing.

I also asked Dr. T., the wonderful holistic chiropractor who had spent years treating me for CFIDS, if he could design a protocol to treat Mark's condition. Dr. T. had an incredible bedside manner that fostered a level of trust and comfort on Mark's part. Based upon Mark's blood composition, Dr. T. created a custom homeopathic remedy, which Mark would take for the next two years, four times daily; he was also treated twice weekly with a cold laser that was designed to gently target his bacterial infections. Dr. T., in conjunction with

Kaaren, provided a range of conservative interventions designed to support Mark's natural capacity to heal.

Via applied kinesiology,[72] Dr. T. was able to determine what foods or supplements would best support Mark's body. Although certain foods looked to be of benefit, as soon as they were consumed a brief number of times on a rotational basis, Mark exhibited significant deleterious reactions. There was a long list of foods that were introduced, only to be discontinued. Fortunately, Mark was able to tolerate two new whole-food supplements that boosted his overall constitution. Irrespective of the challenges, ultimately Mark's striations disappeared and his symptoms miraculously went into remission at the conclusion of his two-year odyssey!

In general, Mark underwent a very successful first year of high school. I felt pleased with the level of professionalism demonstrated by the school staff. Mark was assigned a wonderfully competent social worker and a dually credentialed speech–language pathologist/psychologist. Mark was given the opportunity to enroll in guitar class, drum club, art class, intramural athletics, drama class, school talent shows, and varied theatrical productions, as well as the newspaper club. Mark even won the award for the best acting performance during that school year.

Although Mark's teacher, Mrs. F., was not highly skilled at behavioral management, she had a lovely, nurturing personality. On the other hand, Mark experienced chronic bullying from several classroom peers, culminating in an incident where one particular peer jeopardized his safety by surreptitiously placing two plastic pushpin thumbtacks into Mark's stainless steel water bottle. Fortunately, when Mark picked up his drink to take a sip, he heard a strange rattling sound, prompting him to explore the matter further. He then discovered the risk at hand and was completely protected from harm by a loving Universe overseeing his welfare.

I immediately complained to the administration and the principal acted promptly and transferred the offending student to a different classroom. These experiences prompted Mark to seek a change in environment for the coming academic year. Throughout Mark's school career, he had been on the receiving end of a number of negative interactions with male teachers, though he did manage to forge a fragile connection with one of them. With the hope of learning more, Mark designed a detailed questionnaire for Mr. M. that addressed his teaching philosophy, his classroom management techniques and opportunities for students to learn and progress. After carefully scrutinizing Mr. M.'s answers, Mark took the risk of requesting reassignment to his class for the coming school year. Little did either of us know what the fall-out would be from Mark's bold self-advocacy efforts.

With the exception of our mutual health challenges, Mark's life was progressing in a decidedly positive direction. But neither of us was expecting the next turn in the bend. I received a surprise letter from Jimmy's legal guardian requesting a reunion for the boys. Jimmy spent four blessed days with us during the summer. His return to Mark's life soothed Mark's weary soul and partially restored his loss of faith in a loving Universe.

WHAT I KNOW NOW THAT I DIDN'T KNOW THEN: THE UNIVERSE IS ALWAYS LOVINGLY GUIDING US, VIA SUBTLE AND NOT-SO-SUBTLE SIGNS, MESSAGES, AND IMPRESSIONS. Learning to decipher the language of the Universe begins with focused presence that allows us to be grounded in our bodies, so that we may access tranquility and become acutely aware of our outer and inner realities simultaneously. Focused presence gifts us entry into a world where synchronicities, magic and miracles are commonplace occurrences. Carl Jung defined a synchronicity as two or more events that occur seemingly as a coincidence but carry a special and meaningful message that is unique to the observer. An all-knowing intelligence is continually sending us signs to assist with our higher intentions. We will experience even greater access to healing, alignment of our desires and a multitude of blessings when we ask the Divine for assistance during prayer. Prayer is the practice of opening our hearts and speaking directly to Source, whereas meditation and focused presence entail quieting the mind, so that we more easily decipher and magnetize our answers.

In my view, there is no topic or feeling that is off-limits when speaking to God. It is so because God's embrace is made *solely* of pure unconditional love. God's guidance includes explicit signs, symbols, impressions and downloads that appear in our waking lives or during our dream states. As we enact a consistent mindfulness and meditation practice, we help reverse the atrophy of our senses. As a result, we become more acutely aware of details in our surroundings that would previously have gone unnoticed. These details carry the codes of the Universe. The more we learn to decode this information and act upon Universal guidance, the more we live true to our authenticity and the less likely it will be for our egos to sideline us on an uncomfortable diversionary highway.

The Universe can use anything and everything to deliver a message, from the smallest of insects to a song playing in the background, a massive billboard located on a highway, a coin dropped from the heavens, a key phrase running across our computer screens, or a child in a store who utters a string of words designed for us. Some of us easily connect to number messages, angel messages, spirit animal messages, feathers, flowers, or any nature element. Sometimes it's an idea or set of ideas that are downloaded instantaneously, leading us to quickly jot down every single word of inspiration and sacred instruction. Hundreds of passages in this book were channeled inspirations. We might notice an image that keeps replaying in our minds and as it does, we gain entryway into a more empowered state of being.

Sometimes, we receive a powerful *intuitive hit* in the form of chill bumps up and down the body, tears that steak down the face, an inexplicable queasiness that tells us to immediately leave an environment, or, upon meeting someone new, a feeling of déjà vu that we have encountered them before. These *intuitive hits* potentially lead us to a specific location, connect us with someone special, propel us to read a particular book, push us to enroll in a particular class, prompt us to try a particular healing modality, nudge us to ingest certain foods, et cetera. The list is inexhaustible.

When I first crossed paths with Patrick, the Reiki practitioner, he escorted me through a healing portal. He literally drove me to the next archway of healing – Kaaren's front door. During the next five-year leg of my journey, Kaaren facilitated my improvement on all fronts and even agreed to serve as a catalyst for Mark's healing. As part of my ego's ill-founded attempt to shield me from further devastation, I initially resisted the path being placed right at my feet. However, when a message is repeatedly and insistently delivered, it's wise to heed the call! Not only did Patrick repeatedly and urgently appeal to my intuitive Self but he served as the channel by which I was shown a magnificent Phoenix rising from the ashes. What could be more obvious than that? What more did the Universe need to do? Kidnap me, tie me up, and whisk me away to Kaaren's home office on a magic carpet?

At a number of critical life points, vitally prescient information was delivered via my dreams. Beginning when Mark was four months of age, I began to experience repetitive dreams that were prophetic in nature. The dreams always began and ended the same way and, though the themes in the middle varied a bit, the circumstances were chillingly similar. During the first instance of this reoccurring dream, I felt panic-stricken after realizing that infant Mark had been left alone in his crib, in a room on the top floor of a high-rise hotel. Flooded by fear and guilt, I spent the entire dream frantically trying to return to my son so that I could hold him again in that hotel room. After our separation, I felt bereft, wading through the jungle brush for hours in the heat, as I cut away the thick vegetation with a sickle, all the while clinging to the hope of reunification with Mark.

After hacking my way through the vegetation, I encountered a chaotic wedding party with a bride and groom seated in a carriage. Drenched in sweat, I was then forced to navigate my way through a massive sea of wedding-goers. Next, I entered the maze of the hotel's kitchen, manned by non-English-speaking employees. The employees attempted to evict me from the kitchen, while I ineptly used body language to communicate my desire to find my way to the lobby. I finally arrived in the lobby only to discover that the hotel's elevator system had been disabled. Therefore, I had no choice but to begin climbing the imposing staircase. Partway up my climb, I became so fatigued and depleted that I was forced to crawl, taking one taxing step at a time. My knees and elbows were bloodied from the climb.

Although I repeatedly paused, resting the side of my face against the cool steps, I never had any intention of stopping my ascent. My body had little to no energy reserves left and yet, I still pushed myself to continue the climb. I did so by harnessing the primal fervor that a mother bear would feel in the midst of protecting her cub. When I eventually reached Mark's room, I struggled to pull myself to a standing position, burst through the door and discovered to my utter relief and astonishment that Mark had seemingly slept peacefully in my absence. I rushed to his side and realized that he was in fact still healthy and content.

At the time, I recognized that these dreams held great significance, yet I couldn't uncover their meaning. I didn't *feel* any separation anxiety regarding Mark. I didn't *feel* any trepidation or guilt related to our bond. However, during the next four months, the repetitive nature of this information felt extremely unsettling. Looking back, I feel grateful that I had no real inkling that every single aspect of what I was shown would eventually come to pass! An entire year before my life began to implode, Spirit started preparing and warning me.

My waking life came to reflect exactly what had been forecast in my dreams: Mark regressed into autism, shattering our bond of shared connection and intimacy. Once that circumstance occurred, it felt as though Mark was essentially lost to me. I spent Mark's early childhood fighting through barrier after barrier to ensure our reunion. In the midst of fighting on Mark's behalf, I encountered scores of people who didn't seem to *speak my language* or appreciate my intentions. During the steep climb of those early years, I unintentionally sacrificed my health and vitality. However, in the end, just as the dream had forecast, irrespective of any other reality that would come to pass; *all would be well!* During many dark and despairing moments, I would often reflect back upon the promise foretold in this dream: *in the end, the bond with Mark would be preserved and all would be well!* At times, that promise seemed further and further away, and yet Spirit mitigated my despair by gifting me a message of hope and sustenance that I could always cling to: *in the end, all would be well!*

On the other hand, I regret that I chose to discount the cautionary elements of my dreams that repeatedly admonished me to consider whether the sacrifice of my physical vitality was being made in vain. Just as in our dream life, the Universe sometimes places repeated roadblocks in our path during our waking hours. Overcoming these roadblocks is part of our spiritual fitness plan designed to prepare us to embody a higher consciousness, a higher purpose and a higher mission. As Steven Pressfield so succinctly states, "The more important an activity is to your soul's evolution, the more resistance you will feel to it." Why would that be the case? I believe it is so because these repeated roadblocks are highlighting for us the places inside ourselves where we are living from our ego's old conditioning, rather than from our higher knowing.

Sometimes, these same roadblocks are placed in our path as protection! Just as a parent stops a naïve child from running into the path of a car, God puts the brakes on our insistent desires to race ahead, because we too are oblivious to the danger that is bearing down upon us. The Universe lovingly slows us down or thwarts us because we are far from prepared to handle what we think we desire.

For example, after I invested so much energy into potentially sending Mark away to the facility in Kansas, that option was immediately quashed. Although that facility seemed a cut above the others, how do I know that God wasn't instead protecting us from a reality that wouldn't have served Mark well? After all, I would have been seven hundred miles away during Mark's most heightened suicidal states and I would have been unable to visit more than on a monthly basis. Did the Universe leave him in that "dreaded" junior high school classroom so that he could eventually arrive at the local RTC where he would find brotherhood with Jimmy? Is it possible that Mark's time at the institution was indeed the best of all the options?

Although trusting the process of life is crucial to our well-being, we also hold the intuitive capacity to read the potential flow of energy. As viewed from a specific vantage point in so-called linear time, we are able to examine a snapshot of an expected potentiality, out of unlimited potentialities. However, it's important to emphasize that we are indeed *powerful creator beings,* at cause for our co-creations, and capable of shifting energy to a more elevated path. We have access to vast knowledge that can either validate the footprints we are setting into motion or help us correct course so that we avoid something we do not wish to experience.

Whether the Universe taps us on the shoulder by delivering prophetic dreams; bountiful signs that appear in our waking lives; spontaneous downloads; bodily sensations and symptoms; roadblocks that lead to a higher ground; or knowledge that is conveyed through any of our "claires"[73] (clairaudience, claircognizance, clairsentience, et cetera), we are living in a vast multiverse that is always supporting our higher desires. In any given moment, we only need to awaken and remember that help is always readily available for the asking. With the realization that the Universe is forever working through us and leading us to a more expanded and exalted version of ourselves, we sink into calm and comfort. One way to access this more exalted view is to scale to the top rungs of the *Empowerment Ladder.*

HOPEFULNESS
AND OPTIMISM

"Difficult roads often lead to beautiful destinations.
The best is yet to come."

~Zig Ziglar

Mark enrolled in his sophomore year of high school and was assigned to Mr. M.'s self-contained classroom. I felt a burgeoning hopefulness and optimism as I was under the impression that Mr. M. was a talented, creative and enthusiastic teacher. At the beginning of the school year, Mark started dating Jennifer. Jennifer shared Mark's interests in music, theater and the arts. I immediately liked Jennifer and believed that she was a positive influence on Mark. I accompanied the couple to a variety of community locales.

In November, I learned that my former benign pituitary tumor had reappeared. My neurosurgeon recommended radiation to shrink it, but after visiting the gamma ray knife facility[74] and seeking out other medical opinions, I decided to forego that option. Given what

I had previously lived through, I acted upon my intuitive wisdom that strongly nudged me to take a wait-and-see approach. I had finally begun to tentatively trust my inner compass. By taking back my power, I no longer allowed *every single* temporary outer circumstance to pull me down into an energetic maelstrom. In light of the unexpected turn of events that followed our Christmas holiday, it was fortunate that I was adopting empowering habits.

Unexpectedly, the climate in Mr. M.'s classroom began to dramatically deteriorate in January and February. Mark characterized Mr. M.'s behavior as unpredictable, unreasonable and shockingly explosive. He felt that Mr. M. verbally demeaned and humiliated his students. According to Mark, Mr. M. regularly used threats, intimidation and fear tactics to ensure that his students did not return home and disclose his verbal outbursts to their parents. Despite Mr. M.'s gambits to guarantee Mark's secrecy, once Mark returned to the safety of his home, he disclosed the turbulence in his classroom.

On one occasion, Mark struggled to start a complicated multi-step assignment, Mr. M. berated Mark with the following statements: "You're a quitter. You quit before you even get started. You're not ready for the real world. You're especially not ready to hold a job. You are *the most difficult student* I have ever encountered during my entire teaching career. Your mom fights all your battles for you. And you better not run home today and tell her what I just said either."

In the midst of his tirade, Mark yelled, "Shut up."

"Oh," Mr. M. replied, "so now you're threatening me?"

Mark, being emotionally sensitive, felt devastated and betrayed by the teacher in whom he placed so much good faith.

With flowing tears, Mark asserted, "Mr. M., if I hadn't progressed out of severe autism – if I was a quitter, I wouldn't even be here!"

Mark felt that his lifelong significant efforts weren't acknowledged. As school ended for the day, he was bombarded with suicidal thoughts and felt terrified over how his next set of interactions with Mr. M. might transpire. I had held a number of prior conversations with Mr.

M. about my growing list of concerns. Following these conversations, he immediately apologized to Mark, only to resume his abusive behavior soon thereafter. I truly believed that Mr. M. would have retaliated against Mark if Jane Walker were not present when I exposed his flagrantly inappropriate behavior.

My fear surrounding retaliation stemmed in part from a prior circumstance. After reporting a set of transgressions with another teacher, my serious concerns were pushed aside by the administrators, as Mark continued to be bullied by this teacher. I immediately consulted with Jane Walker about this violation by Mr. M. and felt that I had no choice but to schedule an emergency meeting with her and members of the school's administration so that we could address the psychologically harmful climate in the classroom.

I was stunned to learn that the upcoming meeting for Tuesday was permanently tabled. On Monday morning, Mark entered his classroom and was immediately informed by a peer that Mr. M. "was gone and would not be returning." With little time for the administrators to plan, the classroom aide was promoted to the role of teacher. The aide informed the students that Mr. M. would not be coming back to the school but no further explanations were offered. Additionally, there was no time set aside for the students to process their emotional reactions.

The students were expected to carry on as though nothing untoward had happened. Mark, an Indigo truth-teller, was unable or unwilling to participate in a version of *The Emperor's New Clothes*. He refused to comply with even the most basic instructions and began to verbally incite his classmates to go on strike, unless and until the students were given the opportunity to discuss this circumstance further. Mark tore a page from his notebook and wrote a message of dissent, shades of the lead character advocating for factory workers in the film *Norma Rae*. However, underlying his actions were layers of self-blame, shame, and guilt. Because Mr. M.'s disappearance followed the incendiary interaction during which Mark had screamed "shut-up," he felt responsible for his exit.

At the conclusion of the school day, I received a very angry call from the aide, who was infuriated with Mark's behavior and informed me of a number of punitive consequences aimed at curbing it. I, on the other hand, was angry that the administrators had not bothered to call me during the weekend to inform me of Mr. M.'s dismissal, and concerned that this aide was now in charge of the classroom for the remainder of the year – despite a state law that required a certified teacher to assume that role.

I eventually learned from school administrators that on the preceding Friday, Mr. M. had been let go for physically striking one of his students. This fact did not assuage Mark's guilt and shame. There was an additional reason that Mark felt responsible for Mr. M.'s dismissal. During the fall of tenth grade, Mark had begun to experience ongoing conflicts with Wendi, his assigned home-based support worker. As was often the case, things seemed to run smoothly during the first year. However, as Wendi approached the second year with Mark, she seemed to lose patience with Mark's strong-willed behaviors and his resistance to change.

Mark found it challenging to adapt when the overseeing agency changed direction midstream, tightening up the required expectations for scheduled visits. He did not like working on non-preferred structured tasks, and he wanted to access his preferred community locales, rather than working toward the attainment of life skills. Additionally, the mental health center decided to enroll Mark in a private cooking class. I spent a number of hours communicating face-to-face, by phone and via email with the cooking instructor to ensure that the groundwork was laid for Mark's safety.

Mark strongly disliked his forced cooking lessons and came home on two occasions in a panic, stating that he felt coerced into eating foods that were not on his safe list. While these dynamics were in play, I was in the midst of working with a newly assigned case manager.

Alison and I had formed a magnificent working relationship; however, Kristen, who came across as cold, efficient and militaristic, eventually replaced her. Kristen had been on a leave from the office when Mark's relationship with Wendi deteriorated.

This crumbling relationship with Wendi was now a central focus during psychotherapy sessions. Jane Walker decided to apprise Anna, the stand-in caseworker, of the impact of this strained relationship for Mark. Anna seemed very amenable to hearing Jane's concerns. At that time, I felt a growing sense of optimism that Mark's relationship with Wendi could be salvaged and that the cooking classes could safely be resumed. Once again, however, my optimism would soon be shattered.

During one exceedingly stressful weekend, I ruminated and shed tears over the strain of affording Mark's treatment for chronic Bartonella. My ego temporarily held me in the grip of fear and disempowerment. When Wendi appeared for her shift on Monday, the timing couldn't have been worse. I did not optimally ground my energy prior to my conversation with her, and my Ego lurched forward with my advocacy agenda. In advance of Monday's class, Mark insisted that he was going to be coerced into eating raw sushi, a food group that was *definitely* not part of his food plan. Almost immediately, Wendi reacted with anger and defiance over my need to explore this circumstance. She saw no reason to discuss the matter and things quickly escalated from there, with her raising her voice and me reacting in kind.

"You weren't there," I said, "when I had to race at full speed out of the water park with Mark while his face was swelling and his lips and eyelids were turning blue. Are you willing to assume full and complete responsibility for Mark in the case of an anaphylactic reaction? I don't think you want to agree to those terms."

At that point, Wendi bolted past me into the kitchen and proceeded to shout at Mark. "Mark, you little liar! Why are you telling your Mom these fabrications about the cooking class? I won't tolerate this behavior."

At that point, I asked Mark to go upstairs and I made an additional unsuccessful attempt to de-escalate the interaction and reiterate my concerns. On the surface, calm appeared to be restored. Wendi accompanied Mark to the cooking class. Irrespective of Wendi's comments to the contrary, Mark returned home and confirmed that sushi had been the food of choice on the menu. However, because I had spent much of the week preparing Mark for his class, he wisely and flatly refused to ingest the meal.

When Wendi returned for her next shift, she rushed past me at the front door and refused to make eye contact or return any form of greeting. She repeated *this performance* on the next shift. At that point, I made a phone call to the mental health center to explain that there was an untenable circumstance for Mark, as the key adults were clearly at odds with one another. Rather than hearing my concerns, the table was immediately turned and *I was promptly informed that Wendi had filed a written complaint against me, alleging that I had physically threatened her.*

The following week, an administrator held a phone meeting with Wendi and myself. Because I had not formed a consistent meditation practice, nor had I learned to ground my energy prior to entering into these potentially adversarial circumstances, combined with my physical and emotional depletion, circumstances quickly deteriorated. Entering into this meeting without my own witness/advocate was a significant error on my part! Due to my unconscious influences and my level of exhaustion, I had recreated another experience where people in authority retaliated against me.

The administrator repeatedly bulldozed over my positions and instead outright endorsed Wendi's assertion that I was a threat to her safety. If I truly was a threat, why did the agency continue to send her to my home? I knew that I could not have a worker assigned to Mark who flatly refused to present a united front with me. After Jane Walker learned of these dynamics, she made another urgent call to Anna complaining about the matter. I now see that when energy is moving in a specific direction, it potentially climaxes before being transmuted into something better.

During the following week, Wendi appeared for her shift, brushed past me without speaking and then accompanied Mark to her car. Before I could even relax, both parties were back inside my front door speaking over one another. After piecing the information together, I discovered that Anna called Wendi's cell phone, informing her that her relationship with our family was terminated. Wendi was ordered to leave our premises immediately!

Although I agreed that Wendi needed to exit Mark's life, I felt stunned that this was the way the agency decided to handle this matter. Wendi was observably upset and she wanted nothing more than to quickly depart my home.

She halfheartedly intoned, "I'll see you again, Mark."

I immediately intervened and said, "You know very well, Wendi, that you will not see Mark again. I would appreciate it if you would tell him the truth."

Wendi mumbled some half-baked statements and fled through my door. Mark stood inside the doorway shocked, confused, overwhelmed, and distraught.

He sobbed uncontrollably and immediately felt responsible for Wendi's abrupt exit. Wendi wasn't the only significant person leaving Mark's life. Mark's girlfriend Jennifer, soon to be a high school graduate, abruptly decided to "move on" and broke things off. Mark insisted that he would exhaust all options to win her back, and he would cling to this notion for years, even in the face of a reality that couldn't be clearer: Jennifer was gone for good.

All of these cumulative losses impacted Mark. It would take months of therapy to process the circumstances surrounding the loss of Mr. M. The teacher's comment, *"You are the most difficult student I have ever encountered during my entire teaching career,"* in tandem with Jennifer and Wendi's exits, sent him down a spiral of depression, self-recrimination, and toxic guilt. Mark wasn't the only one regretting his choices. I too wished I had handled my recent encounters with Mr. M., Wendi, and the mental health center quite differently.

Although I was more conscious of the energy I carried into my daily life, I had once again allowed recent circumstances to wear me down and reignite the thought that *I alone shouldered my burdens*. I had not yet released the belief that it was necessary for me to soldier on singlehandedly. I fell back into battle mode and when you show up in your life as a soldier, the Universe will offer up more battlegrounds. When would my ego ever learn to stand down?

The Universe and I were in the midst of co-creating one whopper of a future lesson. My lack of personal balance was ripe to create a heightened version of adversarial circumstances. Tenacity and devotion are virtues. The correct exercise of leadership and authority are virtues. Falling prey to stubborn mulishness, inflexibility and obstinacy is utter foolishness. Before I knew what had hit me, I was back to wearing the fool's hat again and unfortunately it was always Mark who paid a price for my capriciousness.

Mark and I continued to cope with a host of physical challenges. A long list of physicians continued to supervise our care. By February, Wendi had exited Mark's home-based program and the mental health center had slashed Mark's weekly support hours from eighteen hours to five. On the upside, Mark was no longer forced to study under the local "Julia Child" – and Rosemary was still in the game!

By early May, Mark had become so immobilized, depressed and self-denigrating that he was seeing Jane Walker twice weekly for therapy sessions. Unfortunately, all of Jane's valiant efforts to keep Mark afloat were somewhat in vain. During May, Mark underwent a suicide watch that required my full-time supervision. After a meeting with the aide at Mark's school failed to improve the classroom climate, it was decided that Mark would be placed on homebound supervision beginning on May 15.

After weeks of soul searching prompted by Jane Walker, I *very reluctantly* made the heart-wrenching decision to transfer Mark to a new educational setting for the upcoming schoolyear. Although the current expressive arts school had offered Mark a number of advantages, the emotional abuse by Mr. M. undermined my confidence in the assigned officials to manage Mark's needs appropriately.

Fortuitously, the current staff allowed Mark to visit for a half-day in order to say goodbye to key personnel. They also permitted Mark to participate in the end-of-the-year school play and ceremony where he received numerous awards of recognition. Acting with his cast members in the school play drained Mark of his remaining emotional reserves. If only Mark had been able to internalize the recognition that the school offered, he might have been able to realize that he was far from a "worst student" and his depression might have incrementally lifted.

Screening potential therapeutic day schools for the coming year turned into an urgent priority. Simultaneous to that circumstance, there was another iron in the fire. Mark's permanent case manager returned from her leave of absence. Kristen made it exceedingly clear that she did not concur with Mark's homebound plan and twice-weekly outpatient therapy sessions. Although she had never once spoken to Mark or to Dr. Walker directly, she insisted that such a plan was inadequate to address Mark's psychiatric needs. Dr. Walker had evaluated Mark in her office on May 17th and believed that Mark was safe to return to my home.

Nevertheless, during a phone contact on May 18th, Kristen demanded that I immediately take Mark to the local psychiatric hospital for an emergency assessment. Although Mark had been experiencing ongoing suicidal thoughts, he had not verbalized any concrete plans to harm himself. Additionally, he was scheduled to see Dr. Walker during the upcoming evening for a reevaluation of his mental health status. Because I planned on keeping an upcoming physician appointment of my own that had been in the offing for a month, I informed Kristen that I intended to keep my specialist appointment on the 18th and that Mark would be assessed the following evening by Dr. Walker.

I also told her that I would be willing to take Mark for the recommended assessment at the hospital on May 19th. Kristen was made aware that Mark would accompany me to my doctor's appointment, as he was under my supervision at all times.

Kristen asserted, "If you go ahead with your doctor appointment instead of taking Mark to XX hospital for an emergency evaluation, I will make a phone call to State Protective Services on a charge of medical neglect related to Mark's psychiatric needs."

I was infuriated over what I perceived as unreasonable coercion and gamesmanship on her part, not to mention all the years of repeatedly sacrificing my own needs in service to Mark's needs.

However, this was clearly *not* the time to prove that point. Foolishly, I went ahead and consulted with my doctor. I also took Mark to the inpatient unit for the assessment on May 19th. After spending hours and hours there, the evaluating team concluded that Mark was not at imminent risk of self-harm. They also stated that the intensive outpatient day program was not appropriate for his needs.

The social worker asserted, "The day hospital would be too overwhelming for him, given our high census and the streetwise clientele enrolled in our program."

Additionally, Dr. F. evaluated Mark on May 21st, and summarized the visit in writing on his prescription pad: "Mark is safe to currently live at home. He is not at acute risk of harm and does not need inpatient treatment. He should receive homebound tutoring and not return to his current school."

It was quite fortuitous that I had Dr. F's prescription in hand. On May 22nd, a child protective worker appeared unannounced at my front door. This same worker made a return visit on May 29th. Mark believed that he was at risk of being removed from his home against his will. Before the state eventually "unfounded" this medical neglect charge, Mark's entire case file would be lost and two additional workers would reinstate the investigation by re-interviewing both Mark and myself on July 10th and August 4th, causing Mark added anguish.

My ego had not modulated my emotional responses with Wendi; had sent me into an ambush with the local mental health center; and had now handed Kristen all the ammunition she needed to further retaliate against me for the drama that she had not been able to control while she was out of the office. Back in 1994, I couldn't comprehend why the middle-aged women in the autism support group had developed such tunnel vision that they were unable to make simple environmental interventions and yet I had fallen into a very deep hole with the same deleterious patterns of compromised thinking.

I too was at the mercy of my default settings; doing things that were comfortable for me even though they were clearly counterproductive. With the gift of hindsight, I now choose to shower myself with self-compassion and self-forgiveness because I now appreciate the long-term heavy toll on mind, body, and spirit, as well as the *cumulative secondary traumas* associated with caregiving. These costs are often substantial and worst of all, totally invisible to the parties who experience their impact. It was time for me to reflect back on the parable of the frog as my own pot of water was reaching a boil.

At least Mark had temporarily dodged some of the potential fallout – removal from his home and placement in a psychiatric hospital. However, it was only a matter of time until Mark was forced to come face-to-face with one of those contingencies. On June 8th, Mark verbalized a specific plan to end his life and was admitted to the local psychiatric hospital. He spent the next four days there. The hospital medical director was also exceedingly concerned about Mark's safety for an unrelated reason. He decided that the hospital food posed a life-threatening risk to Mark.

Thus, the medical director ordered that *all* of Mark's foods be brought to the hospital. I was exhausted driving back and forth for meal delivery; holding lengthy phone calls with hospital personnel that went on up until midnight, as well as making my own trips to the urgent care center to address a raging bladder infection. Yes, I was pissed off and it showed up in physical form too!

At the conclusion of Mark's hospital stay, he shuffled through the front doors, looking weak and pasty white, with a demeanor that reminded me of a pod person from *Invasion of the Body Snatchers*. Mark had barely slept throughout his hospital stay and was asked to attend a myriad of daily group therapy sessions.

"Mom," he said, "I barely understood a word of what was going on. The patients were talking so quickly and on top of each other. I didn't understand some of the vocabulary and I couldn't follow the conversations. I felt so exhausted and overwhelmed that I was bored out of my mind and I just zoned out. I have never been so bored in all of my life! The hospital is the most boring place ever!"

There had been attempts to adjust Mark's psychotropic medication prior to his hospitalization, during his stay, and afterward; all of which proved unsuccessful. He eventually resumed his original medication regime. Thankfully, Mark was still on the planet. And because of that fact, the tide was about to turn for the better. Within days of Mark's discharge, he walked through his new academy's door to begin his summer session at his eighth school! As a high school junior, he was enrolled in two electives, theater and acting classes!

Mark visited the school prior to enrollment and immediately felt at home there. Mark formed an immediate bond with the principal, Mrs. Fouks, a woman in her senior years who had been at the helm of the school for decades. The school served students with learning disabilities, emotional disorders and very occasionally, children on the spectrum. The school also served a great number of at-risk, streetwise students from Chicago. Although I had some concerns about Mark's assigned peer group, the academy became Mark's preferred school during the next four and a half years. After a very long circuitous route, Mark finally landed in the ideal place!

WHAT I KNOW NOW THAT I DIDN'T KNOW THEN: WITHOUT EXCEPTION, OUR RELATIONSHIPS ARE ALWAYS MIRRORING BACK TO US HOW WE ARE SHOWING UP IN THE WORLD. IT IS THROUGH

THE PROCESS OF FACING WITH COMPASSION ALL ASPECTS OF OURSELVES THAT WE REMEMBER OUR TRUE AUTHENTICITY AND WHOLENESS. We are in spiritual partnership with our children, whether we consciously acknowledge it or not. In *Self-Mastery: A Journey Home To Your ... Inner Self,* Master Hu Dalconzo reminds us that, "A spiritual relationship is formed when two (or more) people come together, *as equals,* for the purpose of spiritual growth."[75] I add to this: *As we heal, we create the climate for our children to maximize their potential healing powers.* Avoiding our own healing is a surefire formula for unwittingly transferring our karmic challenges to our children. It is imperative that we explore the relationship between our unexamined core beliefs and our parenting choices.

> Relationships are assignments. They are part of a vast plan for our enlightenment, the Holy Spirit's blueprint by which each individual soul is led to greater awareness and expanded love. Relationships are the Holy Spirit's laboratories in which He brings together people who have the maximal opportunity for mutual growth. He appraises who can learn from whom at any given time, and then assigns them to each other. ~ Marianne Williamson

We will exponentially accelerate our spiritual growth, *gain perspective about our magnificence,* and understand our wounding by noticing what our children reflect back to us. They mirror core psychological aspects reverberating within – both our healthy, fully realized parts and the shadow or hidden parts of ourselves that urgently need to be seen, healed, and integrated into the whole. In other words, our children are here to teach us every bit if not more than we are here to teach them! Moreover, they want us to experience the greatest version of ourselves joyfully.

As we escort our children through physical life and assist them in having a fully realized life, they are simultaneously escorting us back to the truth of our Divine natures! Our hearts are invariably working in tandem to create a Divine synergistic impact that elevates both parties, and by extension the world. Shakti Gawain taught that mirroring is predicated on the following principles; everything that manifests in our lives is a co-creation and nothing happens by accident! Everything that shows up in our outer reality is one hundred percent related to us. Everything we say, do and feel directly impacts the quality of our lives.[76]

Given all this, we need to honor ourselves by basking in the mirror and appreciating the parts that are the foundation for creativity, empowerment, and thriving. Of course, there will be times when the mirror's glare will reflect harshly, especially when it highlights the shadow parts of ourselves that we would rather discount and deny because our egos have attached shame and condemnation to our less-than-perfect actions. It's important to relax into the mirroring process, knowing that we are safe to trust our children to guide us to exactly where our "hidden treasure is buried." Anita Moorjani asks us to remember; "Everything that seemingly happens externally is occurring in order to trigger something within us, to expand us and take us back to who we truly are."

Consequently, when an experience with our children [or anyone else for that matter] triggers us emotionally, it behooves us to ask the following questions: firstly, what hidden aspect of myself do I share with this individual and, secondly, what shared characteristic, trait, belief system or suppressed pain is my ego driving me to avoid full responsibility for? It's vital that we participate in the mirroring process because at the most inopportune moments our repressed, shadow parts are sitting in wait; ready to mount a *sneak attack*. These hidden personas will either set into motion a reaction characterized by *maladaptive behaviors, a needy attachment driven by yearning,* or they will ensnare us in a *life of quiet desperation*. When these dynamics are in play, we will be unable to fulfill the grandest expression of ourselves and therefore our children will be left without the capacity to envision their own grandest expression.

Thus, triggering events offer us an opportunity for celebration, rather than avoidance or opposition to the healing process. Neale Donald

Walsch admonishes us to "bless your [experience] and be grateful for it. Thank you, God, for this opportunity to announce and declare, to express and fulfill, to become and to demonstrate who *I REALLY AM*."

Debbie Ford, in her classic book *The Dark Side of the Light Chasers: Reclaiming Your Power, Creativity, Brilliance and Dreams*,[77] offers us a brilliant metaphor for understanding mirroring. Imagine that your body contains a hundred different electrical outlets attached to your skin. Each outlet represents a different psychological aspect that you carry. The safe outlets are fully integrated and grounded by an electrical current. On the other hand, the outlets that you have rejected carry a live electrical charge. When something provokes a reaction within, this circumstance ensues because you share the same conditioning, trauma or pain with someone else and therefore you plug right into that person's ungrounded electrical charge or energy field. Here's a helpful prompt to remember: "If I spot it, I got it."[78]

For example, if you tend toward indecisiveness and you are faced with an indecisive child, you share that plug. If you tend toward stubbornness and you are parenting a child that displays chronic stubbornness, you share that plug. If you create unnecessary conflict in your parent/child relationship, you might ask the following question to dissolve that plug: Where am I at war within myself? Additionally, if you have children that see themselves as invisible and you have deep pain anchored to invisibility, that electrical current is active between you. Over the course of my parenting odyssey, the mirror continually offered examples of authority figures retaliating against me. A helpful question would have been the following: How do I betray and retaliate against myself? A further inquiry could have related to my blocked throat chakra: When have I not listened to myself and spoken via my authentic voice?

That said, implementing the practice of mirroring is not as simple as it might seem at face value. Let's assume that some of your children have directed behaviors toward you that fall into the category of intimidation or bullying. What might be at stake is your unconscious programming around tolerating and/or enabling behaviors that diminish you. In this instance, the mirror is asking you to set boundaries so that you can declare your worth and preciousness. Let's consider that some children display a pattern of timidity and you feel irritation and frustration in the face of this pattern. Alternately, you have developed a lifelong pattern of overcompensating for your own timidity by entering situations with boldness and brashness. This circumstance will trigger you if you have not fully embraced your shadow side, the side that wants to hang back and wade into life with caution.

If your children exhibit explosiveness and you have learned to place a straightjacket on your anger, you are potentially being asked to face your anger. In fact, you are carrying an old belief that tells you that it's unacceptable to feel angry and/or you may believe that it isn't ladylike to express it. In this instance, your children are acting out some of your suppressed anger, as they gift you the opportunity to connect with feelings that you have buried alive. If your child's incessant crying *hooks* you, it's worthwhile asking yourself the following: What part of me is longing to cry, to express sorrow, to let loose, and why is my ego stopping me from doing so? In many instances, your children are energy sponges who are attuned to your energy fields and know the truth of your emotional undercurrents long before you do.

How do you know what the mirror is showing you? It is only through a connection with your intuitive Self that you will know, sense or feel, the truth of the mirror's glare. When you quiet your mind and ground your body, you discern the mirror's message. When you slow down enough to ask your higher Self what mirrored projections need to be seen, felt, released and healed, you gift yourself the opportunity to transcend the trans-generational cycles that drain your life-force energy.

Through mirroring, you free yourself from replicating old unconscious programming. Through mirroring, you access your shortcut to healing. For every orphaned personality aspect that you graciously adopt, you move that much closer to *unconditionally* loving and accepting yourself, as you simultaneously support your children toward more fully and unreservedly loving and accepting themselves.

GRACE, PASSION AND ENTHUSIASM

"Sometimes it takes losing everything you thought you
needed to gain everything you ever wanted."

~Mandy Hale

At the academy, Mark not only formed a connection with the principal but with his acting teacher, Eric. During Mark's junior and senior year of high school, Eric served as an exemplary male role model who supported Mark's strengths and, in his unique way, appealed to Mark's higher intentions. Eric was in no way a pushover and he also possessed a remarkable capacity to connect with Mark's sensitive and artistic nature. He encouraged Mark's potential for accelerated learning. Mark felt seen and understood by an important male in his life.

Eric also volunteered to mentor Mark after school and spent his personal time teaching him the basics of film editing, a subject that Mark passionately wanted to pursue. Mark quickly grasped film-editing techniques, thus mastering another outlet for his creative talents, and immediately began creating short film reviews for his YouTube channel. A loving intelligence had arranged new and bountiful blessings on Mark's behalf and I was finally receptive to taking note of the beneficence before us.

Mark also contributed his writing submissions for an adapted screenplay and was cast in a film that was written and spearheaded by Eric's students. Mark loved transitioning to various classes at the academy and finally felt at peace during school. Although he experienced instances of bullying, the school administrators seemed to be invested in promptly addressing the problem behaviors.

Mark also attended his Saturday performing arts classes. Additionally, he auditioned for his first typical dance company and was offered a small part in the Nutcracker Suite. Participating in the Nutcracker was a stretch, but he not only coped with the stress of being thrust into a setting where he did not know a single cast member or adult teacher, he did so without any accommodations for his autism. This burgeoning stress led to some meltdowns on the home front but didn't prevent Mark from expanding his horizons.

During this same time period, Mark was welcomed into the fold at Haley's Playground, a local recreation center for special needs students and, along with Forrest, attended their biweekly teen group. While at Haley's Playground, Mark volunteered to mentor younger children who were more severely impacted by their autism. He possessed a very creative flare and intuitive way of conceptualizing the needs of these children and was often able to find solutions when staff members were stymied by a child's behaviors. Haley's Playground left Mark feeling more confident and lighthearted. In addition, he formed a relationship with his new home-based mentor, Michelle. Although Michelle didn't stay beyond one year, she bolstered Mark's self-belief and exposed him to a number of new experiences.

During Mark's time fulfilling high school requirements, I kept busy spinning a myriad of plates on his behalf. Our state rules did not permit "double dipping," as funding for disabled individuals either funneled through the division for mental illness *or* the division for developmental disabilities. As Mark's time in the state program for mentally ill children approached the ten-year mark, the state threatened to terminate his mental health services. Fortuitously, after waiting ten years hoping to someday qualify for autism-related services on the separate list, Mark's name was pulled in the state lottery system just in the nick of time. Miraculously, the Universe had once again arranged the infinite correlation of details so that Mark could receive key supports. It was a momentous occurrence, and a safety net that would not have been in place without Jane Walker's written advocacy efforts. Since Mark's profile did not fit children served in the developmental division, once again the majority of *local* social service agencies refused to accept him as a client. State funding would be meaningless unless a local agency agreed to step forward.

After contact with every known social service agency provider, I felt immensely blessed to have one agency come to the fore. The board-certified behavioral analyst impressed me from the get-go and the case manager was willing to go the extra mile to keep Mark under the auspices of their system. However, there was an insurmountable roadblock standing in the way – one that prevented Mark from accessing his Medicaid funding source, which was the scaffolding for future services. Mark's ample child support amount was in excess of the sum allowed by Medicaid guidelines.

Prior to the termination of Mark's child support at age nineteen, it was essential that I apply for a monthly medical spend-down dispensation that would reduce his countable child support. I submitted detailed documentation demonstrating that our family's medical expenses were in fact quite exorbitant. The threat of an imminent deadline required me to submit every single medical receipt for the prior six months! I spent the next two days working up to twenty hours a day to complete this mandated project. Once the multiple bins of paperwork were collated, I drove to a Saturday conference lobby where I rendezvoused with Mark's caseworker. Then and there, a handoff took place. Other than the two hours of assistance that had been provided by Forrest's mother, I had single-handedly pulled off an arduous amount of painstaking and detailed work.

As a result, Mark was still in the running to receive state services and could qualify for adult services upon his high school graduation. My efforts would have been in vain without the expertise and advocacy of a wonderful case manager and a creative and committed woman working behind the scenes in the state Medicaid office. Although this local case manager did not remain with our family long-term, she was the exact right person at the exact right moment! Even more astounding, the Medicaid employee's concerted efforts occurred before her scheduled retirement. She went above and beyond to pave the way for our family and, without her tireless efforts, Mark could have been discarded by the state before he even had the chance to get started.

During Mark's junior year in high school, I was also faced with another monumental choice point. Once Mark turned eighteen in February, he would step into the adult role of independently managing his educational, medical and financial affairs! Unless I initiated a legal guardianship over Mark's personhood and estate, he would also be granted his full legal rights, along with the attendant risks of adulthood. In Illinois, guardianship cases are filed in the disabled adult's county of residence. In the United States, guardianship regulations and the terms of restriction vary from state to state. In our case, plenary guardianship would deem Mark unable to adequately manage personal, medical and financial affairs. The court required an extensive physician report documenting Mark's limitations and the rationale for guardianship.

Taking away an individual's rights and freedoms and placing them under a full guardianship is *not* a step to be taken lightly. Once granted, that individual has lost the adult autonomy for decision-making and certain privileges that most of us take for granted. On the other hand, assuming full responsibility for Mark's medical, educational and financial affairs would save him from being forced to do so prematurely.

Many cases of guardianship are very clear-cut and the facts supporting the guardianship are indisputable. Mark's case was a borderline call.

I wrestled with this decision for a considerable period of time, knowing that if I sought guardianship Mark would experience a massive blow to his self-esteem and confidence; it might also rupture the trust he had placed in me. Once I did decide to move forward, a local psychiatrist evaluated Mark and concurred with my decision, preparing a detailed report for review by the judge.

During Mark's time at the academy, I finessed my way through the Medicaid jungle; was granted sole guardianship over him and fulfilled the stringent two-year's worth of requirements to earn my life coaching certification. My deep-dive healing journey, in combination with my intensive training and practicum as a spiritual life coach, had in large measure changed the entire map of my life. Adapting, flowing with the energy at hand, and reclaiming a resilient mindset were going to put me in good stead for upcoming trials. All of those blessings were advantageous as I met the next bend in the road.

Spring arrived, and with it came another terrifying manic episode that disrupted Mark's period of relative stability. This, despite being on a new antidepressant, prescribed by Dr. F. and slowly and incrementally titrated, after the previous one had lost its effectiveness. In the midst of the hurricane, it finally dawned on me that the new medication might have been responsible for escalating Mark's mood. Antidepressants carry the potential to flip the switch, sending a patient reeling through the disordered thoughts of mania.

This particular episode was the worst one that Mark had endured since entering adolescence. I vividly recall the panic that coursed through my body when he threatened to leave our home in the middle of the night. He intended to travel alone to an unsafe neighborhood in Chicago in order to pursue a very irrational agenda. By the grace of God, we navigated our way through another crisis, but we still had to immediately begin scaling down his dose so he could avoid the roller-coaster of side effects.

During this period, it seemed that every known antidepressant posed a risk to Mark's wellbeing. Therefore, Kaaren and I concurred that the properties of a new antidepressant would be delivered to Mark energetically, and only energetically. With Kaaren's methods, Mark's mood eventually stabilized and he was able to successfully navigate through his senior year.

Mark made one new friend at the academy, Sri, who fortuitously lived only three miles from our home. Mark and Sri socialized together outside of school; enjoyed the prom festivities hosted by the school; and, the following year, walked in the graduation processional together. Out of approximately twelve graduating seniors, Mark was the only student who dissolved into tears during the commencement walk. Partings had never been easy for him, and the fact that he planned to return to the transition program[79] during the upcoming schoolyear did little to mitigate his feelings of loss, or prepare him for other changes that were afoot.

Mark's high school graduation day was also marred by a shocking and traumatic event. During the last week of school, Eric unexpectedly informed me of his resignation from the academy and his plan to relocate to Boston. I impressed upon Eric the importance of disclosing the truth to Mark, and followed up with daily emails saying the same, yet Eric remained silent, and I had to watch Mark return from school each afternoon with no idea that his fragile sense of trust and security would soon implode.

At the conclusion of the graduation ceremony, Diane – one of Mark's teachers – and I "cornered" Eric and confronted him about his negligence in this matter. Clearly, he was hoping to make an exit without having to witness Mark's emotional eruption. After our conversation, Eric, Mark, and I walked to a private area in the nature center behind the school. Mark sat upon a sideways log as Eric disclosed his upcoming plans. Mark, as expected, did not take the news well, but burst into uncontrollable sobs and made several anguished statements indicating that he believed that his life was no longer worth living.

Eric encouraged Mark to continue, and suggested that his future purpose might include "paying it forward." He asked Mark to find his own student that he could enlighten with the same life lessons that Eric had previously imparted. It was inspiring advice, but in the moment Mark was too devastated to consider it. Eric also tried to shore Mark up by making what I considered to be an empty promise.

"When the time comes, we will see each other again."

Mark replied, "When will that be?"

"When the time is right."

I immediately felt a pit in my stomach, as I believed that Eric's statements were made to assuage *his* discomfort, rather than to help Mark confront the magnitude of his loss.

"I look up to you," Mark said to him with heartbreaking sincerity, "I hang on your every word and I follow in your every footstep."

Eric responded, "Sometimes, in life, the student needs to lead and the teacher needs to follow."

Mark faced countless other changes as he entered adulthood, some precipitated by his own choices. He was furious over his subservience to a plenary guardianship; he abruptly discontinued contact with both Dr. Jane Walker for psychotherapy and Kaaren for healing sessions. As his guardian, I could have forced Mark's hand but I believed that such a course of action would have been counterproductive. His predisposition had always been to attempt to wield some measure of control, and all too often he had been stripped of all semblance of it. I allowed Mark to assert control in these areas, knowing that Kaaren could continue to work with him remotely. As it was, he was now at the mercy of a merry-go-round of Medicaid physicians and, as a result, also lost his long-term endocrinologist.

After exhaustive efforts on my part, I failed to enlist a new Medicaid psychiatrist, as no one was willing to accept Mark as a patient. Dr. F. generously agreed to halve his fee so that Mark could continue to have continuity of care; however, Medicaid refused to cover the cost of Mark's antianxiety medication that had been of benefit since his days at the RTC. Of even greater concern was the threat that Mark's growth hormone injections would be discontinued, but thankfully he was referred to a specialized Medicaid case manager who helped ensure that this didn't happen for the foreseeable future.

Along with this advantage came a switch to a different manufacturer and ongoing and time-consuming snafus with the new specialty pharmacy. Even against the backdrop of these frustrations, I felt unbridled gratitude knowing that Mark's overall health and wellness had not been imperiled by the hasty and premature discontinuation of this critical medication.

When parenting a special needs child, advocacy efforts will forever run parallel to caregiving efforts! As mothers, we need to realistically accept that new barriers will invariably block our path, requiring us to find a way over, around, or above them. Successfully traversing those barriers is a prerequisite for supporting a child's full potential. Creating experiences that offer joy, relaxation and a respite from the grind is of paramount importance. One such oasis for me was watching Mark branch out into membership with a local community theater group.

After completing his high school credits, Mark auditioned and was accepted as a bit player for one of the summer productions. Little did I know that this springboard would propel Mark to hone his passion for musical theater and build his confidence as a worthwhile, contributing member of our local community.

WHAT I KNOW NOW THAT I DIDN'T KNOW THEN: VIA FORGIVENESS, WE STEP INTO GRACE AND ENTHUSIASM BY FULLY RELEASING OURSELVES FROM THE TOXIC BURDENS OF OUR PAST TRAUMAS. THE PRACTICE OF FORGIVENESS IS A KEY MECHANISM FOR ALIGNING WITH HIGHER CONSCIOUSNESS. Through forgiveness, we unlock the door to our own prison cell and step into the light of freedom. When someone has violated our boundaries via the misuse or abuse of their powers, we place ourselves at risk by energetically carrying their toxicity. By staying stuck in the lower energy of the past, we condemn ourselves to a never-ending feedback loop of shame, blame, toxic guilt and victimhood. By repeatedly rehashing our traumatic experiences, we further entangle our energy with our so-called violator's negative patterns, reinforcing our respective roles as perpetrator and victim. Spiritual teacher Catherine Ponder asserts that remaining in a state of unforgiveness forms an emotional link with our so-called violators that is stronger than steel.[80] Marianne Williamson follows suit: "You can have a grievance or a miracle. You cannot have both." [81]

When we forgive, we choose to *unconditionally accept all aspects of our experiences,* even when we are unable to view those events from a higher perspective. As humans, we may never fully comprehend the reason why certain experiences unfolded as they did. We aren't necessarily designed to understand them. However, we can choose to trust that in a *perfectly evolving universe*, whatever happened was *flawlessly created* for the evolution of our immortal souls, even when we do not possess the foresight or the insight to understand the reasons behind those experiences.

What we "think" about our experiences is merely an opinion formed by our ego-minds; it is those very same opinions that glue us to our painful storylines and our attendant lower vibrations. It is not our job to allow our ego-minds to mete out *Divine justice* to those we believe wronged us. Thus, it was not my job to judge the souls of Wendi, Mr. M., former school officials, my ex-husband, Kristen, other social service professionals, or *even myself*.

Divine justice is assuredly delivered via the *Law of Cause and Effect.* Divine justice operates on the principle that everyone receives in kind the energy that they emit into the world, even when those effects are not apparent to us in this lifetime. From a multidimensional perspective, because everything is potentially happening simultaneously in our multifaceted parallel lives, our tiny little thinking minds cannot begin to comprehend the nature of reality. By hanging onto bitterness, regret, and righteous indignation surrounding the past actions of others or **ourselves**, we greatly inhibit our life force-energy. Unless we learn to forgive *without conditions*, we will carry the burden of repressed, frozen feelings, short-circuit our flow of Divinity, and inhibit our full creative powers.

As Marianne Williamson asserts, "The way of the miracle worker is to see all human behavior as one of two things: either love or a call for love." But how do we *choose* the path of unconditional forgiveness? In point of fact, it is often easier to choose to forgive our so-called betrayers than it is to forgive ourselves. Guilt implies that after reviewing our prior actions, we have decided to judge ourselves harshly for committing those acts and have second-guessed our choices. According to Master Hu Dalconzo:

> Know that at the moment of happening, it was all-appropriate. *If you have learned since then that the act was not what you would choose now* and you feel guilty, know that the act itself has brought you to this understanding. That was all it was meant to do, so it is *cause for joy, not remorse!* [82]

It's vital to shower us with kindness, gentleness and self-compassion, as we embody our earned wisdom and allow the uncomfortable energies to pass through our bodies. We can then tackle life with peace, gratitude, and self-love in our hearts. The body/mind/spirit doesn't know the difference between a movie in our minds and our physical reality. Thus, we hold the power to change any negative energetic signature playing in our quantum field.

Carrying the weight of our past *mistakes* is comparable to dragging a twenty-pound bag of manure around on a full-time basis. Those added pounds stifle our potential and exhaust and harm our bodies. Plus, the stench follows us everywhere! Even when we become impervious to the stench, the stench is still there contaminating everything and everyone in our circle.

Forgiveness does not imply that we are in any way condoning our own or anyone else's prior actions. "Forgiveness is not some sentimental or superficial process! If real harm was done to you, it needs to be legitimized and validated before you will be able to let it go." [83] If someone or a system caused true harm to our children, I am not signaling that acts of harm are acceptable. On a human level, we should not turn a blind eye to the suffering of our children and if we are guided by Spirit to act, we should redress any harm that was committed via appropriate societal channels.

If we felt betrayed by the healthcare system, the educational system, the legal system, the social service agencies, our spouses, family members, our church, our friends, the public at large, God, or even our own children, that is a response that requires validation, so that it can be carefully processed and released. Without a healing process, we consign ourselves to relive our unfinished emotional templates over and over again, robbing ourselves of joy, optimism, and light-heartedness and over time, potentially even our health, stamina, and vibrancy. Our children are in the least advantageous position and will invariably pay the highest price for us unnecessarily allowing our power to leak away.

As Marianne Williamson so eloquently taught, remaining in a state of unforgiveness is like drinking a daily shot of poison, while expecting the party who concocted the poison to die. Unfortunately, in this dimension, some of our so-called trespassers will ***never*** see beyond their blind spots and will never take full responsibility for the real harm that was caused. Sometimes, they have seemingly danced right on, never glancing backward. This fact ***should never stand in the way of us moving forward*** to creating an inspired life. Forgiveness is a ***choice*** that is always available, a practice and a state of being. It is a choice that uplifts and benefits us in a myriad of ways and as new circumstances arise, it's one that may need to be reaffirmed again and again.

We hold the power to integrate our lessons, while no longer remaining enmeshed in how those lessons were delivered. As Carolyn Myss wrote, "Grace is a power that comes in and transforms a moment for the better." By embodying forgiveness, we make room for grace to enter into the cracks in our lives and in ourselves, elevating everyone we touch.

The Hawaiian practice of Ho'oponopono invites in forgiveness. Dr. Ihaleakala Hew Len created a modified four-step healing process termed Self I-dentity Through Ho'oponopono.[84] Dr. Hew Len was a retired psychotherapist who practiced at a Hawaiian State Hospital for the *criminally insane*. Without ever meeting face-to-face with any of the patients, he single-handedly transformed an inhumane and deplorable environment into a place of healing and grace. Regular inmate violence, staff apathy, and high levels of staff absence were replaced by the complete eradication of the facility. Most of the patients were fully rehabilitated and integrated back into society.

Dr. Hew Len accomplished this feat by clearing his own unconscious programming; the very same programming that he observed was a match to his patient's baser drives. He recognized that as a physical being, he was a mixture of both light and dark aspects and he believed that it was his personal responsibility to clear the darkness ***within himself***. His four healing steps contained the following repetitive vocalizations: 1. While visualizing the person you wish to forgive or yourself, choose repentance; *Utter, I'm sorry*. 2. Ask for forgiveness; *Utter, Please forgive me*. 3. Express gratitude; *Utter, I thank you* and lastly, move into step, 4. Reconciliation or connection with love; *Utter, I love you*. Dr. Hew Len wholeheartedly believed, that without exception, if someone or some experience enters our lives, it's ***our responsibility*** to change ourselves by transforming our unconscious minds back to a state of neutrality -- a state where purest love invariably exists.

By doing so, those who cross our paths will potentially be transformed. According to Dr. Hew Len, "the only way to hear the Divine and receive inspiration is to clean all memories." Dr. Hew Len fully integrated and embodied the practice of mirroring and dedicated his life to a practice that began and ended with self-clearing. He then offered miraculous transformation to anyone who entered his awareness. If one exquisite man, via the practice of forgiveness, can change hundreds of criminals with mental illness and a system that was ripe for darkness to rein, imagine what can be done on behalf of your children!

RUNG SIXTEEN

GRATITUDE AND POSITIVE EXPECTANCY

"We can complain that rose bushes have thorns, or rejoice
because thorns have roses."

~ Alphonse Karr, A Tour Round My Garden

Mark returned to the academy for the formalized post-high school transition program he would participate in for the next two and a half years. During year one, he continued taking academic and elective subjects as a high school student. He also spent his lunch hour and special event days socializing with his peers. As the school's official videographer, Mark documented the important academy milestones. Mark even created a short documentary that featured core aspects of the transition program that could be used as the school's marketing tool. Mark's documentary on the September 11th terrorist attacks was shown each year on the anniversary of our national tragedy and gained the respect of the student body.

At the conclusion of the maiden showing, as the theme song played from *Titanic*, one of the more emotionless students found himself on the brink of tears. He approached Mark and said, "You almost had me."

Mark was also given the opportunity to serve as president of the Acting Club; however, he ran into group dissension when several students were not fully invested in creating a completed production. While he lacked the advanced leadership skills necessary to successfully take the helm, standing in as president provided him with a heightened learning opportunity to stretch himself further and gain some astute personal insights. After enrollment in eight different schools, I felt immense gratitude because Mark had finally landed in an environment that was an ideal match for his needs.

During the summer after Mark's first year in the transition program, another miraculous meeting occurred. I sauntered down the staircase to the lounge area adjacent to where the special needs acting troupe gathered. I observed the usual group of parents seated together chatting at one of the tables, then noted an unfamiliar woman seated alone at one of the small tables, facing her laptop. In that moment, I felt guided to introduce myself and asked if I could join her there. She readily agreed and revealed that her talented daughter was also enrolled in the summer session. In the midst of our conversation, I discovered that Jennifer was a gifted vocalist in her own right. She was an opera teacher and ran her own private vocal studio.

I leveled with her about Mark's special needs and asked if she would be willing to enroll him in her studio.

Without hesitation, she stated, "I am more than willing to give Mark a chance to have a trial period in my studio. I am happy to see if we can work together successfully."

Through another amazing synchronicity, I was soon to discover that the Universe had aligned us with the perfect voice teacher for Mark. For the next eight years, Jennifer went on to mentor Mark and continues to fulfill a very important role in his life. As it turned out, Jennifer's daughter was only enrolled in the acting troupe for that one summer session so the Universe worked quickly to ensure that she stepped up as one of Mark's biggest supporters. She went on to include Mark in her recital showcases, carefully prepared him for all his auditions, exposed him to an opera production, and even invited him to perform in front of her college classes.

During Mark's second year, the students were relocated to a building apart from the general high school. Mark disliked the overall change in atmosphere. He longed for the socialization that had been built into his high school experience. Additionally, Mark was still in the midst of grieving the loss of Eric. Though Eric was no longer part of the faculty, there were all sorts of daily reminders that heightened Mark's ever-present sorrow.

Mark also felt the sting of loss because the transition program was comprised of a small number of students who came and went throughout the school day. These students were mastering essential job skills at a number of varied sites. During high school, Mark had detested his vocational assignment – unpacking merchandise and folding shirts at a local warehouse. In light of his apathy about returning to the warehouse, I requested that the academy create a new opportunity for Mark.

I asked that Mark be assigned as an unpaid assistant in one of the elementary classrooms. Fortunately, the principal acceded to my wish and placed Mark in one of the junior high classrooms for one period per day. Mark enjoyed his time there immensely and formed a very close bond with one of the students. He particularly enjoyed assisting with the yearly theatrical productions and filming the academy's yearly talent shows.

During Mark's two-plus years acting as a classroom assistant, he was also assigned to work at a local assisted living center. He was originally assigned to tasks in the dining room but was later moved to clerical tasks and the organization of the storage room. Eventually, he assisted wheelchair-bound seniors by transporting them to various locales within the building. Mark much preferred his time at the assisted living center to his time at the warehouse. However, with his emotional sensitivity, he found it taxing to witness the emotional and physical distress displayed by the residents.

During this same time period, Mark was also adapting to Mrs. E., the teacher who oversaw the transition program. During a prior run-in with Mrs. E., Mark felt that his integrity had been unfairly called into question and therefore his relationship with Mrs. E. did not get off to a winning start. He was trying to establish a fragile sense of trust in her when Janine, a newly assigned home-based personal support worker, came on board.

Janine was a middle-aged woman who seemed more than capable of facilitating Mark's access to community settings. She was also expected to incrementally teach Mark independent living skills. Circumstances looked promising but, as was often the case, within a year her tolerance seemed to be waning, replaced by frustration with her role. In year two, things came to a precipitous head when, without warning, she flew off the handle after I asked her to correct an innocent error on her time sheet. She abruptly grabbed her purse and charged for the front door while I tried to slow her down so that I could discern her future intentions. She insisted that she would resume her assigned work responsibilities, following a two-week personal leave. Naturally, Mark's antenna was already acutely aware that trouble was brewing.

Her promise to return turned out to be an empty one. She not only refused to resume her employment but also flatly balked at holding an exit interview with her employer or an exit phone conversation with Mark so that he could get closure. Once again, he was forced to stand helplessly outside the revolving door as yet another support worker – one of more than seventy over the years – left our home.

In some respects, I wasn't sorry to see Janine go. During the prior year, she had instigated unnecessary drama after misconstruing a communication from Mark. Instead of speaking with me directly and getting clarity about the matter, she reported to the overseeing agency that I was potentially an unfit guardian. Her allegations were an outgrowth of my unanticipated trip to the emergency room to diagnose the unbearable symptoms associated with a kidney stone.

Because this was my first experience with a kidney stone, I could not imagine the source of such unbearable pain, violent sweats, vomiting, and diarrhea. During this crisis, Mark saw "more skin" than I would have preferred, but this was clearly not intentional on my part. I asked Mark for his assistance to call 911. Never could I have imagined the ambush that awaited me at the next scheduled meeting with the professionals. I innocently sat at my dining room table, barely recovered from my ordeal, when the opening shot was fired.

"Mrs. Hasselo, please explain to us why you felt justified walking around naked in front of Mark?"

At that point, I felt completely blindsided; my body reeled with shock and tears stung my eyes as I gripped the sides of my chair, thinking, *What did you just say? What the f#$!?!* It felt like a punch to the gut when staff members from both agencies accused me of displaying grossly inappropriate boundaries and sexual provocativeness toward Mark. Then adrenaline began to surge, changing surprise to anger toward these "professionals" – and Mark, whose careless words and flare for the dramatic had opened me up to this unfair and inaccurate characterization. I was also immediately flooded with fear. Whose words were going to hold the most weight – Mark's, Janine's, or mine?

Although unchecked tears streamed down my face, I mounted the following response, "I feel that this characterization of my conduct is a very low blow, a very low blow, indeed. These accusations are unfair and untrue. I have never 'paraded' around naked in front of my son. I fell ill. I feared for my life. I would not wish this kind of experience on anyone. I know that Mark felt overwhelmed and traumatized, but all of you need to understand that he is not necessarily an accurate reporter of events due to his emotionality and his habit of engaging in cognitive distortions. I hope that you will be willing to reconsider your assessment of the matter and give me the benefit of the doubt."

Once again, the guilt card had been tossed onto the tabletop as they asserted that I had compromised Mark's sense of emotional and physical safety. I was further stunned to learn that in the event of a potential future incapacitation on my part, unless an emergency plan was immediately enacted, I would be viewed as an unfit guardian and they would be forced to take matters into their own hands. They asked for three emergency contacts on the spot, and proof that Mark would receive twenty-four-hour care in the event of an upcoming emergency. I could not provide three emergency contacts in that moment so I told them that I would get back to them on the matter.

I did not in any way object to the idea of an emergency plan being put in place, but I strenuously objected to the tone of the meeting and the insinuation that I had been sexually provocative with my son. Even in the midst of this event, the Universe offered me an immediate emotional tonic. My next-door neighbor agreed to be listed as one of my emergency contacts. Additionally, Dr. F. backed me up, stating that from his vantage point, "Physical illness that is out of one's control is not considered a boundary violation." (Still, I made sure to have a large beach towel handy in my bathroom in the event of any future unanticipated illness!) Thanks to a referral from Jane Walker, I was able to enlist the help of a local private agency that agreed to be on emergency call. Locating an agency with nursing services willing to provide Mark with his nightly growth hormone injection, combined with twenty-four-hour compassionate care, was not an easy or affordable undertaking.

This had not been the first time I had been browbeaten or accused by health care providers and administrators who had the power to impact my circumstances. The difference this time is that I had the tools and the awareness to focus on the silver lining of every cloud, which enabled me to protect my adrenals and bolster my health. The Universe not only nudged me to locate twenty-four-hour emergency care that would put us in good stead for the future, it also delivered to me the apology I felt was long overdue.

Months later, the behaviorist stated, "Mrs. Hasselo, looking back, I see that Janine should have spoken to you directly regarding your health crisis and gathered additional information before reporting distorted allegations to me. I deeply apologize for the way the matter was handled."

This apology placed a salve on my wound and helped me move forward from other instances where I felt the professionals had judged me way too harshly.

Janine was the last home-based worker assigned to Mark – a result of more stringent state training requirements for workers and the inability of the assigned agency to find a replacement for her. This could have been problematic as the provision of services was mandatory in order for Mark's state funding to continue. Fortunately, Mark's other mentor, Rosemary, continued to be an ever-present light. Mark viewed Rosemary as the grandmother he had been denied because his grandparents resided out of state. Rosemary fulfilled eight of the sixteen weekly support hours.

Intermittent kidney stones and other health crises continued to be an ever-present backdrop to my life. However, these crises no longer prevented me from entering a twenty-five-hour-a-week residency program under the auspices of my life coaching school. As a resident, I had the opportunity to deepen my understanding of core healing tools, facilitate teaching segments in various classes, supervise the trainee's work, and assist with curriculum upgrades. During this same period, a publishing company accepted my writing for inclusion in a compilation book – my first. I was thrilled to connect with an amazing group of spiritual teachers and authors. It was essential that I continue pursuing my own deep fulfillment, enrichment and joy – after all, my mission was to model light-heartedness and a capacity to thrive, in spite of any temporary obstacles in my outer reality – and participating in the book definitely fell in that category.

Unfortunately, Mark continued to lurch from one health challenge to the next: continual nosebleeds, urinary tract infections, liver toxicity, and viral assaults, though they were not near as serious or as long-standing as those during early childhood. As he was struggling to manage the physical onslaught, we were dealt another blow when Medicaid denied Mark one of his primary psychotropic medications.

The school social worker, Len, implored me to find another way for Mark's medication to be reinstated. Eventually, I was able to achieve my objective through a Canadian pharmacy that shipped Mark's medication from Great Britain. However, that solution was not timely enough to prevent Mark from undergoing the onset of another frightening manic episode. Subsequently, through an appeal, Dr. F. was able to prevail upon the insurance company to resume Mark's medication.

Despite his mental health struggles in the spring, Mark courageously stepped up to audition for a summer musical theater production and was cast in *Rodger's and Hammerstein's Oklahoma*. Mark took his role in the singing and dancing ensemble seriously and fully dedicated himself to being a proficient cast member. When the curtain rose, my heart swelled with pride as Mark graced the stage in his jeans and cowboy attire. Indeed, throughout the performance, from his exuberant and stunning high kicks to his choreographed fight scene, to the way he belted out his part in the finale, life felt pretty perfect.

It felt pretty perfect because Mark had clearly overcome all odds to find his place of belonging where he could fully express his gifts and talents. I sat mesmerized but it didn't prevent my mind from drifting back to the memory of his intensive years in occupational therapy – the very same years where he worked laboriously on his sensory processing, vestibular, proprioceptive and motor challenges. [85]

During a brief intermission, I happened to strike up a conversation with Sylvia, a very attractive woman seated next to me. She mentioned that she was recently widowed and this event was one of her first forays into the community. As the conversation unfolded, it became increasingly clear that it was no accident that we were seated together. I felt guided to deliver a very timely message.

After some introductory remarks, Sylvia shared the following account; "My nineteen-year-old niece is currently a patient at The Rehabilitation Institute of Chicago.[86] A short three weeks ago, while preparing to leave for college, she had a diving accident, which left her with the devastating aftereffects of paraplegia. Certain family members believe that her recovery is a hopeless undertaking."

As I shared Mark's odyssey, tears pierced her eyes. I stated, "Of course, I don't know your niece's future prognosis, but I do know that the body often holds a miraculous potential to heal. Intensive therapy changed the course of my son's life. I don't think it's a coincidence that we are seated together today or that this topic was broached. I believe you hold the capacity to be her champion as she navigates the healing process. I believe you are there to focus on a greater vision for her life, especially during the periods when she lapses into despair and discouragement. Sometimes, in the midst of adversity, it's hard to see how life is actually coming together but little by little it does come together."

When the curtain arose for act two, I pointed Mark out to her so that she could witness the results of our miracle. As a parent to a child with special needs, it definitely holds you in good stead to savor the high points because other obstacles are often on the horizon.

The cessation of Mark's medication during the spring was not the only factor complicating his mood stability. During the fall of Mark's second year in the transition program, he unexpectedly experienced the sudden onset of another bout of mania. Since his early elementary years, Mark's risk for mania had consistently been heightened during the spring months. This bout, however, seemingly came out of nowhere and was even more intense than his interval in the spring. Dr. F. surmised that the seasonal change had precipitated Mark's symptoms. In addition to his disordered thinking and emotional state, his physical body was also exhibiting signs of breakdown, including a cyst in his mouth. Normally, surgery would have been required to remove it, but thankfully, Kaaren found an alternate solution, "oil pulling,"[87] though it took months for complete healing to occur.

During Mark's last years at the academy, he also fell hostage to continuous handwashing as his preteen fears of environmental contamination came roaring back to the forefront. His hands were raw from excessive bouts of washing, and he used his feet, elbows, shirt and the knuckles of his closed fists as barriers -- preventing the flat of his hands from contacting a variety of surfaces. I watched sorrowfully as he struggled, knowing there was no simple remedy for what plagued him. During his last year at the academy, Dr. F. continued to gradually increase one of Mark's medications to help manage his symptoms.

Fortunately, after Mark's yearlong absence from psychotherapy, he resumed sessions and was referred to Matt, a co-worker of Jane Walker. Another bright spot was Mark's friend Forrest, who continued to provide ongoing compassionate support.

In the meantime, Mark continued to be shuffled from one new physician to another through Medicaid. I spent endless hours trying to enlist a physician network whose primary care physician and endocrinologist would jointly accept his case, as one overseeing medical body was now a requirement. After hours and hours of roadblocks, I connected with a call center receptionist who heard my story and immediately felt moved to assist me. She recommended a specific physician for Mark but alerted me to the fact that there were a very limited number of Medicaid patients accepted by his practice. She offered to personally advocate for Mark to be accepted there and, if successful, she would then advocate for the endocrinologist to accept Mark on his patient roster.

True to her word, this beautiful angel called back and told me that she had managed to create an opening for Mark with both physicians. As my story illustrates, the perseverance of J.K. Rowling is often necessary, coupled with the willingness of the right person, at the right time, to intervene and move mountains to ensure the right result. I now recognized that all along my parenting odyssey the Universe had lovingly aligned me with key people at just the right Divine moments. By doing so, I was learning to focus on appreciation while carrying a mindset that supported faith, hope, optimism and positive expectancy; that in due course, the right circumstances would prevail.

During this same period, the Universe brought another destiny-changing event into my life. My neurosurgeon had continued to monitor the size and placement of my recurring pituitary tumor. Now, he and his partner were strongly recommending focused radiation aimed at the tumor. The list of risks and possible side effects of this procedure are numerous and serious in scope, including damage to the optic nerve. Another potential risk is the destruction of healthy tissue remaining in the pituitary. After undergoing the failure of my pituitary's optimal functioning in 2008, I certainly didn't relish revisiting such an experience.

Through my self-advocacy efforts, I found another neurosurgeon for a second opinion. When I spoke with him by phone, he asked a number of incisive and astute questions, then said, "Something isn't adding up here. You might need to get a third opinion. Come see me and we'll go from there."

When I met with Dr. G., he took a full history, performed a brief neurological assessment, and carefully reviewed my records and scans. Surprisingly, he believed that I had previously been misdiagnosed. The pathology report indicated that the only thing that had been removed from my pituitary was "healthy tissue." There was zero evidence of a tumor.

I had formerly read the report and questioned my original surgeon about the matter. He explained that the tumor had liquefied; negating a sample for the pathologist and that some level of healthy tissue would unavoidably be removed during surgery. At the time, his explanation sounded plausible. However, the current neurosurgeon emphasized the following point: I had never exhibited the physical features of acromegaly and therefore, I'd likely had a pituitary cyst. He recommended a third opinion from Dr. Edward Laws, the foremost expert in the country on pituitary disorders and transsphenoidal operations.

What happened next was nothing short of a miracle. I contacted Dr. Law's office and spoke to a nurse in the practice who answered the phone on my first attempt, listened to my needs, and immediately transferred me to a physician in the practice who also answered my call! I don't think I have ever experienced such an event when calling a physician, even as an established patient in the practice. Dr. Law's colleague spent considerable time learning about my predicament; he also, after informing me that my health insurance was not accepted by the practice, said that I would be required to come to Boston for an in-person exam.

When I explained my special circumstances concerning my son and my personal health challenges, Dr. Law's co-physician, stated, "We will make an exception for you. Send your medical records in their entirety and all of your brain scans and we will give you an opinion by phone!" To say I was gobsmacked was an understatement, especially when I realized they were willing to help by phone without any financial compensation.

Within two weeks of receiving my records, Dr. Law's colleague informed me that my condition had indeed been misdiagnosed. The team was one hundred percent sure that a pituitary cyst was present. They also concurred that I did not present with acromegaly – while they were uncertain as to why my growth hormone levels had previously been elevated, they believed it was nowhere near the expected levels of acromegaly. Their recommendation was "conservative monitoring." Other than undergoing yearly scans to monitor the size and placement of the cyst, they felt fairly confident that I would likely be able to traverse the remainder of my life without any serious repercussions. And there was no charge for their time, expertise, or thoroughness!

Mark was the next one in the family to receive a miracle related to his pituitary condition. After he turned twenty-three, the endocrinologist recommended that he be weaned off his growth hormone supplementation. Even though Mark was five-foot-eleven inches tall, I immediately felt the grip of fear that his immune deficiency might come roaring back.

Mark, on the other hand, seemed to have full faith in the process. He confidently insisted that his body no longer required the hormone.

After the weaning process there was zero evidence of a deteriorating health status, but even better news was yet to come. Without hormone supplementation, Mark's lab work demonstrated that his growth hormone level was within the normal range! Since age eleven, his lab results had uniformly demonstrated that injectable growth hormone was required to bring about a normal insulin-like growth factor-1 (IGF-1) level.

Not only was Mark's first lab marker for IGF1 normal, the same finding was replicated again and again for years without additional supplementation of growth hormone. Mark was no longer tied to the nightly routine of an injectable! That said, those eleven years of injections had led to significant and long-lasting health benefits in a myriad of categories and had been instrumental in creating freedom from one disabling virus after the next. Even though Mark continued to have health challenges, they were nowhere near the magnitude of the first half of his life.

WHAT I KNOW NOW THAT I DIDN'T KNOW THEN: VIA THE PRACTICE OF GRATITUDE, WE MORE EASILY EMBODY A STATE OF GRATITUDE, WHICH ALIGNS US WITH OUR HIGHEST PATH. Gratitude is a mindset, a practice, and an embodied state of being! The practice of gratitude *dissolves all resistance* and *connects us with abundance and aligns us with unlimited miracles.* When we embody gratitude, we magnetize more circumstances into our lives that offer us the elevated experience of gratitude. *Gratitude is the magical bridge between fear and love.* When we source our energy from fear, fear expands and conversely, when we source our energy from the heart, gratitude expands and we magnetize even more circumstances that mirror appreciation. A daily practice of gratitude helps us reduce stress, starts our day with positive momentum, improves our relationships, our mental health, our mindset, our physical well-being, our self-esteem, our capacity to empathize with others, helps us sleep better at night, and is one of our spiritual superpowers.

Appreciation (which is an act or display of gratitude), freedom, and unconditional love fall on the highest rungs of the empowerment ladder. David Hawkins, a renowned psychiatrist who studied states of consciousness and developed a map of consciousness through his experimentation with muscle testing on 250,000 individuals, placed an embodied state of gratitude and appreciation above joy, peace and love, respectively.

What does Wayne Dyer have to say about the importance of your state of consciousness? *"One individual who lives and vibrates to the energy of pure love and **reverence for life** will counterbalance the negativity of 750,000 individuals who calibrate at the lower weakening levels."* Just consider for a moment the magnitude of what our children have come into this life to teach us!

Rita Schiano wrote, "Talking about our problems is our greatest addiction. Break the habit. Talk about your joys." Once you have looked squarely at a challenge and validated the truth of that circumstance and processed and released any lower vibrations attached to that circumstance, it's time to let it go. When your Ego falls back into talking about a dilemma you have already wisely processed, it's a call to pivot and immediately name or record a minimum of three blessings that are present in your life. Even taking note of the smallest blessing matters.

By focusing on your success plans, your micro-movements forward, your dreams, hopes, blessings and answered prayers, you will gift yourself renewed energy. When focusing on your forward momentum, do not forget to turn the lens back upon yourself. What do you appreciate about yourself? What embodied self-attributes do you possess that elevates the world? How does your presence alone elevate the world? What gifts, talents, values and contributions do you bring forward? What big and small efforts have you made that deserve to be acknowledged?

At the beginning of my special needs odyssey, I did not realize the paradox that confronted me – that the grief process and the practice of gratitude could actually co-exist simultaneously. As we watch our children put the utmost effort into mastering skill sets and developmental milestones that most of us take for granted, we come face-to-face with the preciousness of every single human capacity. However, during most of Mark's childhood, I neglected to fully maximize that lesson. I momentarily celebrated his first wave, his first word and his first spontaneous imitation, et cetera – but I rarely slowed down enough to bask in the energy of gratitude. I lived my life like a passenger aboard a high-speed train, heading toward an undisclosed destination with little to no time to take in the passing scenery. I lurched from crisis to crisis and was so immersed in achieving outcomes that I often missed the miracles that were right in front of me!

Surprisingly, we can easily miss our own lives if we are not present to observe the gifts in front of us. *My parenting intensive has taught me that it's the small, fleeting personal moments of connection and intimacy that count! No matter the weight of your circumstances, there is always room to savor the awe-filled nature of your personal encounters.* As Robert Brault so eloquently wrote, "Enjoy the little things in life, for one day you may look back and realize they were the big things." Learning to open your heart, as you enter a deeper reverence for the sacredness of life, while connecting to all the ways that life is mirroring back your essence, is the foundation for blessed receptivity.

There are four steps that will support your co-creation of gratitude. Step one is the practice of focused presence or mindfulness; step two entails enhancing and fine-tuning your observational powers; step three prompts you to bless and appreciate your current and future circumstances; and step four asks you to embrace positive expectancy. In order to complete step one, it can be as simple as coming back to an awareness of your body sensations, while taking conscious belly breaths, as you dial down your mental chatter.

Through the consistent practice of mindfulness, you open yourself to the power inherent in the present moment, where you potentially receive the subtle and overt gifts being offered. A simple exercise for grounding your energy and fine-tuning your observational powers is the 5,4,3,2,1 exercise. You begin this exercise by inhaling to the count of seven, holding your breath to the count of seven, and exhaling to the count of seven. After following this pattern three times, scan your environment and notice five things that you can see. Next, place your focus on four feelings/body sensations. For example, do you feel the wind in your hair, the warmth against your arm, pressure against your feet, or cool air circulating? For step three, notice three sounds, including the faintest sound that you can hear. Next sniff two objects in your surroundings. What do you smell? Lastly, swish your tongue inside your mouth. What do you taste? The options are salty, sour, bitter or sweet. By repeating this practice, you will rehabilitate your atrophied senses and better enter the flow of gratitude.

By noticing your daily blessings, no matter how minuscule, you begin to live at a higher vibration. By recording your daily blessings in a journal or on a square of paper and adding them to *a gratitude jar,* you retrain your brain toward an optimistic mindset, while bolstering your trust in a Universe that lovingly provides. Focusing on your blessings before bedtime is another way of relaxing your mind. Spiritual teacher Amanda Ellis recommends grasping each digit on one hand, while sequentially naming one blessing per digit. Another interesting practice is to record your blessings at the front of your journal and then immediately record your dreams and aspirations at the back of your journal. Then, on a daily basis, you keep notations from the front to the back of your book. As Neale Donald Walsch wrote, "Gratitude in advance is the most powerful creative force in the universe...Expressing thankfulness in advance is the way of the Masters. So do not wait for things to happen to give thanks. Give thanks before it happens."

This principle highlights the need to imagine your success stories and dreams fulfilled and to record those imaginings in your journal.

By visualizing with lavish detail your personal and family-centered goals attained, you will flood your heart with love and bathe every cell in your body with overflowing gratitude, magnetizing even more future desires. *Navigate life as though all your dreams and deepest desires have already been fulfilled!* The universe is designed to be superabundant for everyone, including your children.

Advanced knowledge as to how your desires will be realized is not required! I especially recognized that when I changed the tone of my conversations from blaming, whining, and complaining to acknowledging, blessing, and appreciating, my life began to flow with greater alignment, grace, and ease. The practice of gratitude significantly improved my health, transformed my outlook, reignited my passion for life, and healed my relationship with Mark in a myriad of surprising ways. Just imagine what this simple practice can do for you?

JOY, FREEDOM, LOVE, INTUITIVE CONNECTION, AND EMPOWERMENT

Those worth loving are those who teach you
to love yourself.

Unknown

Mark scaled to even more amazing heights. Mark asserted that being under the auspices of the guardianship court would never define or limit his abilities. He insisted that he would one day live independently and have his guardianship status terminated. In that vein, he has continued to set and accomplish a series of personal goals. More importantly, he comports himself with dignity, concern and compassion for others, humor, reliability, much improved emotional regulation, and a zest for contributing his talents and abilities to the world. Mark has continued to master appropriate coping skills and set healthy self-boundaries, and he has greatly matured in his ability to navigate challenging circumstances. Researchers believe that the male brain matures

by age twenty-five and my experience with Mark reinforces that finding. Mark has not had a reoccurrence of mania for seven bountiful
years! Mark's boundless childhood energy has been channeled into his
adult passion for artistic endeavors.

I fervently believe that Mark would not have been able to continue
toward his highest potential had I not immersed myself in my own healing journey. In addition, Mark's soul contract allowed him to evolve
and grow as a soul who is living out a physical existence. Many of our
children are energetic sponges who easily absorb the frequencies around
them and then operate as though they are those frequencies. Once I
consciously connected with a higher degree of wisdom and light, and
learned to embody more light, Mark eventually followed suit.

While exploring my spiritual ascension, I ardently believed that
Mark was entitled to his own unique process toward empowerment.
I never demanded that he march by my side, yet little by little, he
demonstrated his own curiosity about my core transformational tools
and he very much wanted to harness the principles that undergirded
that metamorphosis. Over time, he became more and more astute
about a variety of healing tools that were outside the realm of societal
conventions. The more he practiced the tools that I have outlined in
this book, the more confident and grounded he became. He felt the
results firsthand and then he was even more motivated to set energetic
boundaries and learn about complementary healing tools.

As I began to form the habit of viewing Mark through spiritual
eyes, I also noted that he often relayed surprisingly accurate spiritual
messages to others. His wisdom and insight were on display, whether
he was sharing an inspirational message, asking someone to listen to a
song with a hidden message or pointing out a subtle spiritual sign during community outings. Here are some examples of Mark's messages:
"Having a loving mother figure is a sign of Divine compassion; The
journey is more interesting than the destination but there are certain
roads you don't want to go down; You can think about the past as
much as you want, but certain parts of your life aren't worth thinking

about as long as you've changed for the better." As Wayne Dyer so eloquently wrote, "See the light in others and treat them as if that's all you see." When you view your children in that manner, the light will be returned to you tenfold, irrespective of how they live in their human bodies.

Since leaving the academy, Mark has performed in six theatrical musical productions. Over the course of his time performing, he has increasingly been given more responsibility. Board members and audience members alike have recognized his work. One director of a summer production wrote Mark a personal message stating that he had been the most committed cast member out of approximately thirty individuals.

In 2016, Mark and I attended a red-carpet event at a local movie theater. Mark and an entire cast of special needs performers were featured in a screening of a documentary film. The film was inspired by a book written by one of the actors living with the effects of severe cerebral palsy. Her imaginative story takes place in a fairy tale setting by the name of "Toyland" and drove home an anti-bullying message.[88] The core story was seven minutes long, followed by the individual actors sharing their poignant experiences, feelings and insights related to being taunted and bullied for their differences.

The screening received a standing ovation and resounding applause; some audience members were even moved to tears. The film was later shown at several local schools and was immediately invited to be included in our community's local film festival. It went on to win "Best Documentary – Short Subject."

Mark, in particular, was lauded for his moving words. Mark said the following in reference to his peers: "These kids have been ridiculed, made fun of and shunned [because of their label]. It's moments like this where they are able to shine. We are essentially saying, 'I am more than just my label. I am more than what you think I am. I am a human being with a personality and nothing is going to stop me'… It's a very wonderful feeling to see these kids show the world that they have potential…They want to be seen and I think that is a step in the right direction."

Another beautiful event took place in the summer of 2017. Mark was chosen to participate in the Surfers Healing Camp for individuals with Autism held at Wrightsville Beach in Wilmington, North Carolina. Mark and I had not been on a vacation since our memorable trip to Kings Island, Ohio. We were long overdue to write a new chapter. Fortuitously, after applying to be selected at the camp, Mark's name was pulled from the massive number of potential surfers in a lottery system. During our time in North Carolina, I met families who had waited ten years to be included in this event. I felt that a loving Universe decided to gift us a much-needed reprieve. Not only did Mark and I take advantage of the historic Wilmington sites for four days, but I was also given the opportunity to spend time with my dear childhood friend, Jane.

Mark and I enjoyed a jam-packed trip. At the oldest opera house in the country, we attended a professional performance of *South Pacific*; Mark successfully learned to boogie board in the ocean; he explored downtown shops full of vinyl records and old DVDs; he toured the bowels of the U.S.S North Carolina, WWII Battleship; he went to the movies; and he took the two-hour Hollywood Walking Tour, which featured Hollywood filming sites and loads of entertainment industry trivia. Naturally, Mark won the "Hollywood Award" for being the most knowledgeable out of the entire tour group.

Then it was time for Surfer's Healing Camp to commence. Mark, Jane and I spent a memorable day at the beach. During the afternoon, it was Mark's turn to take his surfboard out into the ocean. A professional surfer accompanied Mark, helped position his board and timed the waves so that he would have the most optimal chance to stand, get traction and ride atop his board. Because Mark had to navigate getting on the board independently, doing so was quite the challenge! However, as you already know, Mark excels at challenges! He eventually succeeded by making one full pass into the shoreline atop his board! The entire day was simply magical – with the majestic beauty of the natural surroundings, mixed with the faces of the children and families with autism etched with grace, and the kindness and joy of the sponsors.

I also felt tremendous gratitude for having lovely Jane B. by my side, just as she had been, loyally supporting me during my entire mothering journey. Throughout Mark's life, Jane has always modeled complete acceptance and unconditional support toward Mark. Having her unwavering help during the trip was a much-needed break from the responsibility of single motherhood. Jane was there to haul beach equipment, to teach Mark to boogie board, to descend to the lower level of the U.S.S. North Carolina in the one-hundred-degree heat, to chauffeur us around to the sites and help prepare Mark's food, et cetera. The only potential glitch was getting Mark aboard the airplane. It had been years since he had flown and he had developed a fear of flying. Fortunately, Mark handled his time in the air with the application of essential oils for relaxation, paired with tapping on energy meridians.

In April of 2018, Mark landed his first part-time job in a movie theater. As part of the preparation process, I used a virtual simulator that provided Mark with scaffolding to master job interviewing skills. The behavioral questions, in particular, are definitely challenging for anyone on the spectrum. For several years, we worked on the complicated components of confidently introducing oneself and interviewing. I also assisted Mark with his online application.

Although I provided the transportation, Mark took the lead with almost all the other steps. Mark was on his own navigating a work environment that did not provide any additional support or accommodations. Mark was definitely thrown into the unpredictable nature of an entry-level workplace. He faced stressful interactions surrounding an employee who bullied him; adolescent female customers who tattooed themselves illegally in the bathroom; a gas leak in the building; customers raging over a seat confusion; and an assignment to single-handedly assist an elderly woman splayed out on the ground in a fetal position moaning in pain, et cetera. The Universe certainly knew what it was doing because Mark had had a lot of experience dealing with a mother with chronic illness and because he was left alone with this theatergoer to figure it out – he rose to the occasion.

Most miraculous of all, Mark's digestive system began to heal at age twenty-seven and he was finally able to expand his diet! Through another beautiful synchronicity, we were led to a brand-new healing technology. Mark courageously sampled a variety of new nutritiously dense foods. Although he still needed to be careful about what he consumed, he is on his way toward a solid foundation of health and wellness!

WHAT I KNOW NOW THAT I DIDN'T KNOW THEN: THESE MAGNIFICENT CHILDREN HAVE INCARNATED IN MASSIVE NUMBERS TO TAKE A LEADING ROLE IN THE AWAKENING OF SPIRITUAL CONSCIOUSNESS AND SPIRITUAL ASCENSION ON THIS PLANET AND WE ARE HERE TO SERVE AS THEIR DIVINE COUN-TERPARTS IN THAT PROCESS. *Our children are leading us into a new Aquarian age grounded in the values of peace, freedom, unity conscious-ness, sustainability, integrity and heart-centered living.* I opened this book with Truman Capote's paradox stating that more tears are shed over answered prayers than unanswered prayers! We will invariably con-tinue to shed those tears until we elevate our perception; our Divine partnership with our children is staunchly working for us, for our chil-dren, and for the betterment of the world!

There are all kinds of diagnostic, educational, and medical labels to describe our children and there are all kinds of spiritual labels to cat-egorize our children, including, Indigo, Crystal, Rainbow, Diamond, New Children, or, more simply, *Starseed beings of light.* In my view, being *tied* to these labels is just another limiting ideology. Our children have shown us time and again that there is more to their presence here than what appears to be true from our limited human conditioning.

Yet, on the human level, our children undergo a myriad of painful challenges that can impact their minds, their physical signa-tures, as well as, their emotional and/or spiritual states. And yes, our children's pain is often compounded and can devolve into suffering *in part* because there is a mismatch between their pure soul essence, their pure intentions and the environment that does not fully see, honor and support them. By commenting on this dynamic, I am not implying that *you* are primarily responsible for your children's dilemmas. *You are not here to singlehandedly turn the world on a different access point. You are not here to rewrite your child's carefully chosen spiritual fitness program that was outlined in advance of incarnating for very specific purposes.*

Importantly, you are primarily responsible for your own vibrational setpoint and for the way in which you show up for yourself. Your assignment, should you choose to accept it, is to channel the highest degree of light through your various energetic/auric layers, while releasing any barriers that stand in your way. That is the path to self-healing, self-empowerment and self-authenticity. *And while you are in that process, your children are in partnership with you as they propel you forward toward the healing of your heart and the ladder of self-actualization.* Navigating the various rungs of the Empowerment Ladder, in no particular order, will gift you the shortest route toward meeting and integrating all aspects of yourself.

When you observe any energetic disharmony within your children, you are being called to face the rungs of YOUR own ladder. Through your acute observational powers and allowing your heart to lead, you will recognize this energetic mismatch. You might observe this mismatch when your children outright fight anything that smacks of coercion as my son did; you might see this mismatch when your child avoids interactions with you or when he or she flees into unhealthy withdrawal, defeatism and discouragement; you might see this mismatch when your child escapes into self-harm and self-injury or when your child engages in unsafe, aggressive or risk-taking behaviors.

Although we are *not* responsible for our children's creations, it is critical to examine what intentions we have set and what prejudices and projections we have brought to the table as we interface with our children. It matters greatly whether we are willing to do our own honest and radical spiritual self-inventory, so that we may more fully own the instances where our behaviors have missed the mark. It matters greatly whether we have enacted a role of fixing our children's *"broken bodies and psyches."* What I know now is that for every instance that I approached Mark with my crusading fix-it energy – his spirit and light were diminished.

What I know now is the vast dichotomy between curing/fixing yourself and/or your child and instead investing in a healing journey. Fixing/curing begins with the foundational belief that your child is deficient or broken. It's about the ego's need to control the outer reality in order to feel safe. On the other hand, healing begins with the foundational belief that wholeness is already present. Healing happens when we align with that wholeness by removing, rebalancing and restoring what is needed so that we (and our children) can embody our highest templates. The template for wholeness is as vast and unique as each individual inhabiting this planet. As Alison Gopnik wrote in *The Gardener and The Carpenter*, "Love doesn't have goals, or benchmarks or blueprints, but it does have a purpose. The purpose is not to change the people we love, but to give them what they need to thrive."

Our role is one of removing any and all barriers within us, so that our children can more fully express the truth of themselves. Our role is one of inspiring and uplifting those who work with our children so that they can embody our expanded consciousness. Our role is one of anchoring love in a myriad of ways; whether by overhauling the practices that do not support Mother Gaia; the food industry; the chemical industry; the educational system or whether it means overhauling a healthcare system, an employment system, an economic system that is clearly out of alignment with a higher Divine Love. In addition, it might mean overhauling any societal practice that does not offer our children access to the full spectrum of opportunities and human rights.

Notwithstanding any of the above, sometimes parents invariably fall into a deep pit of pain, be it mental, physical, emotional, or spiritual. I, like you, have stumbled as a mother, and I'm sure I will again. I am part of this Sisterhood and I walk right alongside you. And sometimes our pain is compounded because we choose to ignore the following truth: our children are multidimensional beings who are indeed spiritual warriors. Every single child is gifted, whether that *"definition of gifted"* fits our preconceived notions or not and it is our job to look with our spiritual sight so that our children may reveal and express their true spiritual purposes for incarnating.

Some of your children have opted out of the "rat race" and the societal rewards for doing so. Your children are potentially highlighting for you the most essential cornerstone of life… in a word, LOVE! As spiritual teachers, they underscore the emptiness attached to garnering things outside of us. They demonstrate that having more, doing more and being more is not the path toward a consciously awakened life. They implore us to ask the following essential question: how can we embody more love and transmit more love through every single interaction that we encounter?

We will be in a better position to see our children's elevated presence, most especially when they do not rely upon spoken communication or move their bodies in *preconceived ways* that satisfy our ego. It is our responsibility to presume competence and to treat them in a corresponding manner. We will be in a better position to honor their presence when we see them as courage personified. We will be in a better position when we see them as leaders and **our** teachers. Do we currently look at our children and see them as highly evolved beings who have taken on this body in this lifetime in order to orchestrate the vibration of unconditional love and empowerment? Do we also recognize that they are also here to magnify any disparities between purest love and all lower states of consciousness?

What I know now, at my deepest core, is the following: our children, *and every single experience that comes along with them, offers the promise of enhancing OUR lives!* Even the circumstances *that appear* to subtract and dismantle elements from our lives or from our very identities are perfectly enacted to enhance us. That recognition offers us bountiful ease and grace, leading us to voice the following prayer: in union with our light-bearing children, we gratefully and masterfully alchemize every element that has come before, in order to offer up an elixir of life that serves the greater glory of all. And so it is!

AFTERWORD

by Mark Hasselo

As you have read, my mom is a warrior. Just like me, she is a success story straight out of Greek Mythology. I'm specifically referring to the story of Sisyphus. Sisyphus was punished by Hades to forever push a large rock up a mountain, only for it to roll back down again. Just like Sisyphus, my mom found meaning in pushing the boulder. She saw how the boulder was also a teacher – a tool for what she would do later in life.

When I was diagnosed with autism at twenty-one months old, Mom was not offered any tools or strategies to help me, nor was she given any hope that I would improve. In the beginning, very few people wanted to listen to her cries for help. I was alive at a time when people who were diagnosed with autism were no longer being put in institutions for the rest of their lives. She was beyond devastated and her heart was shattered in two. To cope with the harsh reality, she made it her mission to "cure" my autism. But by choosing that path, she lost many of her closest friends, she lost her husband of twenty-two years, and her health was especially compromised. As you have read, anyone faced with a laundry list of problems like the ones mentioned in this book would easily have given up on life and even on their child.

As for me, I can't beat myself up for what happened during my childhood. I want to make something explicitly clear: I am NOT the person you have read about in the earlier chapters. I was not a monster and I was never a bad kid. I had behaviors that I could not control. I hope everyone knows that. When I was young, I was influenced by darkness but I later learned to focus on love and light. To everyone who I have unintentionally hurt, I am very, sorry. I never meant to harm anyone.

By the time I was placed in the residential treatment center, it was the moment of truth for both of us. When I was sent away, my Mom saw it as a way to not only help me, but also herself too. While there, I had to face my darkness and surrender to the part of myself that desired a better life.

My mom refused to let her health condition permanently immobilize her. She saw many professionals, ranging from alternative medicine physicians to spiritual healers. Even to this day, she refuses to let her ME (Myalgic Encephalomyelitis) stop her from trying to live a full life. She is STILL seeing professionals, never giving up hope that one day she will be recovered. We look forward to the day when ME, or Chronic Fatigue Syndrome is not only well known in the public eye, but is curable!

During my lifetime, I have seen my mom at her worst as she plummeted to the depths of despair and dread, I helped to save her life at least twice and supported her through many health crises. Even with all of these traumatic situations that would have driven anyone to the point of insanity, I believe there was a reason that the Universe put us together. My mom and I both fell into the trap of neglecting ourselves and instead putting other people first. I have since learned to concentrate on having a balance between bettering myself and helping others.

I don't believe I would have survived with anyone else besides my mom, as she was the only one who had the ability to understand me on a spiritual level. At first I felt that I didn't need teachers or guides. I thought that I could handle everything myself. I later learned that

I deserved compassion and support from others and that I could also receive unconditional love from the Divine.

For all the kids who are struggling with a neurological disorder, I want you to know that you are not alone. I want you to know that you are *not* your label. I want you to know that autism is a blessing because you look at life and everything in it from a different point of view that very few people are able to see. *People with autism are here to change other people's perceptions on life.* We may have been taught to follow the status quo; we may have been taught that life is all work and no play; we may have been told that life is a cold dark place where no one cares. We may be successful, but at what cost? How are we truly successful?

In my opinion, success is defined by what we have learned in life. Remember, every single special needs child is already successful in his or her own way. For me, life is not about wearing a suit at a high-paying job. Instead, success is about how we've overcome insurmountable obstacles, healed from the wounds of the past, offered self-forgiveness and then moved forward toward our dreams and aspirations. Mom and I achieved that with flying colors.

I am blessed to be in a better place. I have focused on being a more positive person and progressing toward having greater self-confidence. Though I'm a shy individual, and a "hermit" type of person, I have big ambitions and dreams. I want to become a serious actor and film director. I hope to write and direct movies that people NEED to see. One of my dreams is to perform a dance number, sing a solo, or carry a show by myself. I also hope to travel the country, continue to help other special needs individuals, find a life partner and meet the celebrities who have inspired me.

Thanks to my mom, I now understand that despite having autism and bipolar I shouldn't allow my challenges to dominate my life. Even when we live with illness or a disability, we can learn from it. We can't let our conditions stop us from enjoying life. The lessons that we learn on Earth are a permanent part of our spiritual lives.

My mom would really appreciate it if you would talk about this book with your friends and apply the lessons in your everyday life. While I write my future books, I hope you have enjoyed this one.

Peace be with you. Namaste.

ENDNOTES

Rung One

1. As you learn to meet your emotional dependency needs that were not fulfilled during childhood, you will be able to tap into self-knowledge, self-love, emotional honesty and intimacy *with yourself*, thereby showering yourself with self-nurturing, self-compassion, unconditional love and acceptance, while learning to set healthy self-boundaries.

2. Miller, Alice. *The Drama of the Gifted Child: The Search for the True Self*. Basic Books, New York, 1997.

3. Burney, Robert. *Codependence: The Dance of Wounded Souls: A Cosmic Perspective of Codependence and the Human Condition*. Joy to You and Me Enterprise, 2011.

4. Rosenberg, Ross. *The Human Magnet Syndrome: Why We Love People Who Hurt Us,* PESI Publishing Media. Eau Claire, 2013.

5. Nelson, Portia. *There's a Hole in My Sidewalk: The Romance of Self-Discovery*. Beyond Words Publishing, Portland. 1997.

6. A *warrior mother* is a term used in the autism community to denote mothers who will obsessively pursue conventional and holistic approaches to *recover* their children from autism so that they become indistinguishable from their so-called "average peers."

Rung Two

7. Today, ABA continues to face ongoing controversy. Adults with ASD who belong to the neuro-divergent camp have made serious charges that ABA is a form of abuse that leaves clients with extreme forms of trauma. This camp also objects to the idea that children with autism need to be changed and forced to adopt behaviors held by the majority. Practitioners in the ABA camp often deny these charges and make the argument that behavior exhibited by children on the spectrum greatly interferes with quality of life and can lead to ostracism and limited opportunities in adulthood. I believe it's important to keep an open mind about these allegations and to continue to improve any field of knowledge. I also believe that mothers aligned with their higher intuitive wisdom are in a better position to make informed choices for their children.

8. Toe walking is observed in children who have neurological challenges. Some children with ASD consistently walk on their tiptoes beyond the expected time frame of age two.

9. Maurice, Catherine. *Let Me Hear Your Voice: A Family's Triumph Over Autism.* Ballantine Books, New York, 1994.

10. Solomon, Andrew. *Far From The Tree: Parents, Children and the Search for Identity.* Scribner, New York, 2012.

11. Multidimensionality presupposes that aspects of us are experiencing life in a variety of dimensions or planetary/star systems simultaneously. If this theory is true, it means that every choice we make in this dimension potentially influences our other dimensions at the same time, and visa versa. It also means that time is not truly linear, though we perceive it to be so in this dimension.

Rung Three

12. Generalization of skills is an area of challenge for children on the autism spectrum. Generalization means that a child can transfer his knowledge while interacting with a variety of people, across multiple settings and with varied materials. It means that learning has transferred and is understood in all contexts.

13. In today's world, DAN doctors are referred to as MAPS (The Medical Academy of Pediatric Special Needs.)

14. A Herxheimer reaction occurs when the immune system is flooded with toxins produced by an overwhelming amount of pathogens that are being processed and eliminated inefficiently by an overly burdened body.

15. McDonnell, Jane Taylor. *News from The Border*. Ticknor & Fields, Boston, 1993.

16. Boss, Pauline, Ph.D. *Ambiguous Loss: Learning To Live With Unresolved Grief*. Harvard University Press. Cambridge, 1999.

17. −*Autism: The Musical*. Directed by Tricia Regan, Performances by Henry Stills, Joseph Rainbow, Wyatt O'Neil, Neal Goldberg, Adam Walden, Cody Massey, and Shane Doherty. Bunim/Murray Productions, 2007.

18. Nappi, Alison. "5 Lies You Were Told About Grief." Rebelle Society. December 18, 2013. https://rebellesociety.com/2013/12/18/5-lies-you-were-told-about-grief/

19. Singer, Michael A. *The Untethered Soul: The Journey Beyond Yourself*. Harbinger Publications/Noetic Books, Oakland, 2007.

20. Saint John of the Cross-, a sixteenth-century Spanish poet and mystic, is purported to have coined the term "the dark night of the soul," a chronic state of disconnection from Source, your authenticity and personal power, and your ability to *find profound meaning* in the midst of adversity.

Rung Four

21. The adrenal glands, situated above the kidneys, are part of the endocrine system. They produce stress hormones, such as aldosterone and cortisol, leading to the fight, flight, or freeze response in the body.

22. Scott, Sir Walter. *Marmion; a Tale of Flodden Fields.* 1880. Indy-Publish, 2002.

Rung Five

23. The study did not examine the impact of long-term bullying, sibling abuse, homelessness, poverty, accidental injury, crime-ridden neighborhoods, or a host of other childhood traumas. Based on the identified ACES, the researchers found that participants who underwent a higher number of ACES were at higher risk to develop a set of negative outcomes. With an ACE score of 4 or more, the likelihood of chronic pulmonary lung disease or hepatitis increased exponentially and the likelihood of depression increased by 460%. The participants' risk of suicide increased by 1,220%. ACES also put individuals at high risk of being raped, or at high risk of being victimized or becoming the batterer in a domestic partnership.

24. Dalconzo, Master Hu. *Self-Mastery: A Journey Home to Your ... Inner Self.* Renaissance Publishing, Sixteenth Printing, Metairie, 2008.

Rung Six

25. An era when Dr. Leo Kanner and Dr. Bruno Bettleheim propagated the idea that autism was caused by cold, intellectualized, upper-middle-class mothers who unconsciously rejected their children.

26. Dr. William G. Crook is the author of several books on the subject of yeast overgrowth syndrome, including *The Yeast Connection: A Medical Breakthrough. Vintage Books, Random House, 1983, 1986;* and *The Yeast Connection Handbook: How Yeast Can Make You Feel "Sick All Over" and the Steps You Need to Take to Regain Your Health.* Square One Publishers, Garden City Park, 1996-2000.

27. Greene, Ross, W., PhD. *The Explosive Child: A New Approach for Understanding and Parenting Easily Frustrated, Chronically Inflexible Children.* Harper Publishing, New York, 2010.

28. Papolos, Demitri, M.D. & Papolos, Janice. *The Bipolar Child: The Definitive and Reassuring Guide to Childhood's Most Misunderstood Disorder.* Broadway Books of Random House, New York, 1999 and 2002.

29. American Psychiatric Association. *The Diagnostic and Statistical Manual of Mental Disorders, 5th Edition:* DSM-5. American Psychiatric Publishing, Washingon, D.C. 2013.

30. Chopra, Deepak. *The Seven Spiritual Laws Of Success: A Practical Guide To The Fulfillment of Your Desires,* New World Library, Novato, 1999.

Rung Seven

31. Katherine, Anne. *Where to Draw the Line: How to Set Healthy Boundaries Every Day,* Simon and Schuster, New York, 2012.

32. Dienstman, Allison Michelle. "Chakra Healing: How to Open Your Root Chakra: Feel grounded and safe by opening the root chakra." Goodnet: Gateway to Doing Good. July 19, 2019 https://www.goodnet.org/articles/root-chakra-healing-how-to-open-your

33. Broederlow, Christel. "30 Traits of An Empath." The Universal Empath 101. August 2016.

https://theuniversalempath101.com/30-traits-of-an-empath/

Rung Eight

34. According to Carl Jung, a synchronicity is an event that is typically viewed as a "coincidence" but actually carries a specific internal meaning for the person experiencing it. He believed that these coincidences were part of a universe where everything is interconnected.

Rung Nine

35. Functional medicine identifies the underlying causes of dis-ease, using a systems approach that fosters the therapeutic partnership between the practitioner and the patient.

36. Celiac disease can cause short stature as it impairs the body's ability to absorb key nutrients. It is a digestive and autoimmune disorder that damages the lining of the small intestine and leads to an intolerance to wheat, rye, barley, and sometimes oats.

37. A therapeutic day school is a small private school serving children with learning, behavioral and emotional challenges by immersing them in an environment that is highly attuned to their educational, emotional, and behavioral needs.

38. The Observe & Correct Technique is a self-mastery technique that supports individuals in transcending the fear of making mistakes, developed by the Holistic Learning Centers, Inc., of New Jersey.

Rung Ten

39. Dr. Ross Greene's website: http://www.livesinthebalance.org

40. The Magic Foundation is a non-profit organization that supports families whose children have a variety of chronic health disorders, syndromes and rare diseases, impacting a child's growth. They are considered "the global leader in endocrine health, advocacy, education and support." To learn more, visit www. magicfoundation.org

41. Richo, David, *The Five Things We Cannot Change: and the Happiness We Find by Embracing Them.,* Shambhala Publications, Inc., Boston, 2005.

42. Dalconzo, Master Hu. *The HuMan Handbook: A Guide Book For the Inner You.* Renaissance Publishing, Metairie, 2011, p. 75.

Rung Eleven

43. Federal Law mandates that the IEP (Individualized Education Plan) meeting be held at least yearly. The child's educational team, which consists of teachers, social workers, speech and language therapists, occupational therapists, physical therapists, parents, school administrators and other interested parties, is present in order to outline a detailed individualized education plan that is tailored to meet the needs of a child with a disability.

44. An example is Wrightslaw: Special Education Law, 2nd, Edition, by Peter W. D. Wright, Esq. and Pamela Darr Wright. Harbor House Law Press, Inc., Hartfield, 2006.

45. A "D&C" (dilation and curettage), is a surgical procedure where the lining of the uterus is scraped away and removed.

46. ---. *The Untethered Soul: The Journey Beyond Yourself.* Harbinger Publications/ Noetic Books, Oakland, 2007.

47. ---. *Self-Mastery: A Journey Home to Your ... Inner Self.* Renaissance Publishing, Metairie, 2008, p.53.

48. Gray, John. *Men Are from Mars, Women Are from Venus: The Classic Guide to Understanding the Opposite Sex.* Harper Collins Publishers, New York, 1992.

49. ---. *Self-Mastery: A Journey Home to Your ... Inner Self* by Joseph Hu Dalconzo. Renaissance Publishing, Metairie, 2008, p. 56.

Rung Twelve

50. Asperger's Syndrome is no longer included as a diagnosis in the DSM-5, but is still in wide use by many individuals who identify with this label. "High-functioning autism" is no longer in use as individuals on the spectrum are diagnosed looking at the three main features of autism with level one, level two and level three criteria. Level one requires support, level two requires substantial support and level three requires very substantial support.

51. Sensory diets are prescribed by Occupational Therapists (OTs). They are a set of activities that facilitate adaptive responses for children with sensory processing disorders.

52. Colon hydrotherapy is a healing method where purified water is released very slowly into the colon to eliminate built up fecal matter. The benefits are detoxification, restoring digestive health and rebalancing body chemistry.

53. The Emotional Freedom Technique, EFT, or "tapping" is a healing method that is part of energy psychology. By tapping on acu pressure points and reciting accompanying statements, the body is able to release energetic blockages and restore equilibrium.

54. Rhonda Byrne's book *The Secret* and its companion documentary (produced by Byrne and Paul Harrington) became a worldwide phenomenon in 2006. *The Secret* opened a window into the innate power of the Universe, utilizing focused presence via The Law of Attraction.

55. A self-mastery technique developed by Coach Hu Dalconzo, based on the work of Dr. John Gray.

56. The hand points for the 9 Gamut Procedure include the thumb point, located on the side of the thumb toward your body's midline at the base of the nail bed; the index finger located on the side toward your body's midline at the base of the nail bed; the middle finger at the base of the nail bed toward the midline, the little finger located on the side toward your body's midline at the base of the nail bed and the gamut point, located on the back of the hand about an inch down from your knuckles between the little finger and the ring finger. After tapping on the four points on your non-dominant hand and stimulating the gamut point, close your eyes; open your eyes, look down hard to the right; look down hard to the left; roll your eyes very slowly clockwise; roll your eyes very slowly counterclockwise; hum a couple of seconds of Yankee Doodle Dandy; count to five and hum the song again. Then breathe. The 9 Gamut Procedure integrates both hemispheres of the brain and helps dissolve early trauma.

57. Dr. Dawson Church's bibliography lists more than one hundred published papers in peer-reviewed professional journals. This research adheres to the guidelines set for evidence-based treatments, as defined by the American Psychological Association's Division 12 Task Force on Empirically Validated Treatments. Visit his website at www.eftuniverse.com

58. Other EFT practitioners include Gary Craig's website, https://www.emofree.com; Connect with Nick and Jessica Ortner at https://www.thetappingsolution.com/ and Connect with Karin Davidson at https://www.howtotap.com/

59. ---. *Self-Mastery: A Journey Home to Your ... Inner Self.* Renaissance Publishing, Metairie, 2008, p. 59.

Rung Thirteen

60. There are many types of bracing for children with scoliosis, some of which are quite painful, require almost full-time wear, and are quite restrictive. In contrast to 2008, the benefits of bracing are hotly debated.

61. Osteopathy involves the treatment of medical conditions via hands on manipulation of the bones, joints and muscles.

62. A microadenoma is a small benign tumor of the pituitary gland.

63. Acromegaly can lead to the enlargement of the hands, feet and face, a bulging chest, deepening of the voice, and a number of other symptoms, when excess growth hormone is secreted from the pituitary gland.

64. Adrenal glands regulate metabolism, the immune system, blood pressure and the body's ability to mobilize a stress response. With adrenal insufficiency, cortisol needs to be replaced synthetically.

65. It's common for first responders to lack the necessary training and education that helps them identify the behaviors associated with children or adults with autism. Thus, people with autism are at high risk to be seen as non-compliant and to have their behavior grossly misinterpreted and mismanaged during encounters with the police or first responders.

66. Reiki is a Japanese healing method that uses hands-on techniques to restore and reactivate life force energy in the body.

67. To connect with Kaaren, visit her at www.facebook.com/NobleWisdomCommunity or contact her directly at (630) 677-4049. As a mystic, Kaaren possesses the ability to enter into a deep state of consciousness where she connects with Guides, Masters, and Beings from the multiverse. Kaaren practices with the highest degree of integrity.

68. The insulin tolerance test is the gold standard for diagnosing growth hormone deficiency. Insulin levels are raised, signaling the pituitary to release bursts of growth hormone. Levels are measured in the blood at various intervals during a 90-minute period to see if the body is responding in an expected manner.

69. Striations look similar to extensive stretch marks and are associated with chronic Bartonella infection.

70. Savely, Ginger. "Chapter 4." *Insights into Lyme Disease Treatment: 13 Lyme-Literate Health Care Practitioners Share Their Healing Strategies* by Connie Strasheim. Biomed Publishing Group, South Lake Tahoe, California, 2009.

71. Bransfield, Dr. Robert. *ContagionLive: Infectious Diseases Today*, April 4, 2017. www.contagionlive.com Unfortunately, this article has since been removed from the site.

72. Applied Kinesthesiology (AK) is a practice of manual muscle testing to observe either strengthening or weakness of the muscle when diagnosing conditions in the body or testing various remedies for their compatibility with the body.

73. The "Claires" include clairvoyance (clear seeing), clairaudience (clear hearing), clairsentience (clear feeling) clairalience (clear smelling), clairgustance (clear tasting) and lastly, claircognizance (clear knowing).

Rung Fourteen

74. The gamma ray knife radiosurgery uses finely-focused radiation to target small tumors in the brain.

75. ---. *Self-Mastery: A Journey Home To Your ... Inner Self.* Renaissance Publishing, Metairie, 2008.

76. ----.*Self-Mastery: A Journey Home To Your ... Inner Self.* Renaissance Publishing, Sixteenth Printing, Metairie Louisiana, 2008, p. 93.

77. Ford, Debbie. *The Dark Side of the Light Chasers: Reclaiming Your Power, Creativity, Brilliance, And Dreams.* Riverhead Books, New York, 1998.

78. "If I spot it, I got it" is a concept taught as part of the 12-Step Recovery process.

Rung Fifteen

79. Special education students are permitted to access "transition services." These are services that support students in *real world* preparation for a move out of formal schooling and into a post-school life. Transition services were delivered to Mark between his 14th and his 22nd birthdays.

80. Books by Catherine Ponder include *Open Your Mind to Prosperity; The Dynamic Laws of Prosperity; The Prospering Power of Love; The Dynamic Laws of Prayer;* and Open *Your Mind to Receive,* among others.

81. Williamson, Marianne. Quote referring to A Course in Miracles. Facebook, December 13, 2012.

82. ---*The HuMan Handbook: A Guide Book For the Inner You* Renaissance Publishing, Metairie, 2011, p.23.

83. ----.*Self-Mastery: A Journey Home To Your Inner Self.* Renaissance Publishing, Metairie, Louisiana, 2008, p. 77.

84. Vitale, Joe. *Zero Limits: The Secret Hawaiian System for Wealth, Health, Peace and More.* Wiley Publishing. Hoboken, 2007.

Rung Sixteen

85. The vestibular system is a sensory system that coordinates information between the inner ear and the brain and helps maintain balance, coordination, and body adjustments based on spatial orientation. The proprioceptive system perceives positioning in space and sends information to nerves, joints, and muscles to form an adaptive response based upon sensory input decoded by the nervous system.

86. This facility is now called the Shirley Ryan Ability Lab.

87. Oil pulling is an ancient practice that involves swishing a tablespoon of oil in your mouth for approximately fifteen minutes. In Mark's case, heavy metal toxicity was behind his inability to heal.

Rung Seventeen

88. Surges, Billy. *Once Upon A Time Project: Kids in Toyland [Film]* https://www.youtube.com/watch?v=8urtOeHNDaQ&t=1063s

www.ingramcontent.com/pod-product-compliance
Lightning Source LLC
Chambersburg PA
CBHW071144130626
46553CB00004B/1516